ARKANA

MABON AND
THE MYSTERIES
OF BRITAIN

Caitlín Matthews is a writer, singer and harpist. She has studied aspects of Celtic tradition for many years. Through song and storytelling, she is dedicated to the revitalisation of the native mysteries as a practical means of spiritual realisation. She is co-author of the two-volume work on the Western esoteric tradition, *The Western Way* (Arkana, 1985 and 1986).

D0840393

Mabon and Modron

CAITLÍN MATTHEWS

MABON AND THE MYSTERIES OF BRITAIN

AN EXPLORATION OF THE MABINOGION

Illustrated by Chesca Potter

ARKANA

LONDON AND NEW YORK

First published in 1987 by ARKANA
ARKANA PAPERBACKS is an imprint of
Routledge & Kegan Paul Ltd

11 New Fetter Lane, London EC4P 4EE

Published in the USA by
Routledge & Kegan Paul Inc.
in association with Methuen Inc.
29 West 35th Street, New York, NY 10001

Set in Sabon, 10 on 11pt
by Columns of Reading
and printed in the British Isles
by The Guernsey Press Co Ltd
Guernsey, Channel Islands

© Caitlín Matthews 1987
Illustrations © Chesca Potter 1987

No part of this book may be reproduced in
any form without permission from the publisher
except for the quotation of brief passages
in criticism

Library of Congress Cataloging in Publication Data

Matthews, Caitlín, 1952–
Mabon and the mysteries of Britain

Bibliography: p.
Includes index.
1. Mabinogion.   2. Tales – Wales – History and
criticism.   I. Title.
PB2273.M33M37 1987   891.6'631   86–17247

British Library CIP Data also available

ISBN 1–85063–052–6

Lady Sovereignty

EPONA REGINAE SANCTAE
BREHINES NEF A DAEAR AC UFFERN

Is this the land where the sleeper sleeps, the sleeper who shall wake, is he in his island cave – does Briareus guard him yet, are the single standing stones divinities about him? In this charged land of under-myth and over-myth where lord rests on greater lord and by lesser names the greater named are called.... What ageless Mabon recollects ... the axile line of the first of the sleepers?

David Jones
The Roman Quarry

CONTENTS

PREFACE

Into the Otherworld

Since its first translation into English in 1849, the *Mabinogion* has sat rather unhappily on library bookshelves; not quite fiction, not quite mythology, almost folkstory and almost history, it has puzzled readers who like their books clearly categorised.

There are those who read it for its storyline alone, and others who find insights into the wider fields of Arthurian criticism. But while there are scholarly commentaries aplenty for the patient and resourceful student, there is nothing for the general reader in search of instant demystification. Some of its stories are so spare that what is not written becomes an overwhelming obsession for the reader. Why does Rhiannon do nothing when unjustly accused of eating her son? Who is the father of

Arianrhod's twin children? Why is Bran's head cut off and how does it still give comfort to his men? Why does Efnissien cause so much trouble? These questions are not easily answered.

Yet by reference to the subtext of each story and by comparative study of other well-known and accessible stories, we can gain a glimpse of an answer. If the reader is prepared to trust the characters to tell him or her the answers to these and other questions, be sure – they stand ready with the information.

Like the cauldron of Ceridwen, this book has been brewing for a long time. It has come out of deep familiarity with the stories themselves and their parallel sources. It is a workbook, intended for practical work and in-depth study with the archetypal characters of the *Mabinogion* itself.

Since lack of space has foreshortened some areas of exposition, I have chosen to concentrate on the most ancient stories of the *Mabinogion*, the Four Branches – *Pwyll, Prince of Dyfed*; *Branwen, Daughter of Llyr*; *Manawyddan, Son of Llyr*; *Math, Son of Mathonwy* – as well as *Culhwch and Olwen*, and *Taliesin*. These bear a family likeness to each other since they represent a venerable tradition which I have identified as the Mysteries of Mabon and Modron.

These characters make their appearance within *Culhwch and Olwen* and are no more spoken of within the *Mabinogion*, except as a glancing reference, yet they are mysteriously present throughout the other stories as identifiable archetypes of the Wondrous Youth and the Great Mother.

Those who are disappointed not to find the Pseudo-Histories and the Arthurian Romances in this book are directed to R.S. Loomis's *Arthurian Tradition and Chrétien de Troyes*, as well as to other volumes listed in the bibliography. R.J. Stewart's work on the life and prophecies of Merlin[96,97] partially covers the period of the Pseudo-Histories, as well as providing corroborative detail for this book. For those who wish to follow the Grail cycle, the reader is directed to read the works of John Matthews[72,73]: *The Grail, At the Table of the Grail*, and *The Grail Seeker's Companion* (John Matthews and Marian Green, Aquarian, 1986).

A word on the method I have adopted for this book. I have treated the texts of the *Mabinogion* with the respect that tradition has distilled within its complex and fragmentary stories. Where a parallel folk tradition of similar proto-Celtic source is extant, I have not hesitated to use it, setting it side by side with the original story for the sake of comparison.

I am not of the school of folklorists who uphold the distribution theory of oral tradition. It is evident that certain folk themes arise spontaneously worldwide but that these are not derivative from each other, in the main. I have drawn extensively from Irish and Scottish Gaelic sources where these are representatives of a long oral tradition. Irish and Welsh mythologies show a marked similarity, especially within the *Mabinogion*: this may indicate extensive borrowing between the traditions or it may show how both stem from a pre- or proto-Celtic source common to the British Isles.

Where stories are fragmentary or when episodes have been muddled or just plain lost, I have resorted to the closest corroborative sources – the *Welsh Triads*[5] and British historical tradition. Such reconstructions as I have attempted are clearly indicated, so the cautious reader need not be afraid of stumbling into academically boggy patches. These reconstructions are in no way definitive; they are put forward as aids to understanding only.

Readers may be astonished that I have similarly employed Classical mythology in some of the comparisons, particularly in relation to the Mabon theme. Since the cult of Mabon was closely associated with the Romano-British Maponus, which was in turn partially derived from the cult of Apollo, these myths lend corroborative detail to an otherwise meagre file of data. However, most of the Mabon argument is derived from native sources, and the Classical themes are given for comparison's sake. The frequently cited, though seldom explained, association of Rhiannon with Epona has also required some Classical back-up in order to prove their closer acquaintance.

Although the *Mabinogion* was transcribed in the Middle Ages, I have taken for granted the fact that it sprang from a venerable oral tradition of storytelling beyond which lay an even more ancient tradition – that of the British Mysteries. The word 'mystery' is currently understood as 'enigma', but although parts of the *Mabinogion* may require a team of Agatha Christies to unravel 'who done it', this is not how I intend the term.

The British Mystery Tradition was in no wise the highly organised and deeply syncretic religion such as flourished in Greece or Alexandria, but a loosely grouped set of principles, organised on a tribal or local basis, and perhaps latterly finding acceptance over a wider area as successive migrations of new tribes swept over the land. The essential symbols and stories which comprise the British Mysteries were never lost, but merely relabelled when tribal religion was later incorporated and synthesised by both druidism and Christianity. These common, archetypal patterns remain stubbornly embedded within the *Mabinogion*. In this way, we can regard the *Mabinogion* as a treasure trove of such Mystery patterns.

Those who have spent their academic years painstakingly brushing the dust of centuries from these stories may be shocked that I have not only taken them down from the shelves but attempted to use them in a practical context. The problem is that I have never cared for museum exhibits. I like to touch, to handle and know what their makers knew. It pains me to see medieval triptychs tucked into gloomy corners, where once they would have glowed with the devotion of the faithful and been windows to heaven. I like to see household gods propped up by the herb-rack among the pots and pans of a real kitchen, not lodged uneasily with other 'cult objects' in a glass case.

I feel the same about these stories, both for their own sakes and because they are the genuine lode-bearing ore of our native quarries. To understand a tradition, one must enter it, I have discovered. After all, Arthur Pendragon did not enter Annwn in order to arduously acquire some antique plate for his castle walls, but to find and wield the symbols which confer sovereignty, in order to become empowered by the ancestors.

Empowerment is a solemn undertaking and not everyone is desirous of the changes its creates. Readers of this book may not want to have the responsibility of inhabiting these Mysteries. To this end, I have allotted the final chapter to a study of the Mysteries of Mabon and Modron as a living Mystery Tradition. There are many hints for those who wish to deepen their understanding of the British Mysteries by practical meditation, but the general reader need not fear for his or her sanity in these pages – such clues are carefully hidden within the commentaries where they can be ignored or passed over as the author's personal aberrancy.

My only wish for the reader is that he or she enjoy the stories with better understanding, and with some warm appreciation for those nameless storytellers who once memorised and told these tales so that we might read them today.

Caitlín Matthews
23 February 1986

ACKNOWLEDGMENTS

The author acknowledges a great indebtedness to all those scholars who have spent lifetimes studying original texts and without whose translations this book could not have been written.

Especial thanks and love to John Matthews who supplied additional material from his own field of study – the Arthurian corpus – over which body long and heated discussions have raged. It was due to the *Mabinogion* that we met in the first place, and it seems appropriate to acknowledge its power in the shaping of our lives, for without it we might now be pursuing separate careers of engulfing boredom.

To Gareth Knight, Bob Stewart, Wolfe van Brussel and the by now fabled Company of Hawkwood who helped bring Mabon back from the Underworld and who are as worthy and fitting companions as any who entertained the Noble Head: grateful thanks for help, encouragement and assistance. May the Birds of Rhiannon escort you to the Otherworld in harmonious melody at the conclusion of your story.

To Kathleen Herbert, deepest thanks for her translation of the extract on p.162 from the *Gesta Regnum Brittaniae*; this helped anchor one of the crucial arguments of the book. Needless to say, any inherent faults in this argument are not to be laid at her door, but at mine.

Finally, to Chesca Potter, grateful thanks for working with me so closely on the illustrations: she divined exactly what the book needed despite my rather sketchy instructions.

HOW TO USE THIS BOOK

I have assumed that you have bought this book in order to understand the *Mabinogion* more completely; accordingly, I have attempted to give as much cross-reference to parallel texts, traditions and important themes as possible so that a full range of resources is available. This is a vast topic to explore and the serious student is presented with the same problems which beset the archaeologist who has to excavate an important site before the bulldozers move in, noting different strata, isolated finds and other significant information before the soil covers it once more. Chapters 2-7 are arranged so that the reader can read through the story, note interesting or puzzling features in context and refer more specifically, if he or she requires, to parallel sources. To this end, each of these chapters has a short synopsis of the story in which will be found numbered references relating to the following commentary. The synopsis should not be substituted for a full reading of the text, so it will be necessary to have a copy of your favoured translation of the *Mabinogion* to hand. Within the commentary will be references forward and backward to other stories and major themes. The chapter concludes with a discussion of parallel sources and major thematic archetypes.

This explorative study is intended as a workbook which the reader can use as an adjunct to his or her own reading and research. A full list of texts and other source works appears in the bibliography which is indexed in numerical order and cross-referenced in the text.

A GUIDE TO WELSH PRONUNCIATION

The following is only a rough guide for the non-Welsh-speaker. Welsh is pronounced as it is spelt and is therefore more logical than English. Once the reader is aware of these few rules, the seemingly impossible names of the *Mabinogion's* characters will be quite pronounceable.

The vowels, both short and long, are roughly equivalent to Italian sung vowels, with the exceptions of:

u : i**ll**, or French **tu** e.g. Cu'lhwch = Kilhooch
w : l**oo**k e.g. Gw'ri = Gooree
y : p**i**n e.g. Glyn Cuch = Glin Cich
y : also pronounced as in b**u**t e.g. Yspadda'den = Uspathaden

Diphthongs are logically pronounced:

wy : e.g. Pwyll = Pooihl
aw : **ou**t e.g. Llaw = Hlou
oe : b**oi**l e.g. Goe'win = Goywin

Consonants are as in English with the following exceptions:

c : **c**ake e.g. Caer = Kyer
ch : as in Scottish lo**ch**, German Ba**ch** e.g. Gwa'l**ch**mai = Gwalchmy
dd : **th**ere e.g. Llu**dd** = Hlith
f : **v**et e.g. E**f**nı'ssien = Evnissien
ff : **f**at e.g. Fflur = Fler
g = hard g as in **g**et e.g. Ge'reint = Gerynt
ll = hl (raise blade of the tongue to the roof of the mouth, behind tooth-ridge and aspirate huh – this roughly approximates the sound) e.g. Llew Llaw Gyffes = Hlew Hlou Guffes
rh = hr e.g. Rhia'nnon = Hriannon

r is trilled
th = thin e.g. Twrch Trwyth = Toorch Trooeeth

The stress comes on the penultimate syllable of a multi-syllabic word

Wales and the Mabinogion

CHAPTER 1
The Realm of the
Mabinogion

Merlin's Enclosure

For the Welsh to distinguish between myth and history has
always been a difficult exercise.

EMYR HUMPHRIES

Still lives on the ancient speech,
Still the ancient songs endure.

JOHN CEIRIOG HUGHES

1 THE WELSH STORYTELLING TRADITION

It is summer 1983, Caernarvon Castle, North Wales. Within
the castle grounds the timeless stories which form the Four

Branches of the *Mabinogion* are being presented by a bilingual team of actors, musicians and storytellers.[135] They are but the most recent in a long line of storytellers who have helped transmit the *Mabinogion*, from oral and written tradition, into the imagination of new generations. The audience go home in possession of a few fragments of a once mighty Mystery Tradition in which men and women encounter the gods, where animals talk, leaves become gold and where the dead revive. A few may try to read the *Mabinogion* for themselves, puzzled, intrigued and excited by the elusive hints which seem to dodge behind the main story just when revelation seems near. Many readers experience the same mixed emotions.

In order to untangle the complexity of the *Mabinogion* it is necessary to understand that its stories arise directly from a lively oral tradition which, though it has parallels with the European chivalric cycles, ultimately derives from the folk traditions and mystery lore of Britain. It is the descendant of a venerable bardic tradition in which stories, poems, history and ancestral lore were preserved in a professional, though unwritten, manner. We know from Classical and Celtic sources that druids, poets and storytellers taught their skills orally: they were never written down although different forms of writing were in fact available.[71]

Why trouble to memorise the equivalent of a small library at all, it may be asked? To understand this we must realise that one's *word* was one's honour, that it still had the currency of authority, that learned and unlearned alike were equal under its wisdom. The oral education of Celtic society included all levels of learning: legal, genealogical, historical, prophetic and religious – facets which are reflected in the *Mabinogion* itself and which put it outside modern categories of literature. But where once the druidic class had preserved the spiritual mysteries, in Christian times the ancient lore became the preserve of the poet and storyteller – a tradition which was preserved freshly in many memories but which, as time wore on, began to lose touch with its roots. This is how we can distinguish traces of older belief within the stories which have come down to us.

The poet and storyteller who once shared professional status with the druid-kind (a class itself deriving from ancient shamanic tradition, cf. Matthews[71]), and who preserved the old stories, slipped ever further apart. The poet *(pencerdd)* is represented in the *Dream of Rhonabwy* as chanting a eulogy which only another poet could understand: poetry had become technically arduous, its subtleties lost on the listener. Noblemen retained such poets in their households well on into late medieval times in Wales, to eulogise their family and achievements, to relate the complex genealogies by which the poet's lord might trace his bloodline to legendary kings. A *pencerdd* might not sing for common men: his fee was a high one, entitling him to honour and position. It is bards such as these – with an eye to the moneybags rather than their craft – that Taliesin satirises so cruelly: 'they sing vain and evanescent song'.[2]

For ordinary mortals, a *teuluwr* or household poet might suffice, a bard who might sing in the lower hall, while his superior, the *pencerdd*, was singing in the upper hall to his lord and lady. Less honoured even than they, the *clerwr* or wandering minstrel was musician and storyteller to outlying homesteads: he is like the poor scholar in *Manawyddan, Son of Llyr*, who comes from Lloegr, having begged his way: 'I come from England, Lord, from song making', but whose fees amount to a mere pound.

The *cyfarwydd* or storyteller may not have retained the status of the *pencerdd*, yet he never lost his popularity, for his stories were always accessible to his listeners. Like the Irish *seanchai*, the *cyfarwydd* had a store of stories which were handed down from master to pupil orally. Through such an oral tradition, we receive the *Mabinogion* – a collection of stories which had been current for centuries before they came to be written down. Although each story has been given emphases by different storytellers, the results are often remarkably consistent: as the scattered manuscripts from which the diplomatic edition of the *Mabinogion* is derived will tell. Interestingly, errors crept into the stories when copyists lost interest in their weary task. From one such error the word 'mabinogion' is derived (see below).

Set against the formalism of court poetry, the mutations of the stories give a lively variety and colloquialism to an ancient oral tradition. Just as in the Welsh language where initial consonants mutate, where p becomes b, mh or even ph, so the stories of the *Mabinogion* shine with an iridescence of forgotten tradition, hinting at significant episodes yet simultaneously obscuring them. It is true that we have inherited a pied tradition, from storytellers who had lost many of the inner keys, yet memory may yet recall portions which are lost or hopelessly tangled.

The Welsh Triads, which have been collated from many manuscript sources by Rachel Bromwich,[5] give us a glimpse at the complex syllabus of bardic training and help enlighten many dark places in the *Mabinogion*. The triads are mnemonics for recalling stories, e.g. the Three Fearless Men of the Island of Britain, the Three Fortunate Concealments of the Island of Britain, etc. They are training devices, keys to memory which, unfortunately for us, often merely serve to recall stories which are now lost to us and which tantalisingly hint at a deeper tradition. The *Triads*' terse style is due in part to professional bardic secrecy: the lines of each triad were a symbolic key which evoked the story behind the lines. Their subject matter is reflected in the *Mabinogion*, where some of the stories are told and others hinted at.

'Three things that give amplitude to a poet: knowledge of histories, the poetic art, and old verse', says the *Llyfr Coch* – doubtless a Triad which trainee poets imbided at their first lesson.[5] The nature of many of the *Mabinogion*'s stories is historic, of national importance to the listener, but then the *Triads*

> constituted an index of oral tradition formed for the benefit of those whose professional duty it was to preserve and hand on the stories which embodied the oldest traditions of the Britons about themselves – stories which concerned the national past alike of the people of Wales and of the lost Northern territory which was still remembered in the Middle Ages as a former home of the British race.[66]

Where the storyteller parted company with the poet, the loss of many symbolic keys occurred, the mysteries implicit in the tales become more mysterious because they are further removed from their common source. Of these mysteries we shall speak further.

The *Mabinogion* was formulated and eventually written down between about 1100 and 1250 – the very time in which the main Continental chivalric stories were likewise being recorded. Welsh storytellers were still practising their skills when the Breton *conteurs* were influencing the course of European culture: the *Laïs* of Marie de France, the *minnesinger*-cycles of Germany, the romances of Chrétien de Troyes together with the *Mabinogion* are part of the European troubadour tradition, although we must not forget that the *cyfarwydd* drew on ancient bardic skills whose function was educative not merely entertaining.

A partial text of the *Mabinogion* survives in the *White Book of Rhydderch* (c.1300), while the complete text appears in the *Red Book of Hergest* (c.1400). The *Book of Taliesin* is contained in a seventeenth-century manuscript in the National Museum of Wales, itself a copy of a sixteenth-century manuscript: *Taliesin* is not considered part of the *Mabinogion* collection for reasons which will be discussed in Chapter 7. These given dates do not preclude the stories occurring in earlier copies which are now lost to us, nor their derivation from the oral tradition in the manner described above. The Irish tales which correspond in many particulars to those of the *Mabinogion* began to be written down in about the ninth century. It is not known whether one or more hands were responsible for recording the stories, nor whether this person was a *cyfarwydd*. Certainly the *Mabinogion* may have been written while *cyfarwyddiadd* were actively practising and even relating different versions of the recorded tales.

Storytelling did not cease with the introduction of books. It remains a lively tradition within many Celtic countries where impromptu assemblies of people inevitably conclude in mutual entertainment – stories, songs and music. But at some point, the stories of the *Mabinogion* lapsed partially from memory, at least in the oral tradition. Until the first translation of the *Mabinogion* by Lady Charlotte Guest in the nineteenth century, even few Welsh people knew of its existence, although characters from the stories – Gwydion, Math, Arianrhod, Blodeuwedd and Arthur – were remembered as individuals, and recorded in poetry as examples of magicians, false wives and famous kings. Inevitably, perhaps, memories grew shorter and

tales grew more and more embellished with inessential detail.
Notably, in the *Dream of Rhonabwy* the writer concludes:

> this is the reason that no one knows the dream without a
> book, neither bard nor gifted seer (*cyfarwydd*): because of
> the various colours that were upon the horses, and the
> many wondrous colours of the arms ... the panoply ...
> the precious scarfs, and of the virtue-bearing stones.[4]

Lady Charlotte Guest's translation of the *Mabinogion*
appeared in 1849 – in W.J. Gruffydd's opinion, mostly the
work of two scholars, Rev. John Jones and Rev. Thomas Price
who 'devilled' for her.[46] It is to her that we owe the title of
'Mabinogion', which is a misnomer. Lady Guest concluded that
'*mabinogi*' (the Four Branches were called *Pedeir Keinc y
Mabinogi*) was a noun meaning 'a story for children'.
'Mabinogion' appears once in *Pwyll* as a copyist's error; it is
not a real word. However, although purists may complain, the
title *Mabinogion* is retained in this book as a matter of
convenience: it is intended to include the full collection of
stories, both the Four Branches and other tales, including
Taliesin.

Mabinogi is more likely to parallel the Irish series of stories
known as *macgnimartha* – the youthful or boyhood deeds of
the hero. A fourteenth-century translation of an apocryphal
gospel into Welsh, *De Infantia Jesu Christi*, was rendered as
Mabinogi Iesu Grist.[25] Lady Charlotte's explanation of the
term puts these tales in the same category as children's fairy
stories – a far remove from their original purpose.

There is still much scholarly argument over the true meaning
of the title, but we do not miss the mark if we consider the
stories as part and parcel of the Celtic genres of story which
have an authenticated history in Irish tradition: the stories of
the conception, birth, adventures, cattle raids, elopements,
courtships and deaths of heroes.[87]

Many more translations of the stories have appeared since
Lady Charlotte's attempt: a list of these can be found in the
bibliography. Throughout this book, different editions and
translations have been quoted.

2 THE NAME OF THE LAND

The *Mabinogion* is such an essentially Welsh cultural product that few consider it as a source for British mythology. In most minds, Wales is virtually a foreign country with an alien, offputting language. In Welsh minds, Wales is a portion and only remaining outpost of the Island of the Mighty, *Ynys Prydein*, the Island of Britain. Names are important in oral tradition, and the name of the land of paramount importance. A fleeting glimpse at the early history of Wales will show even the most chauvinistic Englishman the rights of the matter. Wales is not an alien land generously taken under English patronage, but a kingdom whose legendary rulers once held sway over what is now English soil. Celtic chauvinism aside, the matter of sovereignty remains of prime importance.

We say that when a monarch reigns wisely that he or she has the sovereignty of the land: this has come to mean that the monarch rules according to the laws which he or she imposes (French: *sovrain*). However, behind this notion is the personification of the land by a mythical female figure, from whom the monarch holds the land by right of his union with her, by his championship of her freedoms and privileges which he lawfully assumes. Land and king must be in harmony, as husband and wife. (A female monarch embodies and personifies the figure of Sovereignty in her own person: the prince-consort polarises and champions her power, but does not wield it himself.)

Throughout Celtic literature, we read of many encounters with the figure of Sovereignty. She is alternatively beautiful or hideous, demands the achievement of arduous feats of endurance and eventually gives herself only to the most worthy.[70] Throughout the *Mabinogion*, she is hinted at: in *Peredur* as the Empress of Constantinople, in *The Lady of the Fountain*, she is Owain's countess, in *Gereint*, she is the lady of the paradisal but deadly garden. Sovereignty is plainly represented by Elen in *Maxen Wledig's Dream*: she is also visible in the figures of Rhiannon, Branwen and Goewin within the Four Branches. These stories will be dealt with in the proper place, but they reveal one of the underlying themes of the *Mabinogion*: the Lady who personifies the land itself, who suffers when it is raped, the one whose favours are sought as fervently as the Grail.

The Romans, who understood the importance and recognition of the *genia locus*, named Britannia as the titulary spirit of Britain, giving her the attributes of Minerva, the spear and shield. Caesar, following Pliny's hint, called these islands Britain, after the tribe of the Pretani, but this is one of many names.

Each country has its inner landscape, its inner name and lady of the land. The British Isles have been through a succession of names. The *Mabinogion* and the *Triads* speak of the Island of the Mighty, *Ynys Prydein*: it has been called Great Britain, not for reasons of imperial grandeur, but to distinguish it from the Lesser Britain, Brittany, which was colonised by the British in the early centuries AD, and with whom the Welsh still share a common bond of blood and language. Today, the island is called the United Kingdom, meaninglessly, or just UK. Somewhere within these titles lie many others, hidden, forgotten – names which are applied only in a poetic way now, but which have their own magic for all this.

> The first name that this Island bore, before it was taken or settled: Myrddin's Precinct (*Clas Merdin*). And after it was taken and settled, the Island of Honey. And after it was conquered by Prydein, son of Aedd the Great, it was called the Island of Prydein

say the *Triads*.[5] This title, *Clas Merdin*, or Merlin's Enclosure, is linked with the Lady of the Land, Sovereignty, whom Kipling describes thus:

> She is not any common Earth,
> Water or Wood or Air,
> But Merlin's Isle of Gramarye,
> Where you and I will fare.[119]

Gramarye is the old form of 'Grammar', meaning magical lore, of which these tales of *Ynys Prydein* are redolent. Merlin makes no appearance in the *Mabinogion*, but there is no lack of enchanters to guard the land and reshape its destiny: Gwydion, Math and the Otherworld kings who sleep fitfully beneath the land. One of these giants, Albion, also gave his name to the land; William Blake breathed new life into the titanic form of Albion in his prophetic poems.[16]

Geoffrey of Monmouth tells us that Brutus, the mythical Trojan leader and ancestor of the British race, had three sons – Locrinus, Kamber and Albanactus – among whom his kingdom was divided. Their names remain the inner names of England, Wales and Scotland: Loegres, Cambria and Alban. Cambria and Alban have all but fallen out of use, but Loegres – Lloegr – is still the Welsh title for England,[37] and of course is the name of England within the medieval Arthurian legends.

Every country has its inner resonance, a name which hints at a mythological hinterland where the ancestral values of tribe and familial cohesion are upheld, despite shifting boundaries and new appellations. C.S. Lewis's book, *That Hideous Strength*, is about this very antipathy of old and new identities:

> There has been a secret Logres in the very heart of Britain all these years; an unbroken succession of Pendragons . . . some of the Pendragons are well known to history, though not under that name. . . . But in every age they and the little Logres which gathered round them have been the fingers which gave the tiny shove or the almost impercept- ible pull, to prod England out of the drunken sleep or to draw her back from the final outrage into which Britain tempted her.[120]

For every separate kingdom which forms the United Kingdom, there is an inner home into which its people yearn longingly to enter. This is not a book dedicated to the reestablishment of Celtic autonomy, but one which deals with the mythological patterns which underlie the *Mabinogion*. Beneath the tribal squabbling which even yet breaks out into terrorism, the land awaits a Pendragon – one who can wield the spirit of the people and tame the dragonish outbreaks of violent faction. Within Merlin's Enclosure numerous tribes are now sheltered: aboriginal British, Roman, Saxon, Norman, European, Asiatic, African and many others, each newcomer bringing his or her native values and customs. Each is welcomed on his or her acceptance by the land, by personal willingness and acceptance of the rules which govern Merlin's

Enclosure – rules which can be garnered by a close study of the underlying stories of *Ynys Prydein*, exemplified most clearly in the rule of the Pendragon, King Arthur – pattern of kings and kingly rule.

Not the Britain of factional division, not the submission of one kingdom to another, but the inner kingdoms of *Ynys Prydein* reveal to us the truth that every court is potentially Camelot, every leader a Pendragon, every subject a knight or lady within *Clas Merdin*. This book presents two challenges: the calling of the Pendragon, and the Naming of the Land with the name of the Mother, the Goddess of Sovereignty. Before these tasks can be undertaken, the reader must be able to distinguish between levels of reality, to travel the landscape of the *Mabinogion* without confusion. To do this we must define the boundaries clearly.

3   REAL WORLD: OTHERWORLD

A country is never composed of a single people, living at one time, with one purpose: it is a stratified society, informed by different levels of time, purpose and inner resonance. The *Mabinogion* is no different: its main characters live within the real world, but they are motivated by internal conflict and personal encounter with Otherworld energies. As in our own society, the birth of the real world from the Otherworld is not complete in these stories: the umbilical cord is still attached – it is possible to travel between the worlds and for the status of one world to affect another. A two-way traffic is possible. Later on in this book some practical methods of encountering the Otherworld are given; these follow the paths which are utilised by the *Mabinogion*'s heroes and heroines, and which correspond to authentic travel-routes utilised in Western esoteric technique.

A detailed analysis of the Celtic Otherworlds is given in both *Western Way vol. 1*[71] and in R.J. Stewart's *The Underworld Initiation*,[98] but for the benefit of the new reader this definition must suffice. The Otherworld is the internal resonance of the everyday world: it exists out of time, simultaneously cross-intersecting *all* time and is thus accessible to visitation from any point of linear time. Within the Otherworld, archetypal forces are perceptible, essential wisdom teachings are available to those who have the correct keys; it is the realm of quest and achievement, of challenge and encounter, of initiation and enlightenment. It is *not* illusory, a figment of imagination or an anthropological invention. It is *not* heaven, hell or analogous to any drug-induced vision. The Otherworld is the mythological reality or symbolic continuum within which we can encounter the archetypal energies of the gods and their acts.

The Otherworld has its own valid reality which is not accessible to the five senses, though it is appreciable by the sixth. It is often spoken of as a state of consciousness, though this is itself an unclear definition, implying a merely psychological foundation for its existence. The Otherworld exists in its own right, is consistent to its own rules and as a visitable reality is not merely confined to the specially psychic people. The incredulous reader who is unwilling to attempt the paths personally may accept the reality of the Otherworld as a fictive one, but will have to come to terms with it on some level since the majority of the stories within the *Mabinogion* weave between the worlds, often within the same sentence.

In the First Branch of the *Mabinogion* Pwyll, prince of Dyfed, sits on the mount of Arberth – renowned magical place, and a distinct gateway to the Otherworld – and his ordinary life starts to assimilate Otherworldly elements very rapidly. In the Second Branch, Bran accepts an Otherworldly cauldron which causes untold trouble. In *Peredur*, the hero ignores the rules of the Otherworld and so prolongs his quest for years. Culhwch can gain his bride only by the achievement of thirty-nine impossible tasks, which lead him and his companions through every level of the Otherworld. These and other examples will be discussed in their proper place.

It is clear that to ignore the Otherworld is to blur the definition of the *Mabinogion* totally. The stories may often be garbled in places, but the *cyfarwydd* is not inventing the magical episodes for the amusement of his audience; he is repeating lore which was commonly understood and accepted. Not one of his listeners would have dared sit on the mound of Arberth at night themselves, for fear of the *Tylwyth Teg* – the household folk or faeries. Titans, giants, faeries, lake-women, magical beasts, the

Mamau – or triplicity of Mothers – were known as inhabitants of the Otherworld and likewise feared and respected. The elder gods were close at the time of half-light; they were associated with certain special landmarks which denoted the entrance to their realm. They lived on in folk memory, often diminishing in stature, but still portents of a larger world which was near at hand. The Otherworld was inseparable from Celtic consciousness, existing as a borderland 'like boundaries between years and between seasons . . . lines along which the supernatural intrudes through the surface of existence'.[87]

And yet, at the same time, one cannot but be aware of the real world within the *Mabinogion*. Many of the stories are onomastic, i.e. they are stories which name places. In *Math*, Gwydion shelters his stolen swine at Mochtref and Mochnant (*moch*=pig) and the Llyn y Morynion (the Lake of Maidens) is where Blodeuwedd's companions drown themselves. In *Branwen*, Tal Ebolion is the place where Bran pays compensation to Matholwch, king of Ireland, for the mutilation of his horses (*ebol*=colt). The Irish *Dindshenchas* give similar lists of stories which have given names to places.

Although Cornwall, London, Kent, France, Ireland and Oxford are mentioned, the scenes, when they do not stray into the Otherworld, are firmly set in Wales. *Pwyll* and *Manawyddan* are set in South Wales, in Dyfed, while the stories of *Branwen* and *Math* are set in North Wales. (The map on p.xviii shows the action of the stories.)

It is foolish to attempt any exact dating of these stories to any particular era since they happen out of time, not within it. The stories themselves are dressed in clothes contemporary to early medieval Wales, but stray garments are clearly of an early date. Pagan and Christian customs overlay each other, as when in the Fourth Branch the spear which is destined to kill Llew can only be forged on Sunday when mass is being said: yet Llew's threefold death is of a much earlier derivation, and related to the pagan kingly-sacrifice. In the pseudo-histories, historical characters like Magnus Maximus appear, while a whole mixed bag of mythical, magical, fantastic and heroic characters can be found in *Culhwch and Olwen*. Harness and armour owe nothing to medieval chivalry, yet neither are they those of Celtic times.

The values of the Celtic world are still discernible: honour, family pride, the laws of hospitality, the custom of fosterage and tribal obligation are foremost in the realm of the *Mabinogion*. These were the currency of everyday life, laws and customs which survived the early British era and which co-existed fitfully beside those of Norman England which sought to superimpose its weight on immemorial Welsh dignity.

Scholars can evidence internal clues and instance references to different Welsh noble houses existent at the time the *Mabinogion* was written down, but this is not of paramount importance to the general reader. The *Mabinogion* has won its own immortality among the stars. The Milky Way is known in Welsh as Caer Gwydion. The constellation of Casseopeia is Llys Don – the Home of Don, mother of Gwydion and the rest of that turbulent family. The Corona Borealis is Caer Arianrhod whose secret citadel is the tower of initiation. Ruler of the heavens and indicator of our true north is Arthur's Wain, or the Great Bear. And, because no king can travel without his poet, Lyra is the Harp of Arthur, Telyn Arthur. Taliesin, the supreme seer-poet, has his dwelling in 'the region of the Summer Stars'.[6]

The realm of the *Mabinogion* is a vast one, spanning real world, Otherworld and overworld. Its stories can likewise be enjoyed on many levels: as folktale, mythology, inner history and, not least, as mystery drama.

4 THE MYSTERIES OF BRITAIN

The question must be asked: how far do the stories of the *Mabinogion* reflect the Mysteries of Britain? By mysteries we mean core-stories which act as personal or cosmic transformers, such as are utilised in the Christian Mysteries, and which helped initiate candidates into the mysteries of Eleusis, Mithras, Cybele and Isis. It is clear that many such traditions can be found in the *Mabinogion* in partial form: the Grail quest, the possession of the sacred head or of the cauldron are all related themes which spill over both into the Matter of Britain cycle and into the esoteric heart of Christianity. Present too is the loss and finding of the Puer Eternus, the Wondrous Youth,

Mabon – a quest which is analogous in effect to the search by Demeter for Persephone in the Classical myth. The descent to the Underworld, or Otherworldly journey which many of the heroes make, is paralleled by the personally transformative journey which the shamanic poet or initiate takes. This intercourse of ancestral and mythic levels with the outer world is more clearly delineated and understood in the *Mabinogion* than it is in our own times, where the spiritual quest is more often squeezed into rigid religious moulds and where the individual's search for meaning and inner refreshment is a cause for embarrassment or ill-natured mockery.

Initiation into the mysteries of any system involves meeting its great archetypes face to face in the reality of the Otherworld. Within the *Mabinogion* this challenge often occurs in the course of a chess game, in the combat of opponents or through the aid of Otherworldly, totemic beasts – all methods by which initiation is effected (cf. Chapter 8).

In considering British mysteries we are looking squarely at a druidic tradition which has been effaced by a diametrically different creed and set of training techniques: certain original elements can be glimpsed embedded in the river of tradition, but mostly the stream is a muddy one. It is not necessary to examine the pseudo-rites of revival druidic sects because these have little or nothing to do with the Mystery Tradition which is under discussion here. Druidic revival was something of an antiquarian pastime whereby authentic genealogical and textual lore was 'worked-up', with the aid of inspired archaeology and comparative religion into nothing approaching the real thing, from the seventeenth century onwards. Its exponents merely cobbled together sundry pieces of druidic driftwood in order to make coracles which would not float. One of these, Iolo Morgannwg (Edward Williams, 1747-1826), was personally responsible for inventing or reinventing much of what passes for druidism today, thus presenting all manner of headaches:

> Since he knew more about Welsh classical literature than any man alive, he could do this with impunity, and over the years he invented so many medieval poems that the chief task of Welsh literary scholarship in the twentieth century has been the disentangling of Iolo's forgeries from the real thing.[74]

It is better to stick to the texts themselves, however mismatched, than to attempt such well-meant pastiche. It is possible to get inextricably entangled in the lost tribes of Israel, druidic fable and Biblical aphorism – a substance as sticky and indigestible as Welsh toffee. The stories of the *Mabinogion* themselves provide a sustaining diet with all the necessary vitamins, if properly chewed, without the need of pseudo-druidic speculation.

If druids cannot help us, perhaps their fellows, the poets and storytellers, can. Originally the professional classes shared a high standard of oral education, specialising in different subjects, yet fellow-initiates of the inner corpus of mystery teachings. The druids were *the* specialists, but their teaching did not come down in written sources. Poets learned the complex metres, rhythms and stanza forms and thus formalised some facets of the mystery teachings, as we can still perceive in Taliesin's poetry – himself the arch-poet, initiate and Son of the Cauldron. Storytellers received a less formal training but dealt with the subject-matter of the mysteries, just as Homer and other Greek poets made the Gods immortal to later generations. Finally it was not the praise-songs of the poets which gave us the insight we need, but the storyteller's skill.

> The old Welsh word for 'story', *cyfarwyddyd*, means 'guidance', 'direction', 'instruction', 'knowledge', 'skill', 'prescription'. Its stem, *arwydd*, means 'sign', 'symbol', 'manifestation', 'omen', 'miracle', and derives from a root meaning 'to see'. The storyteller (*cyfarwydd*) was originally a seer and a teacher who guided the souls of his hearers through the world of 'mystery'.[87]

The storyteller was an initiator then – albeit unknowingly as, with the poet, he became the sole guardian of the mystery teachings when the druidic role was taken over by the priest and monk. The stories of the *Mabinogion* had power to communicate the underlying mysteries to all listeners, whether these were a family gathered about a fireside to hear a wonder-tale at the end of the day or a group of initiates visualising the scenes described by their leader. By the time the *Mabinogion* was written down, these teachings were already being forgotten, or were obscure to their tellers who substituted more plausible explanations or tied a similar pair of stories together for the sake of effect.

The storyteller's skill is quite a remarkable one: in the mind's eye, scenes come to life with vivid detail – and here lies one of the secrets of traditional transmission: inner knowledge of the mysteries does not come down by means of written sources, but by means of symbols, images and music. The reader can test this personally. Quite often, when listening to a lecture or story on the radio, a series of profoundly moving images will flash into the consciousness of the hearer – these may seem unrelated, at least on the surface, to the material heard; yet, if the listener meditates upon these deeply-rooted images, a series of realisations will connect him or her to the true source of the material, recreating it in an original way. In a sense such moments of vision are gateways to the Otherworld.

In this way, singers, storytellers and other performers work from the subtext of their song or script: their conscious minds recalling the words and music, their deep minds communing with the rhythms, images and symbols which are the lode-bearing ore of their artistic quarry. Thus, similarly awakening images, rhythms and symbols are set up in the minds of listeners – in this way, the performing arts are truly initiatory. However, no such transmission is possible if the performer is merely performing by rote, without communion with the sources and key-images of his or her script. All audiences know this and register disquiet or boredom.

The symbolic keys of the *Triads* and certain key passages within the *Mabinogion* work in the same way: they unlock doors to the Otherworld and allow the reader to enter in search of mystery-knowledge. One literally *enters the story*, achieving a unique perspective. This method of mystery teaching is irrefutably authentic: great teachers such as Christ, Buddha and Plato have taught by parable and analogous story. The Classical mystery schools enacted their core-stories, involving both initiates and candidates for initiation. This is why revival mystery rituals do not work: they do not evoke the frisson of creative response because they are not authentically part of the tradition.

The Mysteries of Britain were not uniformly the same from north to south nor from east to west. Names, cults and stories were localised in a tribal way. Linking them together was a common understanding of certain key stories and symbolic tokens: these represented a formalisation of Otherworldly archetypes which could be universally understood among many different peoples. One such story underlies the texts of the *Mabinogion*: it has been called the Lost Fifth Branch, but in actual fact it is rather more like the tap-root of a mighty tree of traditional stories. It is the story or Mystery of Mabon and Modron, wherein Mabon is stolen 'from his mother and the wall' when he is scarcely three nights old. We can read, in *Culhwch and Olwen* how Arthur and his men search for, find and liberate him from his prison, so that he is enabled to find the hidden treasures of Annwn.

The story of the lost child and the sorrowing mother is not merely a nationalistic story, but a universal theme cross-tracking both mythology and religion of all countries and times. The Mysteries of Mabon and Modron are proper to the British Isles, just as the Mysteries of Demeter and Kore are proper to Greece: both happen out of time, in the ever-present reality of the Otherworld. These mysteries have their own exponents and symbolic keys which we will begin to perceive.

As we rehearse the stories of the Four Branches, of *Culhwch* and *Taliesin*, we become aware that a subtle pattern of correspondences will unfold. If we read skilfully and imaginatively, we will begin to uncover the hidden story of Mabon and Modron from among a welter of other tales. And although we can draw on close Celtic parallels, the best evidence for our discovery is to be found within the *Mabinogion* itself.

Mabon and Modron – these names are not personal appellations, but merely titles: they mean 'Son' and 'Mother'. This alerts us to the fact that their mysteries are very ancient, since the absence of a personal name indicates their association with Otherworld archetypes. Some characters within the *Mabinogion* wear these archetypal masks over their own personae so that the empty titles become inspirited with a new life. If we look out for the signs, we can spot the exponents of Mabon: a boy who is lost after birth or who is hidden away to be raised in secret – like Pryderi, in the First Branch, like Llew in the Fourth Branch or like Goreu in *Culhwch*. We can perceive the mask of Modron worn over many features: a woman who loses her child or who has to hide him from danger – like Rhiannon in the First Branch, like the nameless wife of Custennin in *Culhwch*. These are a few examples of how the Mysteries of Mabon and Modron are manifested.

Always we must be sensitive to the way each character interacts with its totemic beast. The association of people with archetypal animals points to an interaction of this world with the Otherworld. One of the important symbolic keys to finding and releasing Mabon is the Initiation of the Totems (cf. Chapter 8), by which his liberators descend the tree of tradition with the help of totemic animals, each of whom stands as guardian to a cyclic age, back to the beginning of the world where Mabon is imprisoned.

As the Mysteries of Mabon and Modron unfold we will begin to be aware of another pattern overlaying it: this pattern is revealed in the Succession of the Pendragons through which many of the Mysteries of Britain are channelled. This central core of our native tradition can be seen manifested through a set of Inner Guardians whose duty is to watch over the mythic or Otherworldly life of the country. The duration of this guardianship varies, but when one guardian steps down, another takes his or her place, the former guardian succeeding to a new and different role.

There is a threefold pattern to this Succession, deriving from inner stories which motivate our cultural heritage: although the *Mabinogion* has been used as a source for these guardians in this book, the pattern utilised here is not the only one which is in operation. The threefold male pattern is as follows:

(a) Mabon – the Wondrous Youth, the Pendragon's Champion, who succeeds to the place of
(b) Pendragon – the King or Poet, the arbiter and ruler, who succeeds to the place of
(c) Pen Annwn – Lord of the Underworld, the judge and sage, who succeeds to the place of
(a) Mabon . . . etc.

The threefold female pattern is discussed in Chapter 9, but corresponds to the male pattern and is polarised fully with it.

It is possible to see many of the *Mabinogion*'s protagonists in these three roles. In the place of Mabon, for example, can be set Pryderi, Goreu and Gwion; in the place of Pendragon stand Arthur, Math and Taliesin; in the place of Pen Annwn stand Pwyll, Bran and Yspaddaden Pencawr. In turn, each role succeeds to the next in the guardianship of the Mysteries. This pattern will become clearer as the stories unfold.

Mabon is everywhere and nowhere, a dream of the child Merlin, an echo of Apollo's lyre, a cry within a prison wall: Modron is visible and invisible, as woman and land, as giver of life and receiver of the dead, as Persephone the abducted and Persephone Queen of the Underworld. *Whoever enters their story shares their story,* becomes Orpheus to Eurydice, Demeter and Persephone, companion to Mabon, child to Modron: they leave it singing, singing. . . .

Mysteries are mighty stories and we are mortal-stock seeking for immortality: our initiation into the *Mabinogion* recreates these stories afresh. It cannot be told – not for lack of words – but because the real mystery must be experienced personally.

And now the First Branch is about to begin; the *cyfarwydd* is seated; the audience settles quietly to listen and share and enter the story of the boy who was lost and found, and of his mother's pain. . . .

CHAPTER 2
Pwyll, Prince of Dyfed

Rhiannon

Ride a cock horse to Banbury Cross
To see a fine lady upon a white horse;
Rings on her fingers and bells on her toes,
She shall have music wherever she goes.
                              ANON. nursery rhyme

And the penance that was imposed upon her was ... that
she should relate the story to all who should come there.
                              PWYLL, PRINCE OF DYFED

1 THE HEAD OF ANNWN

This First Branch is about Pwyll; his Otherworldly wife, Rhiannon; and their child, Pryderi, whose birth is 'literally haunted by all manner of magical mixing-up'.[86] Within it lie some of the most ancient and important themes which link it to the core story of Mabon and Modron who, we will see, are here present in the persons of Pryderi and Rhiannon. The action of the story shifts between the real world and the Otherworld continually: it is this very interaction which gives the story pace and interest. If Pwyll had never gone hunting in Glyn Cuch nor sat on the Mound of Arberth, the Four Branches of the *Mabinogion* would never have sprouted from the British Tree of Tradition. We would be unable to account for the nature of Mabon's imprisonment and Modron's sorrowful captivity, and quite ignorant of the flavour of pork! Fortunately, both in the realm of the *Mabinogion* and in real life, there are those daring explorers who venture into uncharted worlds in order to make our own world a richer, more exciting place.

*1   Pwyll, Prince of Dyfed, went hunting in Glyn Cuch where he encountered a rival hunting party which set on a stag and bore it down. Driving off the other hounds, he set his own dogs on the quarry. 2   A grey-clad huntsman arrived, rebuked him for discourtesy, and threatened to satirise Pwyll. He was Arawn, king of Annwn. Pwyll could make amends by fighting with Arawn's enemy, 3   Hafgan, who was likewise a king in Annwn. To effect this, Pwyll and Arawn had to exchange places, each taking the semblance of the other. At the end of a year and a day, Pwyll had to fight Hafgan, giving him but a single blow.

4   Having changed places, Pwyll went to Annwn where he was welcomed by the court as Arawn himself. He slept beside Arawn's wife, but never attempted to touch her. 5   He fought Hafgan at the appointed time and refused him a second blow. Having defeated Arawn's enemies, Pwyll received the homage of the lords of Annwn, on Arawn's behalf. 6   Pwyll and Arawn exchanged places once more. Arawn found his country well governed and made love to his

* The commentary follows on p.23.

wife, who received his unaccustomed embraces with surprise. Pwyll returned home to find none had missed him. He and Arawn remained firm friends and, because of the substitution 7   , and because Pwyll has been successful in uniting the two kingdoms, Pwyll was henceforth known as the Head of Annwn.

8   While residing at his chief court, Arberth, Pwyll decided to sit on the Mound of Arberth; whoever does so will either be wounded or experience a wonder. 9   Pwyll saw a woman on a white horse pass by. On three occasions he sent men after her, but none of their horses was quick enough. Finally, Pwyll mounted his horse and gave chase; however fast he went, she was quicker. At length he asked her to stop. 10   The woman revealed that she was Rhiannon, daughter of Hefaidd Hen. She had been promised to a man against her will, when all the while she loved Pwyll. He arranged to come to her father's hall a year and a day hence.

11   With a hundred companions, Pwyll came to the feast of Hefaidd's Hall. A suppliant came in and Pwyll promised to grant whatever was in his power to give. Rhiannon was displeased with this answer since the man, Gwawl, son of Clud, was her former betrothed: he asked for her and for the feast. Since Rhiannon had given the feast for the men of Dyfed, it was not in Pwyll's power to give it away. 12   Rhiannon gave Pwyll a bag and arranged a year and a day's delay before she could be given to Gwawl.

At the appointed time, the feast was given, with Gwawl as guest of honour. In came Pwyll, at Rhiannon's prior instruction, dressed as a suppliant. He asked a boon which Gwawl promised to grant, if it was reasonable. Pwyll asked that the bag be filled with food. The bag was stuffed with food, but was seemingly still no fuller than before. Pwyll told Gwawl that only a noble could ensure its fulness by placing both feet in the bag and saying that it had had enough. Gwawl complied and at a hornblast from Pwyll, the men of Dyfed came in, fastened the bag and each proceeded to strike it – 13   a game which is called Badger in the Bag. 14   Hefaidd objected to this treatment. Rhiannon ensured that Gwawl would extract no vengeance. 15   Rhiannon and Pwyll slept together at last and returned to Dyfed.

16   They ruled together for three years, but the people began to mutter about Rhiannon's barrenness and charged Pwyll to put her away. A year later, Rhiannon bore a son. The evening of his birth, he disappeared from the chamber and the nurses, in fear of punishment, killed a puppy, smearing Rhiannon's face with its blood and strewed its bones about the floor. 17   She was unjustly accused of eating her child, but Pwyll refused to put her away since she had at last borne a child. Rather than dispute with the women,

Rhiannon accepted her penance: 18 to sit at the mounting block outside the gate for seven years, to tell her story to all comers and to offer to bear them into the hall on her back.

19 In the meantime, in Gwent, Teyrnon Twrf Liant had a mare which yearly bore a foal each May Eve and which regularly disappeared. He stood vigil and cut off a monstrous claw which came through the window to steal the colt. Returning from his pursuit of the monster, he found a baby boy in the stable, wrapped in rich swaddling clothes. 20 He and his wife pretended that the child was their own and called him Gwri Gwallt Euryn. The boy matured unnaturally fast and was so keen to be with the horses that the rescued colt was given to him.

21 Teyrnon heard of Rhiannon's penance and perceived Pwyll's likeness in Gwri. He took Gwri to Arberth where they both refused to be carried into the hall by Rhiannon. Teyrnon told the story of the boy's finding and Rhiannon declared that she was released, at last, from anxiety (*pryder*). Pendaran Dyfed, Pwyll's foster-father, said this would be a fitting name for the boy: Pryderi. 22 Teyrnon was rewarded for his care and Pryderi was sent to be fostered by Pendaran Dyfed. 23 On the death of Pwyll, Pryderi ruled Dyfed, married Cigfa, daughter of Gwynon Gohoyw.

1 The story begins with a hunt: the pursuit of a beast, often a stag, is frequently the prelude to a mortal entering the Otherworld. Although Pwyll seems to trespass across the boundary between the worlds, his presence in Annwn is obviously required by Arawn. Pwyll's foolhardiness gives him no end of trouble: he sets on Arawn's stag, he ventures to sit on the Mound of Arberth, and makes rash promises to Gwawl.

2 The King of the Underworld and his wild hunt are known by many names: as Arawn, he rides over Pembrokeshire; as Gwyn ap Nudd, he hunts between Glamorganshire and the West Country; while, further east, he appears as Herne the Hunter. He is always accompanied by his white hounds, which have the tell-tale red-tipped ears of the Underworld. Annwn is not analogous to a Classical Hades nor to a Christian Hell: it is not a place of purgatorial torment, but an abode of Other-worldly dignity.[98]

'I will satirise you to the value of a hundred stags', threatens Arawn. The standard Celtic retaliation against insult was the exaction of a compensatory fine, called *sarhad*, or honour-

price, in Welsh. The higher the person's rank, the greater the
sarhad: unfortunately for Pwyll, Arawn is a king. Non-payment
of the fine left the injured party in a position which demanded
satisfaction: he could employ the services of a poet to satirise
his offender. Interestingly, Arawn offers this service himself:
the links between poet-kind and the Otherworld were very
strong, and it is not unusual for an Otherworldly being to have
'bird's knowledge', as inspired poetic colloquy was called.
Pwyll is thus severely embarrassed and obligated to Arawn's
future service.

3   Evidently Hafgan cannot be defeated by a fellow king of
Annwn, but only by a mortal: Pwyll is Arawn's destined
champion. Hafgan's name means 'Summer Song': a hint which
enables us to view this Otherworldly combat by means of a
parallel tradition: the Gawaine cycle of stories.[47] In *Sir
Gawaine and Dame Ragnell*, an Otherworld giant called Sir
Gromer Somer Joure (or Lord of Summer's Day) places Arthur
under severe restriction which can only be countered by
Gawaine – who substitutes himself for Arthur in this story.
Hafgan and Gromer have common roots, without doubt; it has
long been established that Gawaine, and the stories associated
with him, stem direction from Irish tradition in that Arthur's
champion is shown to derive directly from Cu Chulainn.[17]
    Further parallels are apparent from a reading of *Sir Gawaine
and the Green Knight*, where the Green Knight can be
beheaded by one blow but his opponent is defeated by the
second blow. Here Pwyll is instructed to give only one blow,
since the second will revive Hafgan (cf. no 5 below).

4   If we look again at *Gawaine and the Green Knight*, it will
be recalled that Sir Bertilak gives hospitality to Gawaine in a
similar way that Arawn leaves his kingdom in Pwyll's charge:
'treat what is mine as your own', is the implied invitation and
trap. As Gawaine is tempted by Lady Bertilak in the Green
Knight story, so Pwyll suffers the blandishments of Arawn's
wife. Pwyll, scrupulous to the letter of his bond, resists sleeping
with Arawn's wife (cf. no. 6 below). In Irish, and probably in
pre-literate British tradition, it was a basic requirement of
hospitality for a guest to share the bed of the woman of the

house. Numerous instances of this occur in the Irish mythological and kingly sagas where the king's privileges extend to a night with every woman in his domain.

5   The combat between Pwyll and Hafgan is paralleled by the combat between Gwyn ap Nudd and Gwythyr ap Greidawl in *Culhwch and Olwen* (cf. p.100) for the hand of Creiddylad – theirs is the eternal combat between summer and winter for the Queen of the Year. In this instance, Pwyll has come to claim Annwn on behalf of Arawn, yet there may be more than this at stake. Throughout his visit to Annwn, Pwyll is not once referred to by name but is called 'the man who was in Arawn's shape' or merely 'he', which makes for confusion when reading this passage. This uncertainty is further reinforced by the statement: 'by noon of the next day the two realms were in his power'.

6   It has been suggested by more than one commentator that Arawn's wife is none other than Rhiannon.[46] Both women wear the same gold brocade gown. This is not so unlikely as it might seem if we consider the subsequent outcome of the story and see it in the wider context of the Otherworldly woman as fay or goddess who loves a champion, yet first wishes to test his worthiness (cf. Chapter 9). The combat of Pwyll and Hafgan, or of the Green Knight and Gawaine, become understandable in this context: further such combats can be inferred from *The Lady of the Fountain* and *Gereint and Enid*. A discussion of Rhiannon as a type of Sovereignty follows.

7   Although he has only acted as champion of Arawn, Pwyll is nevertheless accorded the title of 'Head of Annwn'. We are told that because of his bravery in bringing the two kingdoms together his old name fell out of use, and Pen Annwn is what he is always called afterwards. The two kingdoms are not the two realms of Annwn, but the worlds of Inner and Outer, between which Pwyll acts as a bridge. All of Pwyll and his family's subsequent actions are influenced by this very Otherworld contact. Those who venture into Annwn in order to effect a change there – whether it be a redemptive act like the harrowing of the Underworld by Mabon or Arthur, or whether

it be the sacrificial action of Bran (Chapter 3) – always suffer a substitution: each hero takes on the attributes of his combatant or of the Underworld King. The effect of this action is clearly seen in the Grail knights of later Arthurian legend: both Perceval and Galahad, as Grail-winners, succeed to the role of Grail guardian. This substitution of champions is a clear motif in the Succession of inner Pendragons – those beings who govern the Otherworldly realm which borders the Island of Britain. In this way Clas Merdin, or Merlin's Enclosure, *is* the very tower of his imprisonment – a willing service on another level of existence (see Chapters 3 and 9). Pwyll is Arawn's substitute and his successor, if we read this story right.

8   The Mound of Arberth can be seen from several standpoints: it is a place of assembly for the people of Dyfed, on which only the tribal officials would sit at arbitrate in times of war or festival; a place where judgements were given and disputes resolved. It is, from the evidence of this and the Third Branch, a gateway between the worlds where strange things happen and so has an unchancy reputation. Pwyll's experience is similar to the Highland custom of 'dreuchainn' whereby to foretell whom one would marry, one would climb a hill on which no four-footed beast could climb: the first creature seen on descending would show the nature of one's intended.[100] The Scottish/Scandinavian story of 'the Black Bull of Norroway' is connected to this theme, and the seven-year penance of the heroine (who has to climb a hill of glass in order to gain her husband) is closely paralleled by Rhiannon's story.[24] The Mound is also 'Sovereignty's Chair' – an inaugural mound where kings are installed.

9   The veiled woman on horseback is none other than Rhiannon – an Otherworldly woman whose antecedents are of great antiquity, as we will see shortly. Her connections with Epona, the Celtic horse-goddess; with the Black Demeter of Phygalia; with the king-making rituals of Indo-European culture and with the Irish Macha, make her a compelling archetype whose legends give us the substance of Modron herself.

10   No one is able to catch Rhiannon except Pwyll, and only when he requests her to stop. She has evidently already chosen him as her consort, which reinforces the suggestion that she has already tested him as a suitable champion. Pwyll has proved himself worthy the title of Pen Annwn – a suitable husband for Rhiannon who is from the Underworld herself. Her father Hefiadd the Ancient plays a negligible part in the story.

11   The order of precedence at feasts and assemblies was always scrupulously determined by stewards among the Celts. Pwyll's prowess has been tested once in the Underworld, but this next test he fumbles badly. Rhiannon's former suitor Gwawl ap Clud (Radiance, son of Light) sounds remarkably akin to Hafgan (Summer Song): this whole episode seems like a continuation of Pwyll's combat. The first combat entailed that no second reviving blow was to be given to Hafgan: this second combat shows Pwyll less than prepared – he gives an answer from which a number of severe blows can be inflicted upon himself by Gwawl.

12   Fortunately Rhiannon is wiser than her betrothed. Her bag, like the many cauldrons and wonderworking bags of Celtic legend, has wonders of its own. It may be akin to Epona's plentiful basket which she is shown carrying on her lap in numerous *bas-reliefs*[68], or her manger at which two foals feed. Pwyll here substitutes for Gwawl, entering as a beggar. This is one of the most famous themes in folkstory: the man who disguises himself as a poor harper and sings for his bride in the Underworld. From Orpheus in Classical times, to King Orpheo in Scandinavian/Scottish story, the retrieving of the bride from Hades has played an important part.[26] Here Gwawl falls into the trap and is put under Pwyll's authority. The way he is enticed into the bag is similar to the way Mollie Whuppie in Highland folkstory induces a giant and his family to enter a totally empty bag in which she has previously been trapped by exclaiming 'oh, if you could see the wonders I can see!'[24] As the salient feature of the Mound of Arberth is 'blows or wonders', the gifts of Rhiannon seem to be either great misfortune or great happiness: a factor which is borne out in the subsequent story.

13   The game of Badger in the Bag is the ultimate insult for a Celtic nobleman. This first branch might well be entitled 'the Mabinogi of the Three Blows' since they play such an important part in the tripartite story: the blow upon Hafgan, the blows upon Gwawl and, lastly, the blow upon Pwyll at the loss of his son and disgrace of his wife. Truly, Pwyll has blows and wonders in equal measure. Interestingly, a similar parallel is found in modern marital warfare: 'the Badger Game' in which a woman seduces a man then cries rape, at which point her husband appears on the scene to blackmail the victim.

14   Gwawl cannot claim *sarhad* here, but Rhiannon exacts no such sureties from Gwawl's family as we see in the Third Branch. It is subtextually apparant that Hefaidd approved of Gwawl and Rhiannon's marriage, since he objects to Gwawl's treatment. Hefaidd can be seen in the light of those giants and Otherworldly kings who are destined to lose their position on the marriage of their daughters and who subsequently place all manner of restrictions upon them (cf. Chapters 5 and 6). Rhiannon and Pwyll make their quick getaway, and do not accede to his suggested delay in the Underworld.

15   Rhiannon and Pwyll sleep together without ceremony. Indeed, the only marriage ceremony in the *Mabinogion* occurs in *The Lady of the Fountain*. In early times, the assembly of the tribal family at a wedding feast was sufficiently effective in publicising the union of a couple. 'And the wedding feast lasted a year and a day', is the frequent conclusion of a folkstory. But Pwyll does not linger, wisely abducting his bride before Hefaidd can trick him into staying away long enough so that he can offer his daughter to another suitor.

16   The barrenness and subsequent unpopularity of Rhiannon, who goes out of her way to smooth enmity by the giving of gifts, parallels Branwen's disgrace (cf. Chapter 3). While the people of Dyfed are keen to applaud Pwyll's prowess in becoming Pen Annwn, they are less excited at the prospect of an Otherworldly bride.

17   The seven-year penance of Rhiannon is the first of her

'imprisonments'. She and Pryderi both have two captivities: they both suffer the misunderstanding of mortalkind as well as the enmity of the Underworld.

18   The abduction of the child and the sorrow of the mother is familiar to us from the story of Demeter and Persephone onwards. The distinct parallels between Rhiannon and Pryderi and Modron and Mabon are further pointed out in Chapters 8 and 9.

19   Teyrnon Twrf Liant (Of the Raging Sea) has parallels with Manawyddan: in Chapter 4 we will further see the connections between the Queen of the Underworld and the King of the Sea. The fate of the child and the foal and their twinned destinies are discussed below. The Otherworld malignancy manifests as a claw on May Eve, Beltaine, one of the Celtic fire-festivals and a day on which the way between the worlds is open. These 'fording-places' – the most feared being Samhain or 31 October, All Hallows E'en – were marked by games and festivals. (See further the story of Macha below.) The claw is reminiscent of the worm Grendel, which Beowulf fights, and even closer to an incident in the Irish Fionn cycle, *Feis Tighe Chonain* (see below).

20   According to the archetypal *mabinogi* of the hero, Pryderi is fostered in a place of obscurity and security. He is given a childhood name, Gwri Gwallt Euryn or Gwri Golden Hair, which protects him against both Otherworld malice and worldly anxiety. His interest in horses is not unnatural in the son of a Horse-Goddess.

21   In Celtic custom, the mother gave the child a name and was responsible for arming him at manhood. Names could be acquired at different times for different uses in Celtic society; there was the childhood name, usually dropped at weapon-taking, and then the manly name, often with the addition of an epithet coined from some daring exploit or peculiar feature. (A number of men bearing these names appear in Arthur's company, see Chapter 6.) In addition, there was the secret name, known usually to the family, but not to enemies.

Rhiannon inadvertently gifts her son with the name 'Trouble' – a hard destiny for a young child. Mabon can have many names.

22   The custom of fosterage was almost universal among the Celts: a child was raised by a noble family and taught household customs and given a general education. Fosterage wrought ties of mutual dependency and trust between different clans, thus blocking possible avenues to clan-warfare. Pendaran Dyfed appears in Triad 26 as Pwyll's foster-father, and the one to whom Pwyll gave the swine which came from Annwn. Pryderi is said to have tended them during *his* fostering.[5] There is a piece of anachronicity between this branch and *Branwen*, where Pendaran is described as a young page-boy left with Bran's son to govern Britain in his absence. Yet among those seven who return from Ireland is Pryderi himself!

23   The end of this story and the Second Branch converge on the beginning of the third, which continues the story of Pryderi's exploits.

2   THE ADVENTURES OF THE MARE AND THE BOY

This branch establishes Pwyll as an Underworld champion, Rhiannon as a representative of the Celtic Horse-Goddess, and sets Pryderi in a long line of heroes whose destiny is interwoven with a totem animal. Pryderi is the only character in the *Mabinogion* to appear in every one of the Four Branches and, as such, his destiny is most clearly discernible. He goes to Ireland with Bran in the Second Branch, suffers an Otherworldly imprisonment in the Third Branch and is finally slain by Gwydion in the Fourth Branch. We know from the *Triads* that he is a herdsman, keeping his father's Underworld swine (a gift from Arawn); he is called 'the Powerful Swineherd because no one was able either to deceive or to force him'.[5] He is also a huntsman, like his father. These twin functions are a feature of Mabon, who also suffers a mysterious and long-term captivity. When he is grown up, Pryderi follows the pattern laid down by his father, yet in his youth he is the son of Rhiannon, whose captivity he shares and whose nature he most reflects. He is the son of his mother, just as Mabon is the son of Modron. While a fuller discussion of this association can be found in Chapters 3 and 9, it is possible to show from Celtic tradition how Pryderi and the foal relate to the conception of the hero and the fate of the land.

In parallel Irish tradition we see how the story of *Cu Chulainn's Conception*, from the Ulster cycle, is dependent upon an early story, *The Debility of the Ulstermen*, in which Crunnchu mac Agnoman was without a wife: an unknown woman, called Macha, came to his house and tended it without speaking, to Crunnchu's satisfaction. On going to an assembly one day, Macha warned him not to speak of her to anyone. At the assembly, the king's horses were paraded, everyone agreeing that they were the swiftest steeds in the land. Crunnchu boasted that his wife was swifter still. He was immediately imprisoned and his wife summoned before the king. Great with child and near her time, Macha was forced to compete against the horses, whom she easily beat, but she expired giving birth to girl and boy twins. She revealed her identity at last as Macha, daughter of Sainreth mac Imbaith (Strange One, son of Ocean), and prophesied that whenever Ulster was oppressed and in greatest need, all Ulstermen should suffer the weakness of a confined woman.[28]

Here Macha is in the place of Rhiannon: an Otherworld woman, forced, by her husband's foolish boasting, to give birth to her children in public. The difference here is that Ulster shares her penance. Macha is unspeaking of her origins, as many Otherworldly brides are; she demands absolute secrecy concerning her Otherworldly abilities and attributes – the infringement of which usually causes the bride to return to her home. Macha and Rhiannon clearly share horsely qualities: the speed at which they both run/ride, in particular. The birth of twins, or of a child and a foal, is a frequently occurring theme in the related stories of Rhiannon and Pryderi.

In *Cu Chulainn's Conception*, the King of Ireland, Conchubor, and his sister Deichtine were in pursuit of a flight of birds yoked with silver. They came to a newly built house where a woman was giving birth: Deichtine helped deliver the baby. Simultaneously, a mare gave birth to two foals. In the morning the baby died; Deichtine lamented her foster-son's death but dreamed that the god Lugh came to her, telling her she would conceive the same child of her own body, and that the twin foals were to be raised as the boy's.[101] The boy was Cu Chulainn – the only non-Ulsterman able to aid the land when the curse of Macha fell upon its men. The twin foals, Dubh Sainghleann and Liath Macha, later yoke his chariot.

Here the story begins with the hunting of Otherworldly birds: the Birds of Rhiannon appear in *Branwen*, and are famed for their ability to cause forgetfulness and induce paradisal bliss in their listeners. These companion-birds make Rhiannon a Queen of Annwn: not a Classical Persephone giving the waters of Lethe to the dead, but a Celtic Persephone whose musical birds give passage to paradise. The foster-son of Deichtine is instantly lost, but will be born of her and will come again in the shape of Cu Chulainn who, with his brave-yoked chariot, will defend the stricken Ulstermen cursed by the Horse-Goddess. As with Pryderi, the foal becomes the companion of the child.

A final variant will clinch the Pryderi archetype; the story of *Feis Tighe Chonain*, an oral tale from Irish tradition. In this, a giant comes to a woman's house and steals her newborn children by putting an arm through the smoke-hole. At her next confinement, the hero, Fionn, with his eleven companions keeps watch. A bitch whelps two puppies as the woman gives birth. The giant returns, is beaten off and the companions track him to a clifftop where six children and the two puppies are found. The giant is killed, the children restored and Fionn keeps the puppies who become his fabled hounds, Bran and Sceolang.[53]

The connection between the destiny of the hero and that of the animal is here confirmed: Cu Chulainn takes the foals as his chariot-horses, Fionn takes the puppies to be his hounds. We are not told in *Pwyll* who is the possessor of the monstrous arm, only that Teyrnon is able to beat it off and rescue both foal and boy. The implication seems to be that Gwawl's cousin, Llwyd of Cil Coed, likewise the predator of Pwyll's family in the Third Branch, means to abduct Pryderi as well as Teyrnon's foal. It would not do to leave one half of the hero's destiny alive, after all. We have no parallel stories which tell of the rescue of the hero by his companion animal – at least, not in relation to the hero's birth: but we frequently come across the helping animals in folk tradition. A fuller discussion of totemic beasts will be found in Chapter 8.

Yet, the reader will argue, there are no stories in which Pryderi and his foal ride to daring adventures. This is because Pryderi *is* the foal, just as his mother *is* the mare which is endangered by his birth. The totemic association of people and animals is a subtle one, operating on more than one level. Rhiannon and Pryderi operate as human beings, yet their innerworld resonances are those of mare and colt. In order to comprehend this mystery we must examine just who Rhiannon really is.

3 THE MARE OF SOVEREIGNTY

Why is Rhiannon associated with horses and what role does the horse play within the symbology of the native mysteries of Britain?

In Indo-European culture the horse or mare has always played a prominent part in king-making rituals. We have Giraldus Cambrensis's shocked account of an Irish kingship rite whereby the king symbolised his union with the land by mating with a mare and bathing in the broth of her flesh: this was in twelfth-century Donegal. Yet a similar ritual, involving a queen and a stallion in a tantric horse-sacrifice,[78] the *asvamedha*, occurs in Vedic tradition. The distance between Donegal and the Indus Valley may seem great, yet we cannot discountenance the evidence of parallel sets of customs in Ireland and India.[87] Part of the *asvamedha* ritual involved a kingly claimant sending out a horse to wander at will: whatever lands it traversed became kingly territory. Similarly, in Ireland, kingly claimants let loose their horses on to disputed land, thus making the universal gesture of the conqueror. The horse or mare seems to have had a central function within rites of Sovereignty.

We have already seen that when the representative of the land's Sovereignty is violated – as in the case of Macha – the land suffers also. Both Rhiannon and Macha are Sovereignty-giving women who resort to their totemic mare-shape when needed: both women are simultaneously revered and disgraced, denoting a duality of function or else a devalued origin.

Scholars have universally agreed in the derivation of Rhiannon's name from the Celtic form *Rigantona* or Great Queen, yet we can also set with this Rhiain (Maiden) Annwn (Underworld) – a title also appropriate to Rhiannon, and one which equates both these titles with those of Demeter and Persephone.

The cult of the Black Demeter, as attested by Pausanius, is also associated with the mare-cultus. We are told that Demeter was searching for the abducted Persephone when Poseidon attempted to rape her. Demeter hid herself among the mares of King Onkios, but Poseidon found her and coupled with her, in the form of a stallion. Demeter assumed her dark form, fled to a cave in Phygalia where she bore twins: a boy named Arion and a daughter called Despoina (which means Mistress). She was depicted in a nearby temple as Demeter Erinys (Angry Demeter) and depicted with a mare's head. Demeter's daughter is therefore both 'Maiden' or Kore and 'Mistress of the Dead' or Despoina. The priests of this cult were called πῶλοι or 'colts'.

We are still not free from the association of the mare with death. The goddess of bad dreams is called Nightmare. Superstitiously, we still instruct our children to call a white horse 'a grey': out of a long-forgotten custom of respect, perhaps? In Wales to this day, the folk custom of the Mari Lwyd or Grey Mary is continued. Every year, between Christmas and Twelfth Night, a company go from house to house with a mare's skull forming the basis of a beribboned hobby-horse; they attempt to gain entry with the Mari by means of a riddling contest which if the inmates cannot answer, causes the door to be opened to the company of the Grey Mare:

> Mari Lwyd, Lwyd Mari,
> A sacred thing through the night they carry.[127]

A legend has it that the Grey Mary was summarily ejected from the Bethlehem stable to allow for the birth of a more prestigious child, and that ever after, she roams for a place to birth her colt. The Underworld Queen of the Dead is present in both Mary Lwyd and Rhiannon: both are outcasts and burden-bearers; both are welcomers of the dead.

Most frequent is the association between Rhiannon and

Epona, a European Celtic Horse-Goddess. The textual evidence for Epona is thin on the ground: she has no legend and her cult can only be deduced from inscriptions which turn up all over Atun, Metz and Worms district, where the Roman legions which spread her cult were stationed. Of Epona we have this fragmentary statement:

A certain Phoulonios Stellos, who hated women, had intercourse with a mare. In time, she brought forth a beautiful maiden whom she named Epona, a goddess of horses.[78]

It seems she was a goddess of abundance, of the newborn and of the dead, of horsemen, fertility and animals. Her feast day, incorporated into the Roman state calendar, was 18 December – fixed between the Consualia (15 December) and the Opalia (19 December). Consus was the god of seed-sowing and was connected with horses, asses and mules: his altar was cleared of earth twice a year on feast days, races were held in his honour, and horses, mules and asses were rested on this day and given garlands. Consus was further associated with Poseidon Hippios. Ops was the goddess of harvest: she inherited the attributes of Rhea. Thus, it will be seen, Rhiannon and Epona really do have connections: Rhiannon and Manawyddan as deities of Underworld and Sea equate well both with Consus and Ops, but also with Demeter Erinys and Poseidon.[2]

Epona's image appeared in stables from Gaul to Thessaly: ostlers offered her roses. The legions in Germany dedicated many plaques to her, where she is shown with a foal following her progress, or with a foal or pair of foals eating from the manger of her lap.[68] Two of Epona's symbols – the key and dog – also mark her as a goddess of the Underworld.[42] The association of Epona was the rose garland and with asses and horses may also give us a new insight into the predicament of Lucius Apuleius who, in *The Golden Ass*, is turned into an ass by mistake. He is destined to remain in this shape until he can consume roses. While in the stable he

noticed a little shrine of the Mare-Headed Mother, the Goddess Epona, standing in a niche of the post that supported the main beam of the stable. It was wreathed with freshly garlanded roses...[9]

but, unfortunately, before he is able to eat them, thieves break in and he begins a long series of adventures in his new shape. It is not until he encounters a mystery procession in honour of Isis, at which he eats a garland of roses, that he becomes a man once more. But this is not before he is vouchsafed a vision of the Goddess and taken under her protection:

> When at the destined end of your life you descend to the land of ghosts, there too in the subterrene hemisphere you shall have frequent occasion to adore me. From the Elysian fields you will see me as queen of the profound Stygian realm, shining through the darkness of Acheron with a light as kindly and tender as I show you now.[9]

Such is the promise of the Queen of the Underworld, whether she be Isis, Epona or Rhiannon: she who lost her own child or who had to hide him from danger, welcomes the confused initiate into her mysteries with the love of Modron, the Great Mother.

The Celtic mania for horses has not lessened, as a trip to any race-course in the world will show. Yet the respect in which the horse was held was not only due to its speed and faithfulness, but a remembrance of the Lady of the Horses herself, the Mare of Sovereignty who bore the burdens of others and who lost her own foal. Such resonances strike us deeply still. After all, was not Pryderi found in a stable, just as Christ's epiphany finds him in a manger, surrounded by newly-dropped lambs? If Pryderi's totem is the foal, then Christ's is the lamb.

If we look at a depiction of Epona certain iconographical features are quite startling. She is seated on the right side of the horse (not the more usual left). She does not ride astride, but sits, like a woman on an ass. Of course the image is familiar: Epona travels into exile, like Mary Fleeing Into Egypt, with her endangered foal, and always, iconographically precise to the last feature, travelling from left to right.

In a tangled web of stories, Rhiannon and Pryderi are but one pair of protagonists. Other parallels, Christian and pagan, Celtic and Classical, have still to emerge. If we are to arrive at a complete mosaic of the Mabon and Modron, other pieces are still to be found and put in the right place. They have shown us the way into the Otherworld, where we shall travel again.

CHAPTER 3
Branwen, Daughter of Llyr

Bran's Head

O Land! – O Bran lie under.
DAVID JONES
In Parenthesis

'Do you want to hear my story?' said the head.
'I've already said so more than once,' I said.
'My story,' said the head. 'You must pay for it, there is a price if I tell it.
'What's the price?' I said.
'The price is that if I tell it you'll know it,' said the head. 'You won't be able to get it out of your mind, it doesn't stop, it just goes on happening with whoever falls into it, maybe you.'

RUSSELL HOBAN
A Conversation with the Head of Orpheus

1   ENTERTAINING THE NOBLE HEAD

Branwen is one of the most poetic and cohesive of the Four Branches, in which it is possible to perceive distinct parallels between Irish and Welsh traditions. Branwen herself suffers a similar fate to that of Rhiannon, being yet another 'foreign' wife of whom the people disapprove, while her brother, Bran, has a long-established role of guardianship. Together they manifest the archetype of Sovereignty and her Champion. Efnissien, the jealous brother, stands in a long tradition of 'disruptive elements at the feast'. Central to the story is the Cauldron of Rebirth, originally brought from Ireland and which returns there to effect the devastating finale of the story.

The fetching, gifting or theft of the cauldron is related to an early Welsh poem, the *Preiddeu Annwn* (The Spoils of Annwn), which we shall be discussing in Chapter 6. This theme gives us the proto-Grail story which developed in such profusion in medieval literature. The guardianship of the Grail or cauldron by the Fisher King is also Bran's function, for the holy vessel is a symbol of the Sovereignty of the land. It is for this reason that Bran is always known by his epithet *Bendigeid* or 'the Blessed': he who guards the Hallows of Sovereignty guards the kingship of the land, and is, thus, in the place of a priest or holy-man. As we shall see later, Bran is a type of the Inner Guardian, one who is to be encountered by the kingly candidate to the seat of the Pendragon.

1   Bran the Blessed was crowned king of the Island. Seated one day with his brother Manawyddan, and their half-brothers 2   Nissien and Efnissien, he saw thirteen ships sailing from Ireland into the bay at Harlech. 3   It was Matholwch, King of Ireland, come to ask for an alliance with Bran by marrying Branwen. Negotiations were concluded and the marriage took place at Aberffraw 4   where tents were pitched, since Bran could not be accommodated within a house.
5   Efnissien, Branwen's brother, arrived to find her already married: 6   in retaliation he mutilated Matholwch's horses. Bran offered a generous honour-price and replacement horses, but Matholwch was not appeased; so Bran gifted him with the Cauldron of Rebirth, into which dead men could be put and would

revive, though they were forever speechless. 7   Matholwch knew the cauldron's original owners who came from a lake in Ireland: the woman gave birth every six weeks to a fully-armed warrior and was a Titan, like her husband. Their behaviour had so offended everyone that Matholwch had ordered their death in a specially built house of iron which was then heated from without. Both man and woman escaped. Bran had received them hospitably, divided their number and set them to work, where they fortified each place in which they stayed.

8   Although Branwen bore a son, after two years, the Irish talked Matholwch into putting her away. She was sent to the kitchens where each day the butcher would strike her on the ear after he had finished slaughtering animals. An embargo was placed on travel to or from Wales. At the end of three years Branwen had taught a starling to speak; she bound a letter to its wing and sent it to Bran at Caer Seint, who read the missive and knew Branwen's disgrace.

9   Bran mustered the men of Britain, leaving seven men in charge in his absence, with his son, Caradawg, as chieftain. The British host sail for Ireland, but Bran strides through the waters, carrying the musicians on his shoulders. 10   Matholwch's swineherds report an amazing sight: a forest moving through the sea with a mountain. Branwen is summoned to solve the mystery: she identifies the wonder as Bran and his men come to rescue her.11   Matholwch and his men withdraw beyond the river Shannon, destroying its bridge, hoping that the magnetic stones in the river will prevent ships from crossing it. Bran makes himself a bridge for his host. Matholwch sends conciliatory messages to Bran, offering to abdicate in favour of his son, Gwern. 12   Since Bran receives this offer coolly, the Irish ask Branwen what will please her brother.

13   A house is built to contain Bran, but on each of the hundred pillars are hung two bags, each containing an armed man. Efnissien inspects the house and when told that the bags only contain flour, crushes the skulls of each warrior.

14   At the feast to acclaim Gwern as king of Ireland, the boy is passed round to each uncle until he comes to Efnissien who seizes the boy and 15   thrusts him into the fire. Bran prevents Branwen from joining her son, and leaps up amid the uproar and bids the Dogs of Gwern to beware of Morddwyd Tyllion. 16

17   The Irish kindle the Cauldron of Rebirth and thrust in the corpses of their dead. 18   Efnissien is struck with shame and remorse and, hiding himself among the Irish dead, is thrown into the cauldron – a living man – stretches himself out and so breaks the cauldron. 19   Only seven men escape from the rout, and Bran himself, who is wounded by a poisoned spear in his heel. He bids

his men cut off his head and bear it to the White Tower in London, with his face towards France, promising that he will be a good companion to his men on their journey, that they will stay in two places for many years in great blessedness, but that they must beware of opening the door towards Cornwall. 20   Returning to Wales with the Head, they disembark at Aber Alaw where Branwen despairs over the destruction wrought because of her. She dies and is buried there.

21   The company hear that the Island has fallen to Caswallawn, that Bran's son is dead, and that only Pendaran Dyfed has escaped.

22   They pass to Harlech where they feast for seven years while the birds of Rhiannon sing to them, making them forget their sorrow. They then go to Gwales and feast in a hall with three doors – two open, and the third closed. For eighty years they remain there – an episode called the Assembly of the Noble Head. 23   Then Heilyn opens the door towards Cornwall and they remember all that has befallen, and feel their sorrow more bitterly than before. 24   They inter the Head at the White Tower, which is called one of the Three Fortunate Concealments: and afterwards called one of the Three Unfortunate Disclosures, since Arthur digs up the Head.

25   Only five pregnant women were left to populate devastated Ireland; these five had five sons who mated with each other's mother, and so they divided the land into five districts. 26   This branch comprises the stories of Branwen's Blow, The Men who Set Out from Ireland, The Assembly of the Noble Head, The Feasting in Harlech, and The Singing of the Birds of Rhiannon.

1   The family tree of Bran is shown in Figure 3.1:

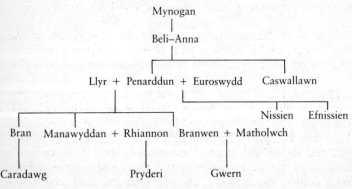

Figure 3.1: *The Family Tree of Bran*

The name of Beli appears as the ancestor at the head of many British genealogies: he is often coupled with Anna. Although they do not appear in this story, it is significant that they have been identified with the deities Belinus and Anu[5] the grand ancestors of the Celtic pantheons. Caswallawn, the shadowy conqueror of Britain, is Bran's uncle; he appears in the next branch also.

2   Nissien and Efnissien – peaceful and not-so-peaceful are the translations of their names – are polarised to no purpose in this story, since Nissien contributes nothing to the action. Efnissien's role as disrupter is readily paralleled throughout mythology and folkstory: like the Goddess Eris who threw the apple of discord at Peleus and Thetis's wedding in Greek myth,[40] like Loki who sows dissension at Aegir's feast in Norse myth[29,79] and the Irish Bricrui Poison-Tongue,[28] Efnissien is fated to wreak havoc on both family and nation.

3   Branwen is named here as one of the three chief ancestresses of the Island of Britain; this is clearly from a lost triad, but we are unable to make much of this puzzling statement without the other two female names. Branwen has no descendants who live to have children, since her only child, Gwern, dies as a boy. Perhaps this lost triad becomes comprehensible if Branwen is seen as one of the many women who represent the Lady of Sovereignty. This is almost the only reason which makes Efnissien's subsequent behaviour understandable (see no. 5).

4   Bran is of Titanic stature; one of the lost giants of the former races, yet his brothers and sister are of normal size. (See section 3 of this chapter for a further discussion.)

5   Efnissien is not consulted about his sister's marriage. His reaction is that of the Jealous Brother of traditional folk ballad,[26] whose sister is courted by a man who asks consent of all her kin, except her brother John who ambushes the newly-weds and slays them in an incestuous revenge. If we consider Branwen as a type of Sovereignty – the royal woman whose blood confers Sovereignty on her husband and children – Efnissien's action is that of a *defender* of Sovereignty. If

Branwen marries the Irish king, the Island of Britain loses its royal line, is Efnissien's reasoning. He is, then, the champion of Sovereignty and the land of Britain.

6   The mutilation of Matholwch's horses is a gross insult to the laws of Celtic hospitality. Bran's generous *sarhad* is not acceptable until the Cauldron of Rebirth is also thrown in: a gift which subsequently devastates Ireland and enfeebles Britain.

7   The man and woman with the cauldron are called Llassar Llaes Gyfnewid and Cymeidei Cymeinfoll: they are clearly Underworld beings and their prototypes appear in the Irish story *The Destruction of Da Derga's Hostel*, as Fer Caille and Cichuil, the likewise unwelcome guests.[28,65]

They and their children are grudgingly received by Matholwch, but hospitably by Bran who finds them so co-operative that he leaves one of their children, Llashar, behind to help govern Britain in his absence. Both giants come from a lake and, just as the cauldron 'gives birth' to armed warriors, so too does Cymeidei give birth to a fully-armed warrior every six weeks. The preparation of the iron house by Matholwch is the same ruse which the Irish king Labriad Loingsech employs to kill his troublesome uncle, though at the cost of burning alive his mother and his jester also.[32] Of all the parallel Irish themes, this is the strongest in the story of Branwen. The iron house also encloses the drunken Ulstermen in the *Intoxication of the Ulstermen*.[28] A full study of the major Irish borrowings and parallels can be found in *Branwen, Daughter of Llyr* by Proinsias Mac Cana.[65] The fact that Bran is able to control the cauldron-folk is significant, since he himself becomes the guardian of the Hallows and an Otherworldly King of power.

8   As with Rhiannon, Branwen's reception is pleasant at first, but she is soon disowned because of the shame her brother has brought on the Irish. During their punishment, both women resort to their totemic beast: Rhiannon to the mare, and Branwen to the starling (cf. Chapter 8). Triad 53 records this as one of the Three Harmful Blows of the Island of Britain: one of the others being the striking of Gwenhwyfar, Arthur's

queen. This further strengthens the idea of Branwen representing Sovereignty.

It will be recalled that King Lear's daughters were each questioned by their father as to how much they loved him, so that he might decide who should have the Sovereignty of Britain. Branwen is the daughter of Llyr, and although this episode is absent from our story, it brings out many interesting resonances for consideration. In the folkstory, *Cap o' Rushes*, which is derived from King Lear and his daughters, the king asks his question, receiving fulsome answers from daughters one and two, but daughter three replies 'as much as meat loves salt', thus causing her father to reject her. She weaves a cloak or cap of rushes and, like Branwen, becomes a kitchen maid, her gentle ways being mocked by the scullions. Cap o' Rushes is only rescued from her predicament by sending a ring baked in a pie to her appointed prince, who recognises it as the jewel of the girl with whom he danced the night before. They are married and reconciled to her father, who recognises her true love by granting her the Sovereignty.

Branwen's role is bewilderingly passive without these parallels to point her true nature. She shows herself resourceful and skilled in the riddling patterns of understanding which grace this story (cf. no. 10).

9   We learn from the text that the sea-passage is shallow between Ireland and Wales, and that the sea has inundated many lands since then. Both land masses were once joined, but at a time some thousands of years before the writing of this story. Parts of the coast are still subject to the sea's incursions to this day, and drowned lands, villages, etc. are the stuff of living folk memory. The influence of Llyr is with us yet.[76]

10   Bran strides with his musicians on his shoulder through the waves. Why this should be so is perhaps indicated by the nature of the following passage which reads like a riddling of poets. Just as Macbeth cannot believe that Birnham Wood has come to Dunsinane, neither can Matholwch fathom the riddling message of his swineherds. Only Branwen can interpret the riddle of the forest as the British fleet, and the moving mountain with two lakes as the nose and eyes of her brother, Bran.

11   Bran says: 'He who would be chief, let him also be a bridge.' This is an important key to Bran and to the Succession of the Pendragons. Inherent in this phrase is the kingly sacrifice which Bran is willing to undergo for the good of his people.

12   Just as Matholwch was not satisfied with the mere replacement of his horses, neither is Bran satisfied with seeing his nephew made king – why should he not be king himself? Just as he once trapped the guardians of the cauldron, so Matholwch plans to destroy Bran in the Iron House. The killing of guests violated hospitality in a way we find hard to grasp now: for the British, as for the Greeks and many other people, the guest was holy, sent by God. Once anyone had eaten and slept in the host's house, that guest was henceforward a 'guest-friend'. Welsh listeners to this story would have been reminded of the massacre at Ambrius where each Saxon was seated next to an unarmed Briton at a feast: on a given signal each Saxon stabbed his neighbour with a knife concealed in his long sleeve. Thus perished most of Britain's nobility[37] as happens also in *Branwen*.

13   The grisly humour of this episode disguises some more poetic riddling. Efnissien is told that the bags contain flour, but in crushing the warriors hidden within to death, he merely supplies the cauldron with invincible fodder against his own countrymen. The Irish dead literally 'rise again', like flour which has been baked. This theme of grain which dies and yet rises again is the subject of one of Taliesin's poems (cf. Chapter 7).

14   According to various translators, Efnissien exclaims, before he casts Gwern into the fire, either 'no one here realises what I am about to do' (i.e. my kin are guiltless of my intentions) or 'everyone here assembled will be outraged by my actions'.

15   Why does Efnissien cast his nephew into the fire? Both Isis and Demeter have stories which tell of their sojourn in a household where they nurse a young baby and attempt to make the boy immortal by holding him in the fire – until so prevented

by the boy's mother.[40] A similar story is told of Achilles whose mother bathed him in fire: he was immortal and unwoundable except for the heel by which he had been held. Such a theory might gain strength from Bran's following remark (cf. no. 16). If Efnissien is motivated solely by malice, then we need look no further. If it were possible to have a 'happy ending' for this story, this feast would have been the point at which to conclude it, with the Irish and Welsh reconciled at the feast of Gwern's succession to the kingship. But if Efnissien is, as we have postulated, the defender of Britain's Sovereignty, then the death of Gwern would render the Irish succession void, Branwen free to marry a British noble, and sufficient British troops on Irish soil to effect a conquest. Efnissien shows his first noble action in breaking the cauldron by his own death.

16   Bran shouts: 'Dogs of Gwern, beware of the Pierced or Wounded Thigh!' He has not, at this point, been wounded so, unless he is prophesying, what does this signify? Firstly, he is addressing the dead Gwern's troops. Secondly, he is speaking of himself as though Pierced or Wounded Thigh was a rightful title, like his epithet of 'Blessed'. As we shall establish below, Bran is a prototype of the Fisher King or Grail-Guardian, who is likewise wounded through the thigh.

17   The scene is now one of utter horror and devastation. The dead are revived, though they are without speech. (The dead may not speak of what they have seen in death's kingdom because they only suffer one death: the initiate poet suffers 'the second death' of initiation and so can speak the riddling tongue of initiates – a language incomprehensible to non-initiates, cf. Chapter 7.) Strabo, the Greek historian, writes of similar rites practised by Germanic tribes; prisoners-of-war are slain over a cauldron by prophetesses – such a scene is depicted on the Gundestrup cauldron.[38] In the Irish story, *The Second Battle of Mag Tured*, the healer, Diancecht, and his children similarly revive the slain Tuatha de Danaan by throwing them into the well named Slane.[28]

18   Efnissien's only redress is to break the cauldron's power by entering it as a living man: he is neither dead nor an initiate

of the mysteries and so has no right to be 'cauldron-born'. However we guess at his likely motivation, and lament his actions, Efnissien's death is a noble one, bringing hollow victory to Britain.

19   Only seven men escape from Ireland: Pryderi, Manawyddan, Glifieu Eil Taran, Taliesin, Ynawg, Gruddyeu ap Muriel and Heilyn ap Gwyn Hen. Likewise, only seven escape with Arthur after he has plundered Annwn in the poem *Preiddeu Annwn* (cf. Chapter 6). Significantly, Taliesin is the survivor of both expeditions, to sing of these exploits to those who come after. The oracular head of Bran is discussed below.

20   The parallels between Branwen and Kriemhild of the Germanic *Nibelungenlied* have been pointed.[65,79] Kriemhild marries the barbaric Etzel in the hope of avenging her husband Siegfried's death. His murderer, Hagen, visits Kriemhild and slays her son which is the signal for mass slaughter, and the burning down of the hall. Although Branwen is rescued by Bran, her heart is broken: Triad 95 speaks of her as 'one of the three who died of bewilderment'.[5] Like the Irish Deirdrui of the Sorrows who looks upon the two kings who are fated to share her body after her husband's death, and who commits suicide, Branwen looks between the two countries laid waste for her and expires of grief. In Geoffrey of Monmouth, we read that Lear's daughter, Cordelia – whom Branwen much resembles – buried her father in an underground chamber dedicated to the God Janus (he of the head which looks both ways). Echoes of *Branwen* are very loud, since Branwen herself is buried in a 'four-sided' grave on the banks of the Alaw. And although Branwen does not commit suicide like Cordelia, the succession of Sovereignty is likewise confused: it is virtually interred with the body of Branwen, and the head of Bran.[37]

21   Caswallawn has usurped the kingship by overcoming the seven guardians left in Bran's stead, by means of his magic mantle of invisibility. (This mantle appears in the list of the Treasures of Britain.) Like the invisible Knight, Garlon, who causes the Dolorous Blow in the Grail legends, so Caswallawn is responsible for causing disaster. Pendarun escapes to become

Pryderi's foster-father in a previous story, although Pryderi is himself one of the survivors: a disparity noticed in the last chapter. Caradawg, Bran's son, is the second person to 'break his heart from bewilderment' like Branwen (Triad 95).

22 The two feasts at Harlech and Gwales (identified as Grassholm, off Pembrokeshire) last eighty-seven years in total: the Assembly of the Noble Head really takes place in the Otherworld where time is not. Indicating an Otherworldly location is the appearance of the Birds of Rhiannon; these are the messengers of hope and Otherworldly bliss who belong to the Goddess. They also grant the gift of forgetfulness: the very same gift which Greek Lethe gives to the dead. Otherworldly birds and cauldrons appear in *The Cauldron of Cu Roi* (see below). These birds sing on the Tree of Knowledge and Memory in the Celtic paradise. The oracular and Otherworldly gift of poets was denoted by the silver branch hung with little bells which was held over the heads of Celtic master-poets as part of their insignia: a branch from the Paradisal tree.

23 Britain is also called 'The Island of the Strong Door' in the *Preiddeu Annwn* – indicating not only the strength of defence against oppression, but also the Strong Door which stands between the worlds: once that door is open, the spell of the Otherworld is lifted and remembrance returns in a painful flood. The Head of Bran remains uncorrupted as long as the door is closed.

24 This passage refers to Triad 37: the Three Fortunate Concealments where:

> the Head of Bran the Blessed ... was concealed in the White Hill in London, with its face towards France. And as long as it was in the position in which it was put there, no Saxon oppression would ever come to this island.

Juxtaposed are the Three Unfortunate Disclosures:

> Arthur disclosed the Head of Bran and Blessed from the White Hill, because it did not seem right to him that this Island should be defended by the strength of anyone but by his own.[5]

The Tower of London, or the White Mount, is still the province of ravens; their disappearance is said to betoken invasion and the conquest of Britain, for which reason their wings are kept clipped. They are the totem bird of Bran, whose own name means quite simply 'Raven'. The concealment and disinterment of Bran's Head has a deeper significance in relation to the British Mysteries. A literal reading of these Triads shows Arthur possessed of hubris, yet in the Succession of the Pendragons, Arthur's visit to Annwn is a necessary one in which he must possess the Hallows of Sovereignty which are guided by the last great kingly sacrifice, Bran himself (cf. Chapter 9). These British Isles have been known since Classical times as the prison or sleeping-place of Cronos, the great Titan of time and transmutation. We shall be discussing Bran as a type of Cronos below.

25   This story appears in the Irish *Book of Invasions* and neatly explains why, anciently, Ireland is split into five provinces.[87]

26   From this medley of titles and from the numerous cross-referenced triads, the story of *Branwen* clearly has primary place in the storyteller's repertoire.

2   GUARDING THE HALLOWS

The richness of themes within *Branwen* makes it difficult for the commentator to survey it fully. The reader will have been struck perhaps by the universal elements common to many European folkstories and mythologies, especially in relation to the Greek legends about Achilles' family, and to both Norse and Germanic cycles.[79] Although Branwen is the eponymous heroine, the story really turns on the possession of the Cauldron of Rebirth – the *Pair Dedani*.

The cauldron is the prototype of the Grail itself: an Otherworldly vessel whose gifts include variously: rebirth, knowledge, spiritual fulfilment, paradisal bliss and magical power, as well as providing physical nourishment. The cauldron is the pagan resonance of the Grail which has been identified with the redemptive symbol of Christ's new covenant. Both Grail and cauldron dispense the draught of salvation, the waters of everlastingness; both are vessels which have an Otherworldly provenance; both are attainable only by people of sovereign power or heroes of daring courage. Death, both physical and spiritual, is written into the scenario of its quest: those who fail are slain; those who win die to the world and are reborn or initiated into a different and Otherworldly condition.

The cauldron in *Branwen* comes from the Otherworld to Ireland and then Wales to become a vessel of contending kings: Matholwch despises its gifts, losing both the vessel and his life. Bran, on the other hand, accepts its gifts generously, to the extent that he lays his life down to become its Innerworld guardian. The Irish employ the cauldron to revive their warriors yet the seven British survivors of the slaughter are nourished by its bounty during the assembly of the Noble Head, when, like the Grail elders, they sit with the Head for company, listening to the Birds of Rhiannon and supping from the cauldron whose draughts keep them alive without ageing.

The appearance of the cauldron and the paradisal birds is a theme of the Irish story *The Tragic Death of Cu Roi Mac Daire* in which we observe resonances between both *Branwen* and *Math*. After the siege of Fir Falgae there was a contention over the spoils: these included the woman Blathnat, the three cows of Tuchna, and the three birds which perched in their ears causing them to give the milk of thirty cows into a cauldron. Cu Roi was given nothing although he had helped the Ulstermen, while disguised in a grey mantle. He therefore picked up the cows, thrust the birds into his belt, put Blathnat under one arm and carried off the cauldron over his back. Cu Chulainn alone challenged him, and Cu Roi buried him up to the armpits in mud, shaved his head with a sword and anointed him with cow-dung for his trouble.

Cu Chulainn then sought revenge on the disguised stranger. For shame of his appearance he did not appear at court but followed a flock of black birds, killing one of them in every country he journeyed through. Finally he came to Srub Brain (Raven's Beak) in the West, near Cu Roi's fort, when he guessed the identity of his opponent. He managed to speak to

Blathnat, with whom he was secretly in love, and together they planned Cu Roi's death. Diverting his men, Blathnat bathed Cu Roi in the river into which she poured the milk from the cauldron as a signal for Cu Chulainn to attack, then she bound her abductor to the bedpost by his hair where the Ulstermen beheaded him.

Cu Roi's poet, Fercetne, asked where Blathnat might be and was told, 'She was only delivered because Cu Roi's head was struck off.' Fercetne seized his master's betrayer and hurled both her and himself over a cliff where they died.[28]

Here the cauldron is an Otherworldly spoil over which rival kings contend. Cu Roi is identifiable with Bran – a Titan of power and magical strength – though his role differs radically from Bran's. Cu Chulainn beheads black birds and realises at Srub Brain who the stranger is; Blathnat is only released by Cu Roi's beheading. The meaning of her name and that of Blodeuwedd in *Math* are identical, as their Delilah-like betrayal suggests: they are both Flower Women, of Otherworld provenance. Fercetne is in Efnissien's place as the killer of Blathnat. Interestingly, the Otherworldly spoils include a woman as well as a cauldron. In the Irish king-cycles, Otherworldly women act as the Lady of Sovereignty, and bestow kingship on heroes, just as we have suggested Branwen does to Matholwch.

In British legend the woman of Sovereignty is rarely present in an obvious sense: more clearly present is the cauldron or other items which form the regalia of Sovereignty, the Hallows themselves. The Hallows, as the holy items of kingly regalia are termed, must be possessed by the rightful monarch who is thus able to administer his lands with Otherworldly discernment and knowledge. This is the fundamental *raison* of *Branwen*; a theme which is further underlined in *Culhwch* and the *Preiddeu Annwn*, where Arthur and his companions journey ostensibly to Ireland to fetch certain objects, though it is clear that Ireland merely stands in the place of the Underworld where these objects are secreted. This is part of the Succession of the Pendragons where the kingly candidate must enter the Underworld and fetch the Hallows from their guardian: a feature which is discernible from early British legend, but which is later replaced by the quests of Arthur's knights for the Hallows of the Grail – the Spear, Sword, Cup and Dish.[72]

What were these Hallows originally? Fortunately we possess a manuscript which lists the Thirteen Treasures of Britain: like the Triads, these items refer to stories we sometimes know little about. They are often confused and repetitious. It is said that Myrddin (Merlin) obtained all of them and that he took them to his Glass House on Bardsey Island where they remain forever.[5] This fits well with Myrddin's role as guardian of Britain: the initiate who has withdrawn from this world into the Otherworld where, like Bran, he keeps a careful eye upon the flow of energy between the two worlds.

The Thirteen Treasures of Britain

1 Dyrnwyn (White Hilt), the Sword of Rhydderch the Generous: if a nobleman drew it, the blade burst into flames. It would come into the hand of anyone who asked for it, but everyone rejected it because of this ability.

2 The Hamper of Gwyddno Garanhir: if food for one was put into it, food for a hundred would be taken from it.

3 The Horn of Bran the Niggard, from the North: it contained whatever drink one desired.

4 The Chariot of Morgan the Wealthy: it took a man quickly to the place of his desire.

5 The Halter of Clydno Eiddyn, which was fastened by a staple to his bed-foot; the horse of one's desire could be found in the halter.

6 The Knife of Llawfrodedd the Horseman: it would serve twenty-four men.

7 The Cauldron of Dyrnwch the Giant: it would not boil the meat of a coward, only that of a hero.

8 The Whetstone Tudwal Tydglyd: if a hero sharpened his sword on it his opponents would bleed to death; if a coward did so, his opponent was no worse.

9 The Coat of Padaen Red-Coat: it was the right size for any nobleman, but would fit a peasant.

10 and 11 The Crock and Dish of Rhygenydd the Cleric: which provided the food of one's desire.

12 The Chessboard of Gwenddolau ap Ceidio: the men were

of silver, the board of gold; the pieces would play by
themselves.

13   The Mantle of Arthur in Cornwall: it made the wearer
invisible though he could see everyone.[5]

Clearly items 2, 3, 10 and 11 serve much the same purpose: a
feature which is shared by the Grail. The Sword of Rhydderch
is the Glaive or Sword of Light – a weapon which is wielded
with great effect in the quest for the Underworld Cauldron (cf.
Chapter 6). The Horn of Bran the Niggard is clearly a
corrupted reference to the cauldron of Bran the Blessed. The
Chessboard of Gwenddolau appears in both *Peredur*, *Dream of
Rhonabwy* and also in *Maxen Wledig* within the *Mabinogion*:
the magical chessboard is a paradigm of the land of Britain
over which the contending sides battle. The Welsh and Irish
chessboard differed from the modern game: the board was
sometimes of 7×7 squares. In Irish the game was called
Brandubh and the pieces were one king and eight opponents.
Brandubh translates as Black Bran; the game was also called
Brannabh which may be a corruption of Bran Naomh (Blessed
Bran). It is tempting to see the Brandubh board as a paradigm
of the Hall at Harlech and Gwales, where the surviving seven
feast with their king. The Mantle of Arthur is worn by
Caswallawn in *Branwen* and used to kill the seven guardians of
Britain and Bran's son.

This list is medieval and does not represent the true treasures,
some of which descend complete into the later Grail stories
while others can be found in the early story of Culhwch
(Chapter 6). They remain echoes of the symbols of Sovereignty,
which must be won by the rightful king from their Inner
Guardian. So why do we consider Bran to be such a guardian
and on what evidence? To discover this we must look at the
textured levels of an ancient tradition where a figure older even
than Bran guards his golden horde in the timeless realms which
lie behind the Island of Britain.

3   CRONOS AND THE SLEEPING LORD

The Titanic stature of Bran the Blessed indicates that he is indeed one of the primordial and archetypal guardians of Britain. Arthur is clearly his successor in the list of mighty ancestors who keep these shores free from oppression: many such guardians follow him. But how did this tradition start, by what authority? And why does Britain have such an important role in the world of the Mysteries?

There is an authentic tradition stemming from Classical sources which indicates Britain as a known Otherworldly *locus*, wherein is chained the last and greatest of the Titans – Cronos. Cronos's father, Uranus, begot many children upon Gaia, but he never let them see the light of day, imprisoning them in the depths of the earth. Gaia helped her son Cronos castrate his father. But Cronos followed the same pattern when he came to maturity, swallowing up the children of his wife, Rhea, as they came from the womb. Rhea bore Zeus secretly and hid him, giving Cronos a stone in his place. When Zeus grew up he liberated his brothers and sisters, and chained Cronos at the outermost edge of the world on the Isles of the Blest, identified as the British Isles.[40, 57] Thus far the Classical story.

In Plutarch's *The Silence of Oracles* there is a report from an official called Demetrius who visited Britain: he had learned many of the ancient religious traditions of these islands including the following:

> There is one island there [in Britain] where Cronos is a prisoner guarded by Briareus in his sleep – sleep was the fetters designed for Cronos, and many daimones lie around him as servants and followers.[60]

In another passage of Plutarch, *The Face of the Moon*, a Carthaginian antiquarian, Sextus Sylla, observes:

> The natives have a story that in one of these [islands] Cronos has been confined by Zeus, but that he, having a son for gaoler, is left sovereign lord of those islands . . . Cronos himself sleeps within a deep cave resting on rock which looks like gold . . . birds fly in at the topmost part of the rock, and bear him ambrosia, and the whole island is pervaded by the fragrance shed from the rock. . . .[11, see also 85]

Not only the scent pervades but the evidence of tradition. Cronos's myth is Greek yet Bran's is British: we cannot say that one preceded the other, but we may conclude that there were parallel or shared traditions. Cronos rules the lost Golden Age – a timeless era which corresponds to the Otherworldly dimension: his very name means 'time'. Zeus stops time by anchoring his father in the cave of sleep, but father and son still interact, according to Plutarch. Cronos's companions are said to give forth utterances of prophetic power:

> but the greatest and those about the greatest issues, they announce when they return as dreams of Cronos; for the things which Zeus premeditates, Cronos dreams.[11]

This passage is central to the theme of Mabon and the Succession of the Pendragons, since it presupposes an interaction between the Otherworldly kingdom of the Sleeping Lord and the realm of the worldly king or ruler.

It is evident from *Branwen* that Bran's effect does not end at death, rather *it starts a new cycle* of occurrence. Bran's head, like that of the floating oracular head of Orpheus,[40] gives council after death and, moreover, is guardian both of Britain from oppression and also of the life-giving cauldron, which is itself a vessel of Otherworldly, or, we might say, Golden Age power. (See Chapter 10.)

Bran entertains his seven companions in the island of Gwales, in a place outside time: Arthur sleeps with his companions under many hills, ready to rise at his country's need; Cronos and his attendant daimones sleep in an Otherworldly cave awaiting their release. Bran guards the cauldron; Arthur guards a golden treasure, it is said; Cronos guards the Golden Age itself and his very presence impregnates the land with the sweet odours of the Otherworld – a place of the ever-living yet also of the mighty dead. The resonances reveal a strong tradition which forms one of the central mysteries of Britain: that of the Sleeping Lord who is wounded, yet dies not; one who passes into the Avalonian realms to await the blowing of the mystic horn in a new age, when he will rise and come again, made young and strong, purged of age. Cronos is the lord of time and transmutation; the Titan who stands at the Strong Door, keeping the destructive enchantments of earlier time at bay.

So too, Bran guards Britain and its Hallows. He is wounded,

like the Grail-Guardian Brons, but he is enabled to pass on to his next phase by the coming of Arthur who wins the Hallows from Annwn and who promises to succeed to Bran's position as Guardian when his time comes. After Camlann and the Last Battle, Arthur goes to Avalon, where his wounds will be healed and where he holds the Hallows in trust for the kingly candidate – the Pendragon – who comes after him. This is why Excalibur – one of many Hallowed treasures of Sovereignty – is cast back into the lake: only so may the kingly candidate win his regalia by means of the Underworld descent into Annwn or Avalon.

If Arthur succeeds to Bran's position of Pen Annwn, who succeeds to the post of Pendragon? The Inner Pendragons are many and nameless, and like those knights who achieve the Grail, are drawn from only the most worthy champions. We must also ask: if Bran is no longer a Pen Annwn, what does he pass on to become?

What changes are wrought in the ancient Titan during his golden sleep? We look to the land of Britain and wonder:

Does the land wait the sleeping lord,
or is the wasted land
that very lord who sleeps?[118]

We must look to the Mabon and his imprisonment if this mystery is to be revealed, else we will never know whether we are merely a dream of Bran/Cronos, or a people unfettered by the subtle enchantments of stale tradition.

CHAPTER 4
Manawyddan, Son of Llyr

The Mouse in the Glove

Sospan fach yn berwi ar y tan,
Sospan fawr yn berwi ar a llawr.
A'r gath wedi crafu Joni bach

traditional, Welsh rugby song

When Bron the Fisher King saw that Perceval would ask
nothing concerning the Grail he was very sad. . . . When
morning came Perceval rose and went through the house
and court but found no one there, and he felt very
sorrowful.

Didot Perceval (c.twelfth century)

1   OF THE HAY-COLLAR AND THE DOOR-KNOCKER

This branch sees the continuing story of Bran's brother, Manawyddan, and his alliance with the family of Pryderi by marriage to Pwyll's widow, Rhiannon. Underlying the charmingly interwoven folkstories of this branch are mighty mysteries which the reader might overlook: these include the imprisonment of Mabon, the Dolorous Blow which causes the Wasteland, and the quest for the Grail or Cauldron. So although this story seems lightweight compared with the mighty matters of *Branwen* and *Pwyll*, this is really a deceptive effect, brought about by a far more self-conscious storyteller/scribe than the one who transcribed the previous branches.

We shall be examining the nature of Pryderi's imprisonment, and that of other famous prisoners who are pressed into servile duties, as well as pointing the parallels between the raising of the Enchantments of Dyfed and the quest for the Grail.

If the story has the shifting opacity of an object under water we should not be too surprised, since its chief protagonist, Manawyddan, son of the Sea, is a renowned shape-shifter in Celtic tradition. In an Irish story he is Manaanan, the king of the Otherworld paradise – which is an island in the Western seas – from whence he comes to gift mortals with the Cup of Truth.[28] His Otherworld greatness is considerably muted in this branch, where he becomes an ageing mortal weary of earth's sorrows, though still cunning and resourceful enough to defeat the enchantments which beset the land and his adoptive family. The alternative title of this branch, *Mabinogi Mynnweir a Mynord*: the 'Story of the Hay-Collar and the Door-Knocker', reminds us that the underlying theme is the imprisonment of Mabon and the punishment of Modron, and is a restatement of the events from *Pwyll*.

1   After the seven returned to Britain from Ireland and had buried Bran's head at the White Mount, Manawyddan exclaimed that he alone had no place to lodge that night. Pryderi comforted him with the thought that Bran's cousin, Caswallawn, was now king, but Manawyddan could not share a house with the usurper of his brother. Pryderi proposed that Manawyddan return to Dyfed and marry his widowed mother, with whom goes a dowry of seven

cantrefs. 2   Rhiannon is agreeable to the marriage and, after
feasting, Pryderi goes to Oxford and pays homage to Caswallawn.
    3   One night, Pryderi and Cigfa, Manawyddan and Rhiannon sit
on the Mound of Arberth. A mist descends, thunder sounds and
when the mist rises they find the countryside bare of people and
dwellings. They are left to support themselves as best they can. After
two years they grow weary and 4   go into England to live by a
craft. Manawyddan makes saddles with Pryderi's help, but they are
so well enamelled and of such good quality that no other saddler
can sell his own products. The saddlers agree to kill their rivals, but
they are warned and travel on. In another town Manawyddan
makes shields, and the resident shieldmakers are similarly done out
of business. They escape and become shoemakers. The resident
cobblers cannot compete against their rivals' gold-buckled shoes
and they escape once more. 5   On each occasion, Manawyddan
restrains Pryderi from taking revenge on their rivals, saying that
freedom is better than imprisonment, and that Caswallawn would
hear of it.
    They return to Dyfed and support themselves by hunting as
before. 6   They encounter a pure white boar which lured men and
dogs to follow it. They chase it to a castle which has newly
appeared; Pryderi enters it, despite Manawyddan's warnings.
7   The castle is empty inside but in its centre there is a marble
fountain with a golden bowl on a marble slab, attached by chains
which reach into the sky. Entranced by the workmanship, Pryderi
lays hands on it and finds his hands stuck to the bowl and his feet to
the marble slab. 8   Manawyddan waits for his return all day and
goes homeward where Rhiannon berates him for leaving her son
there. She goes to the castle and becomes similarly stuck to the bowl
and slab: thunder and mist strike again and the castle vanishes.
    9   Cigfa and Manawyddan are now alone. Cigfa weeps for fear,
and Manawyddan swears pure friendship to his step-son's wife.
They return to England, having lost their dogs and being unable to
hunt any more, where Manawyddan 10   lives as a shoemaker once
more, much to Cigfa's disgust. The other cobblers threaten him and
they return to Dyfed, settling at Arberth where Manawyddan farms.
11   He sows three fields with wheat, inspecting each every night in
turn to find the stalks empty of grain. He stands watch on the third
field and sees a host of mice descend on the grain. He is unable to
catch any save one which is slower than the rest, which he confines
in his glove. 12   He hangs it on a peg and informs Cigfa that he
will hang the offender: she is horrified at his concern with such
vermin.
    13   Manawyddan sets up a miniature gallows on the Mound of

Arberth. 14   A poor scholar passes by, much to Manawyddan's surprise, since no living being has been seen in Dyfed for seven years, and offers to ransom the mouse with a pound. Manawyddan refuses. A mounted priest passes by and offers three pounds for the release of the mouse. Lastly comes a bishop with his entourage who offers seven pounds for its release: at Manawyddan's refusal he increases the offer to 24 pounds. He then asks Manawyddan's price, which is the release of Rhiannon and Pryderi, the removal of the enchantment on Dyfed and the identity of the mouse.

15   The bishop replies that he is Llwyd ap Cil Coed, cousin of Gwawl ap Clud, Rhiannon's former suitor, and that the enchantments are his, in revenge for his cousin's insult. The three fields have been ravaged by his court, all of whom he turned into mice, but his wife was pregnant and slower than the rest. Manawyddan makes him further swear never to repeat the enchantments on Dyfed, that Rhiannon and Pryderi are to be free of further reprisals, and that he himself is to be so exempt. The mouse-wife is released at the same time as Rhiannon and her son. The land is restored to more than its former bounty. 16   It is revealed that the punishment of Rhiannon has been to wear about her neck the hay-collars of the asses after they have been hauling hay and that Pryderi has had the knockers of the court-gates about his neck, and that this is why this branch is called *Mabinogi Mynnweir a Mynord*.

1   Manawyddan is named in the Triads (no. 8) as one of the three disinherited chieftains, 'because he would not seek an inheritance'. In Irish legend, Manaanan, although later associated with the Tuatha de Danaan, is not mentioned as one of their number in earlier texts. He is a man apart in this story because he will not be part of Caswallawn's triumph over his brother, Bran.

2   Caswallawn is a usurper by means of his cloak of enchantment: this garment puts him with those enemies of Britain who put the land under enchantment (see below). In Geoffrey of Monmouth, Caswallawn is called Cassilivaunus who replaces his elder brother Lud or Lludd, the founder of Lud's Town or London: just as in *Branwen*, Caswallawn replaces Bran, whose head is buried under the White Mount.[37] There are significant parallels between Manawyddan and Caswallawn which suggest a hidden or lost story, since both men are named in the Triads as two of the Three Golden

Shoemakers. In this hidden story, which can be guessed at from the Triads, Caswallawn disputes with Julius Caesar over a maiden, Fflur (Flower), and pays homage to Caesar in order to secure Fflur's safety. Fflur appears to be another representative of Britain's Sovereignty, she is championed by Caswallawn, just as Cigfa is by Manawyddan, or Branwen by Efnissien.[5]

Rhiannon's marriage with Manawyddan makes her husband a landed man once more: the association of the Queen of the Underworld and the Lord of the Sea has already been noted on p.34 where Rhiannon has been shown to correspond to Demeter Erinys. So too does Manawyddan correspond closely to Poseidon.

3 The fateful Mound of Arberth becomes operative once more. When Manawyddan and his adoptive family sit there they contact the malevolent Otherworldly power of their ancient enemy. This action corresponds closely to the way the Grail knight sits upon the Perilous Seat and so causes the Wounding of the Fisher King and the wasting of the land. This is discussed more fully below. Curiously, Pryderi gives the actual administration of his lordship over to Manawyddan: this substitution parallels that of Pwyll for Arawn in the First Branch.

4 A Celtic nobleman did not work at servile tasks, yet Manawyddan works in leather for the making of saddles, shields and shoes. The tanner's trade was only slightly less smelly and ignoble than the fuller's, and dealing in hides was considered as shameful for a nobleman as pig-herding, an occupation totally barred to those of gentle birth. (Even the provision of pig-sties had to be out of smelling or viewing range of a nobleman's house according to Irish law.) Yet, as we will see in Chapters 5 and 6, the pig plays a central part in both *Math* and in *Culhwch and Olwen*. Manawyddan is the master of any craft he picks up and Pryderi is his reluctant apprentice. As neither Rhiannon nor Cigfa are mentioned here (and as Cigfa would most certainly lodge the strongest objections to her husband performing menial labour, if her later remarks are anything to go by) we may assume that the women are either lodged separately from the men, or do not travel with them.

5 Pryderi bears his servitude with ill grace, determined to seek a nobleman's revenge against craftsmen. He suffers loss of face here but also later, despite Manawyddan's words of warning, imprisonment in yet more servile bondage.

6 As Pryderi's father was lured into the Otherworldly realms by means of a white stag, so Pryderi himself is lured by means of a white boar.

7 The theme of becoming struck to an object is well known throughout folk tradition; however, in this instance, the cauldron and its castle relate directly to the Grail story and the achieving of the Grail knight, as we will see.

8 Rhiannon and Pryderi now undergo an almost exact rerun of the events in *Pwyll* where they suffer abduction and servile imprisonment together. Like the British warriors cast into the cauldron in *Branwen*, they lose the power of speech.

9 The storyteller has given Cigfa a very medieval modesty in the face of this situation. In Irish legend, Manaanan has the reputation for being a night-visitor of women, and fathers many heroes: a fact which the storyteller might well have had at the back of his mind.[87] This incident parallels the chaste friendship of Pwyll with Arawn's wife in the First Branch. Here Manawyddan substitutes for Pryderi, as Pwyll did for Arawn.

10 Here is the reason why Manawyddan is called one of the Three Golden Shoemakers (Triad 67), since he ornaments his shoes with golden buckles. Similarly, he ennobles an ignoble profession for one of his rank by employing precious dyes and enamel or *Calch Llassar* – a craft learned from Llassar Laes Gwfnewid, the Underworld being who brought the Cauldron of Rebirth from the Irish lake.

11 Just as Teyrnon in *Pwyll* lost one foal every May Eve, so does Manawyddan lose each of his three fields of wheat: both men keep watch on the final occasion.

12 As Gwawl was tied in the bag in *Pwyll*, so Manawyddan

imprisons the mouse in his glove. The Irish Manaanan was famed for his possession of a crane-bag – a marvellous receptacle in which its treasures were visible at high tide, but which appeared empty at ebb tide. These treasures correspond to the Hallows of Sovereignty or of the Grail, and to the Thirteen Treasures of Britain.[91]

13 The fateful Mound of Arberth reverts to its original role as a place of assembly and judgement: all the ills, enchantments and blows emanate from this Otherworld gateway and here at last, they are resolved by Manawyddan, the arbitrator. We have already mentioned the connections between Bran and Cronos, yet Cronos ruled the Otherworld, according to Classical tradition, with his brother Rhadamanthys, Lord of the Dead and of Judgement. Manawyddan stands in the place of Rhadamanthys rightfully, since he is now married to the Queen of the Dead, Rhiannon, the Underworld Mistress.

14 Manawyddan provokes one of the Mound of Arberth's strange properties: either to give blows or show a great wonder. He witnesses the latter – the appearance of people after seven years of deserted countryside. It is possible that in earlier oral versions the disguises of Llwyd might have been a wandering bard, a druid and a judge. Manawyddan bargains ruthlessly for the release of his wife and step-son, for their release means the lifting of the enchantment.

15 The true connections between the First and Third Branches are clearly apparent. Gwawl, Rhiannon's former suitor, who promised not to revenge himself on Pwyll has been vindicated by his cousin Llwyd. Just as Gwawl was struck by he knew not whom in *Pwyll*, so Pryderi and Rhiannon are stricken with a Dolorous Blow by being imprisoned in the Otherworld, while their land suffers enchantment.

16 The land is restored from Wasteland to its accustomed fertility at the moment of Rhiannon and Pryderi's release. Their notable and shadowy imprisonment is deeply connected with the Mabinogi of Mabon and Modron (cf. Chapter 9). The theme of the mule without a bridle became widespread in later

French romances: while the bridle is missing the enchanted person cannot resume his/her former shape.[58,63]

2   THE ENCHANTMENTS OF BRITAIN

Part of this story's mysterious action takes place in the Otherworld, in the Hollow Hills, which is where the unwary find themselves if they travel unprepared. Just as we know little about the possessor of the great claw which attacks Teyrnon's foal, so also we are ignorant of the place of Rhiannon and Pryderi's imprisonment. Throughout the first three branches magic mists and mysterious disappearances abound, yet the influence of the Otherworld is not evil in itself. Pwyll gains the friendship of Arawn and himself succeeds to Arawn's title; he marries the Underworld woman, Rhiannon, whose magic singing birds bring refreshment and forgetfulness to Bran's surviving companions. Yet beneath this friendship is set the constant enmity of Gwawl, Rhiannon's intended suitor. The Otherworld gateway bestows wonders and blows impartially.

The arch enchanter of the land of Dyfed is Llwyd ap Cil Coed, cousin of Gwawl, who causes mist to appear and engulf the land, people to disappear and the mysterious castle with the marble fountain to appear. He, like his cousin, is an Otherworldly lord of great power. We have already noted how Caswallawn is called an enchanter because his mantle of invisibility helped him slay Bran's son: he likewise causes devastation of the land in *Branwen*. The appearance of both men in the Third Branch doubly reinforces the enchantment that is upon the land. The mist and the mantle of invisibility seem to be of the same provenance: both render the countryside waste and empty of people. Yet the enchantment of Dyfed is brought about by Pryderi and his family sitting upon the Mound of Arberth.

There are two stories which help point the parallels between this branch and the themes of Grail, Wasteland and the descent into Hades for an Otherworld bride. (This last theme relates to Pwyll's quest for Rhiannon, by which the tangled web of enchantments are set upon the loom.) These are the tale of *Theseus and Peirithous* and that of *Perlesvaus* or the *Didot Perceval*.

Peirithous the Lapith was said to be a son of Zeus who, disguised as a stallion, mated with Dia. He made a pact of friendship with Theseus and invited him to his wedding. But the Centaurs who also attended the feast were unused to wine and one raped the bride, Hippodameia (Horse-Tamer). Her bridegroom Peirithous and his friend Theseus leapt to her rescue, cutting off the ears and nose of the offending Centaur. After Hippodameia's death, Peirithous and Theseus sought daughters of Zeus as brides. Theseus sought Helen of Sparta, and then helped Peirithous to obtain Persephone, accompanying him to Tartarus where Hades received them and bade them sit on the chair before them. They sat, unsuspecting, on the Chair of Lethe, of Forgetfulness, which welded itself to their flesh, and from which they could not rise. They remained in torment until Heracles came to complete his last labour, when he was permitted to release Theseus, but not Peirithous who had blasphemously attempted to seize the Queen of the Underworld.[40,57]

It would be impossible to superimpose this Greek legend over the Third Branch and bring forth direct parallels, yet it is possible to see a tangled relationship between Pwyll/Pryderi and Peirithous whose family retains an interest in ladies of an equine nature or Underworldly disposition. The disastrous marriage feast resembles more the feast of Gwern's succession in *Branwen*, when so many men are killed: there is even an echo of Efnissien's mutilation of Matholwch's horses, in the mutilation of the Centaur. The trip to Tartarus in order to obtain Persephone ends in the two friends stuck firmly by their backsides to Lethe's chair, from which only Theseus is finally released. Peirithous remains a prisoner. This echoes the way Rhiannon and Pryderi are stuck to the golden bowl in the Otherworldly castle. Pwyll's attempt to marry Rhiannon brings him also to the Underworld where he must defeat by guile a rival suitor, and from whom he extracts humiliating terms. Yet Gwawl is aptly revenged on Pwyll's son and widow.

To pinpoint the moment at which the Enchantments of Dyfed begin, we must return to the First Branch where Pwyll sits for the first time on the Mound of Arberth. Two features recur when anyone sits there: thunder sounds and a mist descends – the Otherworld reaches out and impinges upon the

world of every day. Such features also occur in the story of
Perceval where, on arriving at Arthur's court, Perceval seats
himself on the forbidden Perilous Seat:

> As soon as he was seated the stone split beneath him and
> broke with such an agonising sound that it seemed to all
> that the world might sink into the abyss. And ... there
> issued such a great shadowy cloud that for more than a
> league they could not see each other.[95]

The voice from the cloud exclaims that Perceval has performed
the rashest act ever known in that, by sitting in the Perilous
Seat, he has barely escaped destruction. Bron, the Fisher King,
cannot be healed of his wound until the best knight should
come, seek the Fisher King's court, and answer the Grail
question. Only then will he be cured,

> and the stone will be reunited in this place at the Round
> Table and the enchantments will fall which at present are
> in the land of Britain.[95]

Perceval, after many adventures, does find the Court, but fails
to answer the question and when he awakes he finds the
countryside empty of people, just as Pryderi and his family do
on the Mound. However, he does eventually achieve his quest.
Bron gives the Grail into Perceval's keeping and all hear the
melody which issues from the vessel. Bron then dies, leaving
Perceval to guard the Grail, the stone seat is reunited and the
enchantments of Britain are relieved. Perceval is given the title
of the Fisher King.

Bron, as we have said, is a later resonance of Bran who
likewise guards a cauldron and who awaits a successor. By
sitting on the Perilous Seat the stasis between the worlds is
ruptured, and the true cause of the enchantments is known.
Pryderi likewise succeeds to his father's role of Pen Annwn, but
only after he has been proved worthy by humiliation and
imprisonment. Bron, like Bran, is a willing prisoner, chained to
mortality by his unhealing wound – itself a paradigm of the
land's condition – the unbearing, Grailless land laid waste by
enchantment. But only in the castle of the Grail can the truth be
made known. The chained cauldron of the mysterious castle
where Rhiannon and Pryderi are imprisoned is not of this

dimension. One of the best-crafted Grail stories will help us see its function more clearly.

In *Perlesvaus*, Perceval, nearing the end of his quest, is taken to an Otherworldly island, to a hall hung with depictions of Christ and his disciples. Thirty-three men enter, each dressed in white with a red cross on their chests. As they sit down to eat, Perceval saw:

> a golden chain descending and from the middle hung a golden crown . . . it was attached to nothing save the will of Our Lord. As soon as the masters saw it descend they opened a great wide pit in the middle of the hall . . . the greatest and most lamentable cries ever heard rose up from below; and when the worthy men heard them they raised their hands to Our Lord and all began to weep.[20]

The chain is withdrawn after the meal and the pit covered up. The crown is intended for Perceval who is told that he will be made king of the Isle of Plenty, the former king having succeeded to a greater kingdom. The conditions of his service state that he must see 'that the isle is well provided for; if you do not, the crown will be taken from you and you will be placed on the Isle of Need, whose people you heard crying in this hall'. At length, Perceval becomes the Grail Guardian and departs on a ship for his destined kingship.

Striking here are the resonances between this Otherworldly company of Grail initiates and the Assembly of the Noble Head. Although there is no cauldron of gold, the masters wash in a great golden basin before the chain descends, attached, as in *Manawyddan*, to the thin air. The vision which Perceval sees is directly related to the Succession of the Pendragons: those worthy guardians of Sovereignty whose part is to ensure the bounty of the land. Those who serve faithfully, will be allowed to succeed to another kingdom, while those who fail will be as those lamentable souls in the pit who, like Mabon, the immemorial prisoner, grieve unceasingly. In *Perlesvaus* there is no hypocritical rejoicing in the fate of these prisoners, rather compassion and a willingness to end their torment. Such is the fate of the Titans who exceed their role and become the scourge of their land, like Cronos: yet there is hope even for him in succession of the ages. Taliesin wrote

Perfect is my seat in Caer Sidi,
Nor plague nor age harms him who dwells therein.
Manawyd and Pryderi know it. . . . [101]

Are they both masters at this feast, who contemplate unendingly the mysteries of the Grail and the Noble Head?

The parallels between Perceval and Pryderi show that both men are rash in their actions, inconsiderate of important tasks and correspondingly humiliated in their failure. Yet while Perceval is a prisoner of his own ignorance, he is not physically imprisoned like Pryderi. Unlike Perceval, Pryderi is himself a ruler of a country at the beginning of the story, although he has passed the kingship into the hands of Manawyddan. He has sat with the other six survivors about the Head of Bendigeid Fran, and known the sorrow of mortality and remembrance when the Otherworldly door was opened. If Pryderi was ever connected with the quest for the Grail or Cauldron, then that episode appears only in relation to *Branwen*. Although, according to the Irish translation of Nennius, Manaal is the keeper of a perpetual cauldron.[63] In *Manawyddan*, Pryderi is an immature ruler, who needs the cautious support of Manawyddan, his step-father. Surely, few characters can have had more fathers than Pryderi who is born of Pwyll, brought up by Teyrnon, fostered by Pendarun, lastly gaining Manawyddan for a step-father. It is only within the last branch of *Math* that he appears as a mature ruler, and even there he is easily duped by Gwydion – yet another enchanter. Gruffydd has suggested that Manawyddan and Teyrnon Twrf Liant (Lord of the Raging Sea) are doublets of each other and that Teyrnon, not Pwyll, is really the father of Pryderi. His theory centres on the derivation of Rhiannon and Teyrnon's names from the Celtic Rigantona (Great Queen) and Tigernonos (Great Lord) – these names are titles, just as Mabon and Modron's names are. Certainly, Manawyddan is a substitute father since Pwyll has succeeded to his destined role as Pen Annwn, Lord of the Underworld. We have also the evidence of Pausanius to cement the union of the Sea God with the Queen of the Underworld (cf. p.34).

Poseidon raped Demeter while they were both in the shape of horses, so that she gave birth to twins. The wooden statue of Demeter Melaina at Phygalia showed her with a mare's head, with serpents and other animals issuing from it. In one hand she held a dolphin, the symbol of Poseidon, and in the other a dove, a symbol of Persephone. Try as we might, we cannot escape the mare and her foal. One further story will show how Pryderi's servile punishment accords with both that of Mabon and that of another god, Apollo.

3   THE POWERFUL HERDSMAN

We are not told precisely what Pryderi's punishment was while he was enchanted by Llwyd: we only know that the door-knockers or hammers of the gate were about his neck – this seems to be symbolic of a punishment, *not* the punishment itself.

So what can this punishment have been? There may be a hint at this in Triad 26 where we are told of

> Pryderi son of Pwyll, Lord of Annwfn, tending the swine of Pendarun Dyfed his foster-father. These swine were the seven animals which Pwyll Lord of Annwfn brought, and gave them to Pendaran Dyfed his foster-father. And the place where he used to keep them was in Glyn Cuch in Emlyn. And this is why he was called a Powerful Swineherd; because no one was able either to deceive or to force him.[5]

This descriptive yet eliptical triad both reveals and obscures something of our story. Let us leave it to one side for a while and consider clues from a Classical tradition – *Apollo's servitude to King Admetus*.

In this story, Apollo had to do penance for an act which is variously described as:

(a) the slaying of the oracular serpent, Delphyne
(b) the slaying of Zeus's smiths and herdsmen, the Cyclops
(c) tricking Thanatos (Death) out of a destined victim.[35,57]

For each of these outrages, Apollo's penance is identical:

> Zeus would have hurled him to Tartarus; however, at the intercession of Latona (Leto) he ordered him to serve as

thrall to a man for a year. So he went to Admetus, son of Pheres . . . and served him as a herdsman, and caused all the cows to drop twins.[8]

The name Admetus means 'invincible', and is one of the titles of Hades – the Greek 'Pen Annwn'. This period of servile bondage seems to have been part of Apollo's cult when, according to the Delphic religious calendar, Apollo is said to be absent in the land of the Hyperboreans – the place beyond the North Wind, associated with the Celtic Paradise or Elysium where Cronos was similarly put out to grass.

Plutarch interpreted this yearly absence as Apollo's annual descent to the realm of the dead – a necessary event in his cult's calendar. We notice that it is only at Latona or Leto's advice – the mother of Apollo – that he is spared the torments of Tartaros: instead he is punished by servile bondage to a Lord of the Underworld.

Is it possible that the punishment of Pryderi was of a similar kind? He is the son of Pwyll, Pen Annwn and a Lady of the Underworld who was abducted from the Land of the Dead by trickery: a transgression committed by Pwyll, but revenged upon his son. But in what manner can Apollo and Pryderi have any possible connection?

To anticipate the argument in Chapter 9, we can note that Pryderi stands in the place of Mabon, as an embodiment of Mabon's power. Further, that Mabon/Maponos was closely identified with Hyperborean Apollo. The connection with Pryderi and the immemorial prisoner, Mabon, is deftly given in the *Preiddeu Annwn* poem by Taliesin which states:

> Complete was the prison of Gwair in Caer Sidi,
> According to the story of Pwyll and Pryderi.

Gwair is one of the names of Mabon – the prisoner who must be released. So famous was this theme that the comparison between Gwair and the stories of Pwyll and his son could be drawn upon by poets to indicate the nature of Mabon's imprisonment, in the Underworld castle of enchantment.

If we look again at the alternative title of this branch, the *Mabinogi Mynnweir a Mynord*, and contemplate the nature of Rhiannon and Pryderi's imprisonment, we will note a few interesting facts.

'Pryderi has had the knockers of the gate of my court about his neck, and Rhiannon has had the collars of the asses, after they have been carrying hay, about her neck. And such have been their fetters.'

There is a mystery hidden within this part of the story which only the initiate poet could penetrate: the asses have been carrying *gweir* or hay, in a literal sense, but it is Rhiannon, whose dual penance is to become the pack-mare and portress at the gate in both First and Third Branches, who is really *the bearer of Gweir* – Pryderi, who is a type of Mabon.

The collars which fetter them to the Underworld are the chains by which the Golden Cauldron is attached to its lord – the chains of enchantment which make them both prisoners and porters at Llwyd's gate. As the *Preiddeu Annwn* goes on to relate of Gweir:

> None before him was sent into it
> Into the heavy blue chain which bound the youth

indicating that Gweir's imprisonment was the first, but by no means the last, of its kind. Present also within this poem is a mysterious reference to a beast which is guarded, and whose destiny is closely woven with that of the prisoner.

Pryderi's totem beast is the foal which is bound up with his birth and conception: but on his father's side, he inherits the swine of Annwn, which are the gifts of Arawn to Pwyll, in token of their everlasting friendship. As we have been told by the triad, it is Pryderi, not Pwyll, who is one of three Powerful Swineherds: further we note that the swine are given in trust for Pryderi to Penndaran Dyfed, and that these swine are the magical seven in number – the same number of men who are redeemed from the visit to Ireland with Bran as well as from the Harrowing of Annwn with Arthur (cf. p.107).

We can only speculate, given these facts, that Pryderi is indeed such a one as Apollo: he undergoes a necessary sojourn in the Underworld as a prisoner, tied to a task which is normally demeaning to one of his nobility, but which establishes his willingness to 'stand at the gate' between the worlds of the living and the dead. Destined to be a sorrow to his mother, Gwri Golden Hair leaves behind his childhood to become Pryderi, 'Anxiety': a name arrived at by his mother's first utterance upon being reunited with him, and confirmed by Penndaran Dyfed whose herds he guards. Lastly, he becomes one of Three Powerful Swineherds whom no one can deceive because he has already suffered his term in the realms of the Underworld. The scene is set for Pryderi's last appearance and for a new Mabon to appear.

CHAPTER 5
Math, Son of Mathonwy

Blodeuwedd, the Flower-Bride

Few there are who know where the magic wand of Mathonwy grows in the woods.

ANON.
Daronwy

Did he and his back-room team
contrive this gleaming spoil from fungus by Virgil's arts in Merlin's Maridunum?

DAVID JONES
The Anathemata

1   THE ENCHANTER'S NEPHEW

In this the Fourth and final Branch of the *Mabinogion*, we take leave of Pryderi and witness the birth of another hero – Llew. The First and Fourth Branches are not only the longest stories, but also the most complex, interweaving forgotten tales with unexplained themes which tantalise the reader. These branches are connected by a circuitous chain of cause and effect: Pwyll befriends Arawn and receives the Underworld swine as a gift; Gwydion steals them by trickery in order to cause war and to satisfy his brother's lust. And so one hero perishes and another is conceived.

In the other branches the conflict has been between this world and the Otherworld, or between Britain and Ireland, but here Gwynedd and Dyfed, North and South Wales, are opposed. The events of the *Mabinogion* seem to leap from Otherworldly into real time where the tawdry enchantments of Gwydion are motivated by lust, greed, pride and jealousy, and where the ancient values of kingship and sacrifice, as typified by Math, are in decline.

Gwydion and his brothers and sister are children of Don about whom we have no information: scholars have pointed the parallels between this family and that of the Irish Tuatha de Danaan, or the family of Danu – a similar, shadowy ancestress whose descendants' names match those of Don's almost exactly. In each case, both families are known as children of their mother, not their father – except for Arianrhod who, according to Triad 35, is the daughter of Don by Beli. This same triad makes Arianrhod at least a half-sister of Caswallawn and perhaps hints at other familial connections which do not necessarily become plain from the family tree derived from this branch.

1   Math ap Mathonwy was Lord of Gwynedd and Pryderi was Lord of Dyfed. When he was not at war, Math had his feet held by the footholder, Goewin – an appointment which only a virgin could maintain. 2   Only Gwydion and Gilfaethwy, Math's nephews, were able to go on circuit in place of their uncle. 3   Gilfaethwy lusted after Goewin, yet she was never out of Math's sight: accordingly Gwydion planned to help his brother by raising war. 4   He

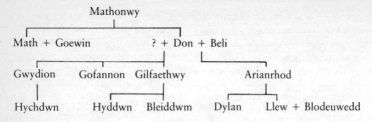

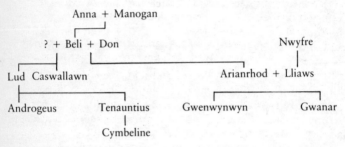

(a)   Family Tree Derived from the Fourth Branch

(b)   Family Tree Derived from Triad 35 and Geoffrey of Monmouth

Figure 5.1: *The Family Tree of Don*

petitioned Math to let him go and ask for the pigs which Pryderi had and which came originally from Annwn.

5   Disguising themselves as poets, Gwydion and Gilfaethwy sang for Pryderi and, for their fee, asked for the pigs. Pryderi was bound not to give any away until they had bred and increased their number twice. Gwydion then created by his magic thirteen steeds and twelve hounds, and offered to exchange these and their accoutrements for the pigs. Taking the swine, Gwydion and his host returned home. But his enchanted gifts resumed their former shape – namely mushrooms. They were pursued by Pryderi's host and arrived in Gwynedd to find their kinsmen marshalling for war.

6   In the uproar, Gilfaethwy raped Goewin. War was joined between Gwynedd and Dyfed. 7   Pryderi suffered a defeat and gave hostages to Gwynedd, then, to prevent needless slaughter, he offered

to fight Gwydion in single combat, to decide the outcome of the
war. Gwydion won by magic. 8   Returning to the court, Math
found that Goewin was no longer a virgin: he immediately offered
her marriage in reparation, and then forbade his people to give
shelter to or feed his nephews, who were forced to submit to his
judgement. He struck them with his wand, turning them into deer:
Gilfaethwy into a hind, Gwydion into a stag, and bade them live,
mate in the wilderness and produce young, returning to court in a
year's time. At the year's end, both returned together with a fawn
whom Math changed to a human child, then he further enchanted
his nephews – Gwydion into a sow, Gilfaethwy into a boar. A piglet
was born of this union and similarly made human. The last
enchantment saw Gilfaethwy as a bitch wolf and Gwydion as a
wolf: they returned with a cub. All three children were raised by
Math.

9   The nephews were forgiven. Math asked their advice about
the succession of the footholder. 10   Gwydion suggested Arianrhod,
his sister. As a test of virginity, she steps over Math's wand and
immediately births a yellow-haired boy. On leaving the court, she
drops something which Gwydion picks up and hides. 11   The child
is baptised Dylan; he makes for the sea and swims away.
12   Meanwhile. Gwydion finds that what he has put into the chest
at the foot of his bed has become a boy, whom he puts out to
fosterage until he is four years old.

13   He takes the boy to Caer Arianrhod where his mother
refuses to name him and lays a geise on him that none shall name
him but herself. Gwydion then returns with the boy in a boat, both
disguised as shoemakers. No shoe will fit Arianrhod until she
presents herself in person. She sees the boy cast a stone at a wren
and exclaims: 'The fair-haired one has hit it with a skilful hand.'
The boy is then named Llew Llaw Gyffes by Gwydion and both
resume their true shape: Arianrhod then swears that none shall arm
him as a man but herself.

Disguised as poets, Gwydion and Llew travel to Arianrhod's
castle again where Gwydion summons up the illusion of an enemy
host. Arianrhod then arms Llew herself, but Gwydion lifts the
enchantment and she swears that Llew shall never have a wife of
humankind.

14   Together Math and Gwydion fashion a woman out of
flowers, called Blodeuwedd. Math gives Llew estates in Ardudwy.
One day, while Llew is absent at court, Blodeuwedd sees a hunter
and offering him hospitality falls in love with him. They plan Llew's
death. 15   Feigning anxiety about the cause of Llew's death, Llew
tells her the condition under which he can be slain: only with a

spear that has been fashioned on Sunday while mass is said; he cannot be killed inside or outside, neither on horse nor on foot. This can only be accomplished if a bath is made on the river bank with a roof-frame over it, then Llew can stand with one foot on the edge of the bath and the other on the back of a goat.

Blodeuwedd informs Gronw, her lover and then, a year later, begs Llew to show her how difficult such a death would be to calm her anxiety. 16   He complies and Gronw casts the spear, killing Llew, and taking both Blodeuwedd and Llew's estates. Llew disappears in the shape of an eagle. 17   Gwydion scours the land to find him, and eventually comes to a cottage where a swineherd is having difficulty in penning or guarding his sow. Gwydion follows her to under a tree in Nantllew where she feeds on rotten flesh which falls from an eagle in the tree top. 18   He sings three englyns to entice it down, and then strikes the bird with his wand. It is the wasted body of Llew, whom he takes back to the court to be cured.

19   In revenge, Gwydion pursues Blodeuwedd. Her maidens all drown in a lake, while she is transformed into an owl, doomed ever to hunt by night. Gronw asks if he can pay compensation to Llew: it is refused. 20   Llew demands that Gronw suffer the same stroke as he had from Gronw, under the same conditions. He allows Gronw to place a stone between his body and the blow, but Llew pierces both the stone and Gronw. 21   Llew eventually succeeds to Math's kingdom.

1   The post of footholder was named in the Welsh laws: the *troedawc* was entitled to rent-free lands and perquisites. 'His duty is to hold the king's feet in his lap from the time he begins to sit at the carousal until he goes to sleep, and it is his duty to scratch the king.'[45] It was clearly a position of honour roughly equivalent to the present lady and gentleman of the royal chamber. Goewin also seems to exercise one of the privileges of Sovereignty in that while Math's feet are in her lap, the land is not at war. There is a venerable tradition of young women who serve aged kings: King David had Abishag to give him heat in his old age (I Kings 1, 1-4) while, in the East, young women are taken into the beds of sages as a test of continency and as a means of absorbing the life-giving Sakti or female power. (Gandhi followed this practice.) In medieval poetic tradition there was clearly a variant story in which Arianrhod was Math's footholder, since she is described as sharing Math's bed in a poem by Lewis Mon (c.1480).[45]

2   In the succession of Celtic kingship, it is the king's nephew, not the king's son, who has precedence. The blood of the mother, not the father, confers royal status, hence the king's sister produces the heir. Matrilinear succession is clearly an ancient practice which is still observable within Arthurian tradition and within the *Mabinogion*, long after the introduction of primogeniture among the Norman kings governing England and Wales. As we will see, it is Arthur's nephews who figure largely in the heroic stories of his court, while his son, Medraut or Mordred, is his opponent.

The custom of going on circuit was followed by all professional classes: druids, judges, poets and kings went on circuit to inspect the good government of the land, to administer justice, settle disputes, tell stories, etc. This custom helped spread responsibility for feeding the court, whose provisioning must have been gargantuan. Although Math is the maintainer of the realm, the active role of administrator of justice has fallen to his nephews.

3   Math is able, like the Coraniad in the story of *Lludd and Llefelys*, to hear news on the wind. While he is attended by his footholder, he is omniscient, rooted in the very heart of his land. Yet Gwydion is able to divine Gilfaethwy's complaint very easily. Gwydion is virtually Math's successor, both in magic and cunning, yet he lacks Math's stability. He exemplifies the sterile black magician within this story: one who destroys because he cannot create anything out of love.

4   The pig was a beast of great importance to the Celts, both as a staple food and as an Otherworldly totem. The many cuts from the pig were served to selected heroes at feasts to honour their exploits, yet also, there is the curious ban on having anything to do with their herding. We have seen that Pryderi is named as one of the Three Powerful Swineherds, one in contact with Annwn and the sometimes overwhelming Underworld powers. The older gods and heroes always have this Underworldly connection and act as door-keepers for those who travel to these realms (cf. Chapter 8). The hunting of the boar by the boy born in a pig-run is the theme of *Culhwch*: a quest which is analogous to the Harrowing of Annwn to gain its

treasures. Gwydion wishes to have the Underworld's treasures for his own people and, like Arthur and others who travel to Annwn, is willing to steal them at the cost of many lives.

5   Here is yet another of the many substitutions which afflict Pwyll's family. Pwyll changed places with Arawn in the First Branch. Manawyddan refused to exchange the mouse-wife of Llwyd for a retinue of horses and greyhounds in the Third Branch. Unfortunately, Pryderi is not so cautious: he accepts Gwydion's enchanted offer and so breaks his promise to Arawn. However, the pigs are a dangerous commodity, bringing with them the terrors of war and Otherworldly disruption into the lives of the men of Gwynedd.

6   The rape of Goewin is the rape of Sovereignty, since war is joined and the land set in uproar. Although Goewin is the one raped, it is Arianrhod who bears the children (see below).

7   As a hostage to the peace, Pryderi gives Gwrgi Gwastad as a hostage to the north. This name is suspiciously like that of Gwri – Pryderi's childhood alias. The text also tells us that Gwrgi is a youth: he and his companions are freed at Gwydion's suggestion from their imprisonment after Pryderi's death. With Pryderi's ignoble death, his story, which has bound the Four Branches together, transfers to another level of consciousness: he takes on an inner guardianship of which we will speak further. The combat between Pryderi and Gwydion echoes the earlier combat between Pwyll and Hafgan.

8   Math's redress and punishment are both radical. Goewin is restored to her former honour, becoming queen in fact. Gwydion and Gilfaethwy both suffer the punishment of greed and lust by becoming animals themselves and bearing children to each other: they are both seen by the court while in this condition, just as Arianrhod is later shamed.

9   Presumably Math has spent some three years minus his footholder; a discrepancy which the storyteller conveniently glosses over.

10   Arianrhod has been translated as Silver Wheel; Gruffydd further suggests that, since she is often spelt Arianrad, it may also mean Silver Fortress.[45] She is an Otherworldly queen and has archetypal connections with Ceridwen as the mistress of initiation (cf. Chapter 7). She seems to have undergone a curious rationalisation into an enchantress of malign intention in this story. The tangled sources for this transformation from possible footholder of Math into a wicked mother are dealt with in more detail on p.86.

Tests of chastity were much beloved of medieval conteurs but here Math's wand rather Freudianly becomes the weapon of Arianrhod's undoing. She is, of course, one of the royal women from whom the rightful heir can descend, since she is Math's niece. Math's wand has the ability to shape-shift a subject into revealing its true nature, as we have seen from his transformation of his nephews: here he effects a twin birth suggesting that Arianrhod's inner role is not one of virgin footholder. The mystery of the children's father is never solved in the story, though, subtextually, many have observed an incestuous union between Gwydion and his sister. One child is nearer term than the other – if we are not to consider the second 'small something' as the placenta which Gwydion magically incubates and turns into Llew.

Triad 78 names Arianrhod as one of three fair maidens: one of the others is Creirwy, the daughter of Ceridwen, so we may make a possible link between the two women and see them as the maiden aspect of the Triple Goddess of whom Ceridwen manifests the mother.

11   Dylan's lost story is known only from a similarly lost triad which is here referred to as one of three unfortunate blows: his death at the hands of his uncle, Gofannon, is partially reconstructed on p.87.

12   Gruffydd cites many instances in folklore where the placenta is considered to be the double of the child.[45] Gwydion shows himself incapable of creating anything himself: he always has to use some kind of raw material to effect his enchantment, as when he creates horses and their comparisons from mushrooms and leaves. The story of Finn Mac Cumhall's

secret upbringing is particularly relevant to Llew's and is given on p.87. The rapid development of Llew is parallel to that of Pryderi, and indicates that we are witnessing a new hero in the mould of Mabon.

13 The triple geise or prohibition upon Llew strongly prevents his acknowledgment among society since without a name, arms or a wife, he would be a non-entity. Since Gwydion has taken away her own reputation or name, Arianrhod refuses to name Llew. Her reluctance to name him is perhaps also due to the fact that he is the child of her brother. The incestuous parentage of the hero is well-attested in Celtic folklore.[87] Such a union produces a special child with superhuman abilities: yet he is generally outcast by being thrown into the sea, as in the case of Mordred or Taliesin. Here, of course, it is Llew's brother, Dylan, who takes to the sea.

The name of Llew, like the naming of Pryderi, is taken from his mother's first expostulation. Both Llew and his Irish counterpart, Lugh, are renowned for their skilful aim: Balor names Lugh in exactly the same way as Arianrhod (see below). Llew's killing of a wren – traditionally an oracular bird – is analogous to Lugh's slaying of Balor, who is Math's Irish counterpart. If we consider Math's omniscient hearing, the slaying of the wren makes more sense. The killing of wren was an Irish folk custom which corresponded to the winter death of the Old Year or King, when the Wren-Boys would go about singing a carol, showing the dead wren hung from a pole, and demanding payment in the immemorial way of itinerant players. Llew and Manawyddan are named as two of Three Golden Shoemakers (although it is Gwydion who makes the shoes here) in Triad 67. The third, Caswallawn, is somewhat of a mystery, since his story has been lost. Yet he too marries a flower-bride, like Llew, in Fflur. There is probably an ancient tradition of Llew and shoemaking since the Gaulish god Lugus was the patron of shoemaking.[45]

Since Llew and Lugh both have associations with the spear or sword, it is likely that the arming of Llew would have mentioned this weapon in an original version of the story. As it is, Llew's skill is transposed to the first geise, and his spear to the third part of the story where he is killed by it: this weapon seems also to have been the cause of Dylan's unfortunate death (cf. p.87). The arming of the son by the mother was an important part of Celtic society where young men 'took valour' or were recognised as marriageable men of adult status. By denying him this right, Arianrhod dooms Llew to perpetual youth.

14 This last geise is the most difficult to accomplish and beyond even Gwydion's skill. It is Math who is skilled in creation. The creation of Blodeuwedd from the flowers of oak, broom and meadowsweet is well annotated. It appears as an interpolation of the *Cad Goddeu* poem, attributed to Taliesin.[2] While Math's great enchantment can create a body, it cannot ensoul his nephew's intended wife. She is totally Otherworldly, incapable of human morality and, hence, unworthy of Gwydion's harsh punishment.

15 The old ruse of feigning anxiety over the possible cause of a husband's death is employed by Blodeuwedd: her betrayal of Llew is like that of Blathnait's (cf. p.50). No one inquired whether she loved Llew, she is merely given to him. A late Welsh story relates how the wife of Huan plotted to kill her husband. His father, Gwydion, eventually found him in Caer Gwydion (i.e. in the stars), where his son's soul had flown. He turned the daughter into a bird. The story is called Huan's Deceiving: *Twyll Huan*. A tylluan is also Welsh for owl. This story gives corroborative evidence that Gwydion is Llew's father, not just his uncle.[45]

16 Llew very stupidly breaks his own death-geise by accomplishing two of the three conditions for his death. It is interesting that, although he is given the geise of namelessness, lack of arms and wifelessness, he should be aware of the death-geise. Since Gwydion incubated him and partly created him, this information was also vouchsafed to him. Such impossible conditions are common in folklore where the protagonists have to appear neither sitting nor standing, neither clothed nor naked, neither running nor walking etc.[41] In this instance the conditions are clearly as follows: neither inside nor outside, neither riding nor on foot, with the additional

condition of being neither clothed nor naked, since a bath-tub is mentioned. Llew straddles it half-clothed: we may wonder whether an original detail had him clothed in a fishing-net, but such watery details have all been transposed to Dylan, his brother.

17   As once Teyrnon watched anxiously for his foal's safety, as once Manawyddan watched the burgeoning of his crops, so Gwydion follows the progress of the sow in order to find Llew. Llew does not die of Gronw's blow, but is transformed into his totem bird, the eagle. In times of stress and under the influence of the Otherworld, the characters within the *Mabinogion* revert to their archetypal shapes. Here the appearance of the sow is doubly significant since Gwydion, in his earlier transformation by Math, appeared as a sow and so knows all the ways of this beast. The sow, the most ferocious and dangerous beast, is the fearsome or dark aspect of the Goddess, and so may be seen as an extension or representative of Arianrhod, who wishes her son's destruction in this story.

18   The three englyns are worth examination and meditation. Gwydion here employs the authentic magic of the poet, rather than the tawdry enchantment of his magic. He uses music to attract the astral form of his nephew/son back from the edge of death to the threshold of life once more. He stresses the real world location to him, and identifies the eagle as Llew, thus helping him to bring his soul from the state of limbo between the worlds where he is trapped.

19   The revenge of Gwydion upon the body of the woman he helped to create is without mercy or compassion. Blodeuwedd is transformed into an owl, a night-hunting bird which other birds shun. Alan Garner's great reworking of this branch, *The Owl Service*, revolves around this very point of revenge or mercy: 'she wants to be flowers, but you make her owls', cries the crushed and penitent descendant of Gwydion, Hugh Half-Bacon, who has lived through the triple destruction of Llew, Gronw and Blodeuwedd times without number and witnessed his own loveless defeat.[110]

20   Llew's revenge has the tempered quality of his great-uncle, Math. He allows Gronw the shelter of a stone when he casts the spear, for the reciprocal blow, though this in no way alters the inevitable outcome of his death at Llew's hands.

21   Since Arianrhod denies Llew a bride, he cannot become a true king, wedded to his Sovereignty. Blodeuwedd is an Otherworldly woman, and in this human world of the Fourth Branch, can confer nothing on her husband. Llew's own birth was caused by the loss of Goewin's Sovereignty and by his mother's loss of reputation: his subsequent sufferings are a working-out of a hard destiny in which he will eventually succeed to his great-uncle's throne and his uncle/father's magic.

2   ONE-EYE AND THE SKILFUL HAND

All the signs indicate that the Fourth Branch is of later composition than the other three. The world of Gwynedd, though still replete with enchantment, has less direct contact with the Otherworld, and though there are still many ancient themes buried within it, this story has the greatest number of rationalisations of character. Because of this aspect, it is the one which most readers find easiest to identify with. The terrible rejections and revenges exacted here are wholly human and, as such, the most tragic and unendurable. The only persons for whom Gwydion shows any love – Gilfaethwy and Llew – suffer from his jealous love; and those who oppose the objects of his affection – Pryderi, Blodeuwedd and Gronw – are subjected to terrible revenge and merciless death.

   This branch is composed of three connected stories: the theft of Pryderi's pigs and the rape of Goewin; Llew's childhood and lifting of his geises; the betrayal of Blodeuwedd. Beneath these tales are even more ancient ones which we are able to uncover by the help of many Irish folkstories to help solve the mystery of Dylan's death, Arianrhod's lover, and the nature of Gwydion and Llew's relationship. We are indeed fortunate that so many variant stories directly relating to the birth and destiny of Llew's Irish counterpart, Lugh, survived within the oral tradition. A common tradition underlies the families of Don and Danu: the Irish evidence for this was recorded at a much earlier date than the transcription of the *Mabinogion*, but this does not necessarily make it older in essence. The surviving folkstories, relating to Balor and his grandson, Lugh, are correspondingly very late, from the point of transcription, since J.F. Campbell and Jeremiah Curtin recorded the oral tales of Ireland and Scotland in the last century.[24,30] These stories are also relevant to our study of *Culhwch*, since it draws on the same oral tradition.

Gruffydd, in his monumental study of *Math*, has fully demonstrated the stages by which common Welsh and Irish themes synthesised into each other, so we will content ourselves with a brief retelling of the relevant Irish stories. The main source is *Balor on Tory Island*.[30] King Balor lived on Tory Island because it was prophesied that he would be killed by the son of his only daughter: to this end he imprisoned her in a tower on Tory with twelve women to guard her. Opposite on the mainland lived a smith, Gavidim, who owned a magical cow – the only such beast in all Ireland – which could fill any vessel with milk.

Balor wanted the cow and sent his agents to fetch it, but they were refused. The three sons of Ceanfaeligh came to Gavidim to have swords made for themselves; each promised to take turns in guarding the cow. Fin, the youngest brother, was responsible for losing the cow, which was captured by Balor's agents. Gavidim demanded its return of Fin whom he threatened to behead. Fin asked the help of an Otherworldly man called Gial Dubh (or Mathgen, in another variant). Together they went to Balor's castle where Fin was submitted to impossible tasks which Gial Dubh achieved magically. He helped Fin sleep with Balor's daughter, counselling him also to sleep with the twelve guardian women so that they might not warn Balor out of jealousy of each other. Fin achieved the cow and returned it to Gavidim.

Before the end of the year, Fin returned to Tory and rescued the thirteen children which the women had borne. Twelve fell overboard and became seals and the thirteenth was Balor's grandson who did not thrive until taken back to his mother's breast. Gial Dubh created a magical forest about the island to hide the child from Balor, but a wind blew it down, and Balor killed Fin. Not knowing himself to be Balor's grandson, the boy determined to kill his father's murderer. In another variant, the boy becomes the gardener's assistant and because he is able to pick up many apples, Balor cries out: 'Tog leat Lui Lamfada' – 'Take them away, Little Long Hand': and so he receives his name.

Lui kills Balor's agents and escapes from the island. Balor pursues him to Gavidim's forge where Lui waits with a red-hot spear. Balor had an eye in the middle of his head which he kept shielded with nine shields that the world might not be blasted: as he raised the last shield, Lui struck him in the eye. Balor then knew the identity of his opponent as his own grandson and requested Lui to behead him and place Balor's head over his own, so that he would know everything and become invincible. However, Lui cast the head down where it made a hole in the earth deeper than the deepest lake.

Many recognisably similar aspects between this and the Fourth Branch are apparent, but the characters and their motivations are totally dissimilar. Gavidim the smith is Gofannon. Gial Dubh is Gwydion who helps Fin with his magic: the variant name of Mathgen for Gial Dubh equates the magical roles of both Math and Gwydion in one character. Balor and Math are totally dissimilar: Balor appears again in the *Mabinogion* as the Cyclopean giant, Yspaddaden, in *Culhwch* where again his death is dependent upon his daughter staying unmarried. Balor's daughter is analogous to Arianrhod: both women are associated with their dwelling in a tower. Math's testing of Arianrhod's virginity here makes more sense if, in an original source, Math was in the position of Balor. In *Balor*, the daughter is impregnated through magical means: she bears a son by Fin, and her women each bear a child who swims off into the sea, just as Dylan does. In another variant, the smith Gavidim fosters Lui and it is he who forges the famous spear of the hero, which in *Math* becomes the weapon of both Llew's downfall and Gronw's death. In both instances, it is Gial Dubh or Gwydion who is the enabling magician who obtains the magical cow/pigs, and helps impregnate the imprisoned daughter.

Gruffydd has shown that Goewin was a late interpolation into the Fourth Branch and that Arianrhod originally fulfilled the sustainer of Math. Tudor Aled, a fifteenth-century poet, spoke of Arianrhod like this:

> woe to him who looks upon her. . . . Over her . . . is a keeper as strong as the wall . . . there is her father with his eyes upon her . . . the lissom lady dare not jump on to the cliff.[45]

Lewis Mon (1480) wrote comparing his love with Arianrhod:

> My plaint concerning a maid is greater than that of Math Hen, son of Mathonwy. The arm of a chaste white-armed maiden was every night his pillow, Arianrhod white as snow; that man might not live without her.[45]

Which demonstrates that knowledge of other variant stories were still circulating long after the first transcription of the *Mabinogion*.

Arianrhod's tower, Caer Sidi, has passed into the Mysteries of Britain as the magical tower of poetic initiation and also the Otherworldly Caer of transformation and death. Folk tradition speaks of the inundation of the tower into Caernarvon Bay, where a reef of stones can be seen at low tide.[13] This legend is very like that of Kaer Ys in Brittany where the pride of Ahes, a woman not dissimilar to Arianrhod, causes its inundation.

Arianrhod is described in the triads as Beli's daughter. Beli and Balor are derived from each other. In Irish legend Balor becomes the restrictive grandfather giant whose Cyclopean eye blasts all he looks upon: while in Welsh legend, Beli becomes a renowned ancestor, whose name heads many genealogies. If we refer to the family trees on p.74, we will see that Beli's wife or mother is named as Don or Anna: both names derive from a common Celtic source and, while later medieval commentators have tried to pass Anna off as identical with St Anne, mother of the Blessed Virgin, it is evident that the lady in question is really Danu, Don or Anu, the ancestral Goddess of both Irish and Welsh peoples.[5,91] Arianrhod has clearly inherited all of Balor/Math's characteristics from a lost original: she restricts her own son in an inexplicable manner, putting upon him geises which were once probably issued by Balor/Math. Of her own imprisonment and secret wooing, *Math* is silent: what remains is an unattractive enchantress whose malignancy is total.

The birth, conception and upbringing of Dylan and Llew are strongly related to that of Finn Mac Cumhall whose own upbringing was kept necessarily secret. Finn's mother bore two children, the second of whom was hidden by her brother Gobhan Saor in a tree-trunk or among a magical enclosure of trees. *Gobha* is Irish for smith, and clearly relates to Gofannon's role as foster-father of Dylan, while the hiding of the child in a tree equates to Gwydion's hiding of Llew, or the hiding of Lui by Gial Dubh in the magical forest. In a folkstory relating to Finn, it is told how Finn's father had to temper the sword he was making on the first thing which came through the smithy door, such was his skill at making deadly weapons; at such times, Finn's mother hid her son away and sent in a dog to the forge that the sword's venom might be spent on the beast and not the boy.[45] This perhaps gives us the necessary clues to Dylan's own untimely end. Gofannon, the master-smith, was doubtless the forger of Llew's famous sword or spear in the lost original.

The following tentative reconstruction should not be considered as definitive, but as one possible means of understanding the complex mysteries hidden within this story.

Math's rule was destined to end when his daughter married. To which end she was imprisoned in a tower on an island. Math desired the magical pigs of Pryderi and sent his agents to fetch them. The youngest of these, Gilfaethwy, aided by the magic of Gwydion and the smithcraft of Gofannon, determined to supplant Math by sleeping with his daughter, Arianrhod. Gilfaethwy slept with her, while Gwydion slept with her women. When it was time to rescue the children Dylan slipped into the sea, whereupon Gwydion gifted him with the ability to turn into a seal, so that the boy had two natures. The other boy, Llew, was weak, requiring his mother's milk. Gwydion disguised himself and the boy as gardeners and gained employment on the island of Math where the boy was hidden among the trees.

Math suspected that his daughter had borne a child and submitted her to a test of virginity. On finding she was no longer virgin, he swore a destiny on her son that he should have no name, that he should bear no arms. Then he transformed the boy's father into a beast. Yet Math himself named the boy

by remarking on his great dexterity and good aim, so that the
boy was called Llew of the Long or Skilful Arm. Further, Math
desired that a spear be made for him which should have great
venom and kill the first thing which entered the smithy door
while it was cooling. Gofannon set up the forge for such a
weapon but, after it came from the anvil, Dylan returned to his
foster-father's forge and was accidentally slain in place of Llew,
for whom Math intended the spear.

Llew then caught up the spear and killed his grandfather,
who swore a final destiny that Llew should have no woman of
mortal-stock for his wife. Gwydion was able to make a woman
from flowers but she was inhuman and she betrayed Llew with
another man. Gwydion sought the stars for his foster-son until
he found his soul. Llew was revenged upon his wife and her
lover but, having no offspring, he died and Gwydion set him in
the stars as the hero with the spear or sword of light who fights
for those imprisoned beyond hope of release.

Lui, Lugh and Llew are strongly related to hero Llwch
Lleminawc, whose brilliant sword of light wins the treasures in
the *Preiddeu Annwn* (cf. p.107). His name has been associated
with the Celtic deity Lugus, who is remembered in many place-
names, e.g. Lugudunum (Lyon) and Luguvalium (Carlisle).
Throughout Celtic legend, Lugh/Llew/Lugus is a sun-god whose
skills rank him supreme among the gods. His name is now lost
to modern pantheons, but not his power to which St Michael
now succeeds. T.C. Lethbridge's study has shown that many
places once associated with Lugh were rededicated to
St Michael during the Christian era.[59] The bearer of the flaming
spear still thrusts down into darkness those things of ancient
evil, and releases prisoners with his sword of light.

But it is not only as a Christian saint that Llew has survived,
but also in the person of Lancelot, the queen's champion, who
is raised by the Lady of the Lake. In almost all versions of the
Arthurian legend, this Lady is unnamed, yet in Layamon's *Brut*,
she is called Argante, in which we see an echo of Arianrhod
who also inhabits a sea-girt island. Arianrhod and Llew, like
Rhiannon and Pryderi, stand forth as the latest contenders for
the titles of Modron and Mabon. Both women are shamed by
their child's birth; both children are lost, raised in secret and
return to perform great deeds.

If the Arthurian overtones seem a little strained, we have only to consider that in *Lanzelet*, a German twelfth-century poem, Lancelot's foster-mother, the Lady of the Lake, is named as Modron whose son, Mabuz, becomes an evil magician in this story.[105] Further we can play a permutation game in which Arianrhod, Gwydion and Llew become Igrayne, Merlin and Arthur, but once one enters the vast field of Arthurian sources, it is easy to find correspondences – it is a virtual treasury where gold is so common, one can stuff one's pockets full and still come back for more.

The Fourth Branch is as rich a field as the *Mabinogion* hunter could wish for, in which the young sun-god suffers a small eclipse only to rise brighter on the morrow and perform more splendid deeds of valour.

CHAPTER 6
Culhwch and Olwen

Hunting the Boar

My lords, a proven sooth it is that seven times was the Court found in the seven Cloaks of the story. But as yet ye know not what this may signify . . . the seven Cloaks are in truth the seven Wardens, Each of these Wardens in his turn will tell you how he found the Court, and before hand ought it not to be told.

Elucidation de L'Hystoire du Graal

Bring the sword of light that can never fail to cut or give light, the bread that can never be eaten and bottle of water that can never be drained.

J. CURTIN
Coldfeet and the Queen of the Lonesome Isle

1 TASKS AND HEROES

With *Culhwch and Olwen* we leave the canonical Four Branches of the *Mabinogion* and enter a wider, more archetypal world; nevertheless, this story draws upon many ancient sources which are parallel and complementary to the Four Branches. *Culhwch* is virtually a compendium of stories ironed out to read as one sequence. Embedded within it can be discerned genuinely traditional portions of original storytellers' presentation. These are found in the riddling dialogues of Culhwch and the Porter, the repetitive utterances and sequences, as well as in the great artistic wordplay which describes Culhwch and Olwen themselves. Repetition of phrase and descriptions are a feature of orally-transmitted stories; landmarks to guide the teller from one passage to another. We find them in the *Iliad* and the *Odyssey* where Homer draws on oral tradition, right down until the present *seanchais* who are the last guardians of the Irish storytelling tradition.

Compared with the medieval constraints which have fallen upon the retold Four Branches, *Culhwch* has all the humour and immediacy of a folkstory. It ranges from high tragedy to burlesque. We meet Arthur's court which is made up of heroes from so many levels of tradition that we are surely within the Otherworldly realm itself. Beasts, birds, men and gods, witches, maidens, queens and enchantments mingle in this most complex of tales. The list of Arthur's court, giving the names of no less than 250 individuals, is very offputting to non-Welsh speakers, and this is a shame because some of these characters are very revealing; others have merely nonsense or riddling epithets tagged on to their names.

Although this seems the most Welsh of stories, we should not be surprised to encounter distinct Cornish and Irish elements. Culhwch bears a strong relationship to both Tristan and Lugh, as we will see. But the major themes are those central to the British Mysteries: the Harrowing of Annwn by Arthur to fetch the Hallows; the finding of Mabon, with the help of the oldest animals – a theme to be discussed more fully in Chapters 8 and 9; and the defeating of the restrictive giant, which highlights Arthur's place in the Succession of the Pendragons.

1   Cilydd ap Celyddon Wledig married Goleuddydd ferch Anlawdd Wledig. While she was pregnant she ran mad; near her time, she returned from the wilderness and gave birth to her son in a pig-run. He was subsequently known as Culhwch or Pig-Sty. Goleuddydd fell ill and before her death forbade her husband to marry again until a two-headed briar grew on her grave. For seven years her tutor trimmed the grave, but at length he forgot and Cilydd found such a briar growing thereon. 2   Cilydd then fought the neighbouring King Doged, married his widow and also took his lands and his daughter. The new queen demanded of an old hag if her abductor had any children; on learning that he had Culhwch, she bade Cilydd recall him from his place of fosterage. She then suggested to Culhwch that he should wed her daughter, but he refused. She put a destiny on him that he might marry none save Yspaddaden Pencawr's daughter, Olwen.

3   Immediately, Culhwch conceived a love of Olwen, so that his father sent him to Arthur to ask his help in obtaining her.
4   Culhwch was prevented from entering the hall by Glewlwyd, Arthur's porter. 5   Culhwch threatened to satirise Arthur and lay waste the country by his complaint, unless he gained entry. He was let in and demanded of Arthur the rights of a king's heir 6   and that Arthur should trim his hair for him. Arthur realised their kinship instinctively and promised 7   to grant whatever Culhwch asked, save only his personal gear and his wife. 8   Culhwch then demanded Olwen in the names of all at Arthur's court.

After a year's search, she was not found. Cai, Bedwyr and others with Culhwch went to a far land and met 9   a giant herdsman on a mound called Custennin who had been dispossessed by Yspaddaden. 10   Culhwch gave him a ring which Custennin took home to his wife. She realised instinctively that Culhwch was her sister's son. The company came to Custennin's house where Cai was nearly killed by the wife's joyful greeting. 11   The woman revealed her (unnamed) son who was hidden in a cupboard for fear of Yspaddaden, who had killed twenty-three of her sons. The boy became Cai's charge. The woman then arranged for Culhwch to see 12   Olwen who comes to wash her hair every Saturday night at their place.

13   Olwen told Culhwch that she could not marry him, having given her promise not to disobey her father, who would die if she married. She bade Culhwch accept any task or promise which her father might exact. 14   The company came to the hall and asked for Olwen's hand. 15   Yspaddaden must raise his eyelids with forks in order to see his guests, and he cast a poisoned stone spear at them; Bedwyr flung it back and pierced the giant in the knee.

They came again and were delayed by the answer that Olwen's great-grandparents must be consulted first. Yspaddaden cast a second spear and Menw cast it back, catching the giant in the chest. On the third occasion, Culhwch cast back the spear and caught the giant in the eye.

16 At last Yspaddaden heeded their request and set Culhwch thirty-nine *anoethu* (impossible tasks) of which fourteen are achieved within the ensuing story. 17 These were (listed by their number in the catalogue of tasks):

TASK:			
		39	to get the sword of Wrnach, the giant
		28	to release Eidoel ap Aer, Mabon's cousin
	18	26	to release Mabon ap Modron
		36	to get the hounds of Rhymhi
		7	to sow the fields with linseed, that a veil might be spun of it for Olwen's wedding
		30	to get the leash made out of Dillus Farfawg's beard
	19	22	to get the whelp, Drudwyn
		32	to summon Gwynn ap Nudd
		27	to get the leash of Cors Cant Ewin
		16	to summon Gwrgi Seferi and Odgar ap Aodh
		15	to get the tusk of Ysgithrwyn, chief boar
	20	14	to obtain the cauldron of Diwrnach
	21	21	to hunt the Twrch Trwyth with the help of the assembled helpers
		18	to obtain the blood of the pitch-black witch, daughter of the bright-white witch with which to anoint Yspaddaden's hair.

These tasks were accomplished in the order as shown above.
22 Then Yspaddaden was shaved, according to his request, with the comb and scissors which were between the ears of the Twrch Trwyth. He gave his daughter to Culhwch who, by the help of Arthur and his men, had fulfilled all conditions. Goreu son of Custennin then beheaded the giant, and Culhwch was possessed of Olwen and her father's castle.

1 This preliminary story of Culhwch's birth establishes his totemic name: Pig-Run or Pig-Sty which, at first glance, appears outrageous or merely comic. However, it is Culhwch's destiny to defeat the two great boars, Ysgithrwyn and Twrch Trwyth. As we have already stated, the pig played a great part in Celtic life both as a staple food and as a totemic creature of the Underworld. The combination of pigs and madness is a joint

theme which subtracks Celtic literature. Merlin, in his madness, addresses his lamenting prophecies to a pig in Coed Celyddon, thus showing himself to be one of the great swineherds or guardians of the totem beasts (cf. Chapter 8). Here, Goleuddydd gives birth 'for fear of the swine'.

If pigs come from the Underworld, then their guardians, swineherds, often have an initiatory significance as Underworld way-showers. They show the way to health and prosperity, as instanced by King Bladdud's finding of the hot springs over which the city of Bath was founded,[99] or by the swineherd who discovers the mysterious location for the Eoghanacht kings of Cashel in Ireland.[21]

Culhwch is found in a pig-sty, just as Pryderi is found in a stable: each hero's destiny is bounded by this totemic association just as the Irish hero, Diarmuid, whose destiny is woven with that of a white boar.[87] Culhwch acquires no other name, although he does gain a helper, Goreu, whose role is bound up equally with both Culhwch winning Olwen and with the destiny of Mabon, as we shall see in Chapter 9. There is a secret and undisclosed association between Culhwch and the mighty Twrch Trwyth which may be hinted at in *Cormac's Glossary*, a tenth-century Irish tract. In Irish, *torc* or *orc* and *triath* mean 'boar' and 'chieftain', respectively. We read: '*triath* is the name of a king, *orc triath* is the name for a king's son'.[21] In Celtic times the pig was valued, yet the trade of pig-tending was disgraceful for noblemen. The role of swineherd is connected with both madness – it is often the trade which banished or temporarily deranged heroes take up – and with exile: yet, as we have seen, it is a role which bestows hidden insights and often riches. Part of the kingly candidate's training consists in servile labours in many myths from Apollo to Pryderi. Culhwch is no exception to this rule: he has to perform strange and impossible labours to placate the giant; he has to kill the Twrch Trwyth which, according to the Irish gloss, means King's Son. The connections between our hero, the boar and the giant will be traced on p.111.

2   Doged's widow enacts the role of the jealous stepmother in this story, determined to further the rights of her own child. Like Arianrhod, she lays a marriage geise upon Culhwch. Her

dialogue with the old hag survives as late as the nineteenth century in the Irish folktale, *Black Thief and King Conal's Three Horses*, which parallels Culhwch almost exactly up to this point.[30]

3 Culhwch is, according to the story, only seven years old at this point. His new-found adulthood is accelerated by two actions: the realisation of Olwen and his love for her, and his shaving at the hands of Arthur. He loves Olwen the moment she is named and, as in *Maxen Wledig's Dream* where Maxen cannot rest until he finds Elen, so Culhwch sets off on his quest. The description of his ride to the court, like the later description of Olwen, is one of the masterpieces of Celtic storytelling embellishment.

4 The pattern of question and answer between Culhwch and Glewlwyd is very ancient indeed. It parallels almost exactly the exchange between Irish Lugh and the porter in the court of Nuadu of the Tuatha de Danaan, as told in *The Second Battle of Mag Tured*. Culhwch arrives at Midwinter to Arthur's court in need of help but he is shut out. Glewlwyd, extolling the great deeds of Arthur, states that he has never met a more worthy man than Culhwch throughout the two-thirds of his life.

5 Culhwch threatens to raise three shrieks which will blast the land's fertility – a very serious challenge to the rightful upholder of Sovereignty, King Arthur. In *Lludd and Llefelys*, a dragon cries every May Eve and similarly blights both land and animals. The theme of wasteland is slight within *Culhwch*, yet the unrestricted Underworld powers of Twrch Trwyth threaten to blight the Island of the Mighty. When Arthur aids Culhwch, he is strengthening his own realm (see p.104).

6 Culhwch is one of Arthur's many cousins. The cousins and nephews of a king were of greater importance in family precedence and succession than the king's sons. The family tree in Figure 6.1 will show some important links which are very revealing.

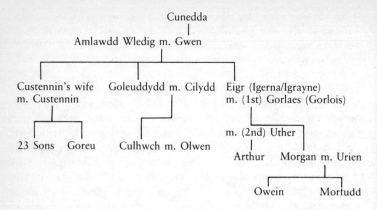

Figure 6.1: *The Family Tree of Culhwch*

It will be seen that Arthur's mother, Eigr, as the Triads call Igerna, is the sister not only of Goleuddydd, Culhwch's mother, but also of Custennin's unnamed wife. These three sisters are none other than the 'famous Cornwall sisters' of later Arthurian romance whose magical arts weave the fate of Arthur like the *Parcae* or Fates.[5]

Culhwch's shaving is a rite of passage into manhood, administered by the most senior and most noble of his kin – Arthur himself. Hair and shaving is another theme of this story: Culhwch is shaved by Arthur, Olwen washes her hair in the house of her foster-mother, a leash is made of Dillus's beard, and Yspaddaden demands extensive barbering with a variety of implements.

7   Triad 93 describes Culhwch as one of three 'who specified their dependency from Arthur as their gift'. Arthur promises help, exempting only his ship, mantle, sword, spear, knife and wife. An almost exact catalogue of these items is given by Geoffrey of Monmouth: Arthur has a golden helmet whose crest is a dragon, a shield called Pridwen across his back, on which is painted a likeness of the Blessed Virgin. His sword, Caliburn, is forged in the Island of Avalon, and his spear is called Ron.[37] Clearly, *Culhwch* and Geoffrey's *Historia* have definite links.

8   Culhwch's request leaves out nobody in Arthur's retinue. From the list which follows, it is clear that Arthur's court is of an Otherworldly nature since famous Arthurian heroes are mentioned in the same breath as immortals, kings of adjoining lands, poets and survivors of Camlann (at which Arthur himself was borne away to Avalon). Monsters and nonsense people abound, such as the daughters of Bwlch, Gyfwlch and Sefwlch – Plague, Want and Penury. The storyteller and his successors have included many characters from the entire Arthurian court, as well as favourites from other traditional stories current at the time. It is exceedingly valuable to study the names listed, as a fuller picture of the Dark-Age Arthur can be built up.[73] Several names are mentioned more than once: noticeably that of Llwch Llenllawg, of whom we will speak later.

Nearly every branch of the *Mabinogion* is represented by one character, but most important are those men of special skills who are the enablers of Culhwch's quest. Each of these possesses a unique and Otherworldly skill and these men form Culhwch's inner band of human helpers (cf. p.102).

9   Custennin is Yspaddaden's herdsman and porter. The text implies that these lands and the fortress once belonged to Custennin who says, 'Because of my wife, Chief Giant Yspaddaden has ruined me.'[3] We are not told what manner of claim the giant has on Custennin's wife nor why she has caused Custennin to lose his lands. But it seems likely that she is somehow kin to Yspaddaden – possibly his sister – in an older frame of reference. Both she and Custennin are described in titanic terms. The roles of herdsman and foster-mother, which they jointly fulfil, are deeply involved in the initiation of the hero and heroine (cf. Chapter 8). A similarly awesome herdsman figure appears in *The Lady of the Fountain* where his role as guardian of the way between the worlds is clearly shown. Custennin's fortunes are in decline and can only be rescued by his remaining son, Goreu.

10   The mysterious riddling dialogue between Custennin and his wife is quite baffling until we look at other parallel stories. Custennin pretends he got the ring from a washed-up corpse,

but his wife immediately knows this is not so and, like Arthur, she immediately realises a deeper sense of kinship between herself and Culhwch. In *The Second Battle of Mag Tured*, Eri, a woman of the Tuatha, conceived her son, Bres, after lying with a man who came out of the West in a magical boat. He left her a ring and bade her give to none other than the one it should fit. When Bres grows up and becomes the King of the Fomorians, he demands to know of his father: Eri gives him the ring, which fits perfectly, and sends him to his father.[28] Further to this we have the testimony of the Tristan legend, so close to Culhwch's own upbringing. Here Tristan's mother gives a ring to her husband when she is near to death after giving birth to Tristan; she bids him show the ring to King Mark so that he will know that the child is his sister's.

It would seem, then, that Culhwch gives his mother's ring as a token and Custennin's wife, being sister to Goleuddydd, immediately recognises it.

11 In this episode, where Cai is nearly strangled by the woman's greeting, we see Cai in his accustomed role as buffoon, deflecting the danger of the Otherworldly powers. However, he accepts Custennin's son in the spirit of true fosterage. The terms of his service imply that the boy's life will be as long as his own. This is important if we consider Cai's later action of freeing Mabon and carrying him away on his back. Goreu and Mabon have very close relationships and may be seen as aspects of each other. Both are hidden or imprisoned, both do deeds of great glory. Cai is their enabler and so has an important role in the Succession of the Pendragons. Heroes do not become kings without the help of such willing enablers.

12 Olwen and Culhwch are never described in mundane terms: they are the peerless protagonists of this story. Olwen's name means 'White Track' after the white clovers which spring up behind her as she walks. It is clear that she is Flower-Bride, like Blodeuwedd or Blathnat (cf. p.50). Her relationship with Custennin's wife is very close; whether it is as niece or foster-daughter is not entirely clear.

13   Although she is the giant's daughter, Olwen is not a giant herself. Like Bran and Branwen, who have similarly disparate sizes, Olwen and her father come from very different levels of proto-Celtic story. Olwen is a Flower-Woman whose Sovereignty is of an Otherworldly order, while Yspaddaden is a Titan of negative Underworldly restriction. The motif of the Giant's Daughter is discussed on p.102. Although Olwen does not follow the pattern of other giants' daughters in this story, by actively helping her suitor, it is possible that she does give magical help to Culhwch and his helpers. Sworn never to disobey her father's orders, Olwen knows that her marriage will mean his death.

14   The fort is ringed by nine gates, at which nine porters and nine mastiffs wait – all are killed by Culhwch and his men. Yspaddaden's court is therefore analogous to Annwn itself and to the complex descent which Arthur's men and Culhwch are making (cf. Figure 6.2).

15   Yspaddaden is clearly a Balor figure, even down to the baleful one eye: from Odysseus and the Cyclops onwards, this motif is a constant in many cultures. The giant has a stone spear, the barbarous weapon of a native Titan. Yet the poisoned spears which are deadly to mortals are as mere barbs to giants: like a cartoon baddy, Yspaddaden complains with exaggerated peevishness at the inconvenience caused by having spears in his knee, chest and eye.

16   He sets Culhwch thirty-nine impossible tasks (*anoethu*); tasks which are clearly stories in themselves. Only fourteen are actually achieved in this telling. The early tasks (nos 1-14) involve the provision of food, drink, music and clothing for the wedding. Of these, only tasks 7 and 14 are achieved: the veil for Olwen, which is made with the help of an ant colony whom Gwythyr ap Greidawl saves from a fire, and the cauldron of Diwrnach, which is none other than the cauldron of Annwn. Tasks 15-39 concern the assembling of men, horses and hounds in order to obtain the comb and scissors between the ears of Twrch Trwyth, and the tusk of Ysgithrwyn: with these last items Yspaddaden will be shaved and his hair will be

cut – signalling his imminent death. The obtaining of these things is totally dependent upon Culhwch's ability to assemble men of appropriate gifts, abilities and aptitudes to accomplish the *anoethu*.

17 In task 39, which is performed first, the sword of light is won from Wrnach, a fellow giant of Yspaddaden's ilk. The dialogue between the porter and Cai is exactly the same as between Glewlwyd and Culhwch. Custennin's son, hitherto unnamed, wins his name, Goreu, 'the Best', by his exploit of crossing three courtyards and defeating their guardians. Just as Culhwch became adult at Arthur's court, so Goreu becomes a man in the court of Wrnach.

Task 28 consists of freeing Eidoel ap Aer, Mabon's cousin, and without whom Mabon cannot be found.

18 The freeing of Mabon (task 26) is accomplished with the help of the totem beasts. This important episode is told fully in the *Song of Mabon* (p.187) and is discussed in the context of the mysteries in Chapter 8.

19 Task 32 involves getting Gwynn ap Nudd, but this is delayed because of the dispute between him and Gwythyr ap Greidawl over the possession of Creiddylad. This ancient theme of the fight of the Summer and Winter Kings over the hand of the Spring Maiden is deeply rooted in the British Mysteries. To some extent, Rhiannon is fought over by Gwawl and Pwyll, according to this pattern. The combat between Tristan and the Morholt over the hand of Iseult merely reinforces the links between this story and that of Culhwch. This combat is also a feature of later Arthurian romance where Guinevere is abducted by Melwas of the Summer Country from Arthur who plays the part of the Midwinter King.[49]

Gwynn ap Nudd is King of the Underworld, and plays the Winter King here, while Gwythyr's antecedents are unknown; however, his epithet, Greidawl, derives from 'scorch' and so he is likely to be the Summer King of this fray. Creiddylad is none other than Cordelia in disguise – her father is Llydd Llaw Ereint (King Lear); he is a doublet of Nuadu of the Silver Hand who loses the Sovereignty because of his disability. In order to judge between the kings, Arthur rules that every May Day her champions shall contend for her, but none shall win until Judgement Day, until which time she remains with her father.

The doubling of boars, giants and heroes in this story is doubtless confusing, but they appear on different levels. Ysgithrwyn's tusk (task 15) is only one of the implements which will deal Yspaddaden his death.

20 This task is closely associated with the Harrowing of Annwn by Arthur. Although the cauldron of Diwrnach (task 14) is in Ireland, we may see it as a resonance for the Underworld. In Celtic legend, neighbouring islands are often recognised as the abode of the dead, whence they are ferried by a grey-clad, hooded boatman. The ship of the dead sails still in Celtic imagination in both Brittany and Cornwall, as well as in many other places. A fuller discussion of this task follows.

21 Task 21 sees the pursuit of the Twrch Trwyth and his seven piglets. Arthur sends Gwrhyr, who knows the speech of beasts, to parley with the swine; he learns that the boar was once a king, the son of Prince Taredd, condemned to boar shape for his sins. This legend has a direct parallel in Irish tradition where a druid, Cian Mac Cainte, bewitched his pupils into beasts of the chase and would hunt them himself, in the form of a hound. The Children of Turenn struck him with his own magic wand and turned him into a black pig, whence the *Clad na Muice* or Black Pig's Dike in Northern Ireland – the great defensive earthwork which can be seen today – which was thrown up by the fury of Cian the druid in his rampage across Ireland, until he plunged into the sea off Donegal – where the dike ends.[48]

As with Matholwch's cauldron in *Branwen*, which also came out of Ireland, the boar Twrch Trwyth represents the potentially destructive power of the Underworld when it is let loose in Britain. Because it is an unbalanced force, only the most ancient archetypal characters of Arthur's court can catch and subdue it. It is chased from Ireland, to Wales, down the Severn and into Cornwall, whence it vanishes into the sea.

22 The shaving of Yspaddaden is done by Caw of Britain,

another giant of British mythology. Yspaddaden is killed, not by Culhwch nor Arthur, but by Goreu, Custennin's son, who avenges his father's disgrace and his brothers' deaths. The retributive and satisfactory conclusion of the story hides one of the major patterns in the Succession of the Pendragons: that of the substitution by one character of another's role (cf. Figure 9.1, p.164).

2   PIG-STY AND THE HOUND OF LUGH

The sources for *Culhwch* are so numerous that they would fill a book, never mind a chapter. The three main sources or parallel texts derive from folkstory as partially integrated tradition, from the legend of Tristan and from the mythos of Lugh.

Central to the story is the theme of the *Giant's Daughter*, which may be summarised as follows. The hero's father makes a bargain with an Otherworldly power before the boy's birth so that he is destined to difficulties and possible imprisonment. He falls in love with the giant's daughter, while employed by the giant. He may win her only by performing impossible tasks, e.g. mucking out a byre left dirty for seven years, thatching a roof with birds' feathers. He is aided by the giant's daughter, who has her father's magical powers, or by companions whose abilities are unusual, e.g. able to drink a lakeful of water or eat a barnful of food. (This theme is known as *Six Go Through the World*.) Or else the hero is aided by animals whom he has rescued. Having achieved the tasks, he must identify the daughter from a roomful of identical-looking women; she is identified by some disfigurement caused in the completion of the tasks, e.g. a finger-joint is missing. They are married and then pursued by the giant who is overthrown by his own enchantments. Often it is necessary to find the hiding place of his heart or soul, which is then broken along with his power. The hero is very often driven into service by the giant because his father has remarried and the stepmother wishes to dispossess him in favour of her own children.[30,53]

The *anoethu* which Culhwch performs to win Olwen are clearly akin to the labours of Hercules. The power of Yspaddaden resides in his hair and so he must be shaved, like

Samson, before his destined death. The *Giant's Daughter* motif occurs in world folkstory, but it is from two particularly Celtic sources that we find the closest parallels.

We have already mentioned the Cornish connections of *Culhwch*. Not only is the hunt of the Twrch Trwyth completed in Cornwall, but traces of that most Cornish hero, Tristan, are readily apparent. The *Tristan* legend has its parallels in the Irish *Diarmuid and Grainne* story, and must have one of the widest distributions of any Celtic story, since it appears in Welsh, Icelandic, Danish, German and even Serbo-Russian texts. There are only fragments of the Welsh texts, but these are very revealing.[49]

Tristan is here called Drystan and his father is Tallwch or Talorc. We will remember the Irish gloss which tells us that *orc triath* is the name for a king's son which makes Tallwch 'first or chief boar'. We should not be surprised that apart from his father's name, Drystan has closer connections with pigs. He is named, with Pryderi, as one of the Three Powerful Swineherds (in Triad 26) who tended the swine of March ap Meirchyawn (King Mark) while the swineherd went with a message to Essylt (Iseult). The Triad alludes to an expedition on the part of Arthur to steal these pigs, without success; but the story is now lost.[5] What is interesting is that Drystan becomes *a substitute swineherd*, and that he elopes with Essylt to Coed Celyddon – the very place where Merlin addresses pigs in his madness. This story also corresponds to the details of the Summer and Winter Kings' combat for the hand of the Spring Queen. Arthur hears both sides of the argument from Drystan and King Mark, both of whom want Essylt, ruling that she should go to Drystan when leaves were on the tree, but to Mark when the trees were bare. Essylt's reply may well indeed be that of Creiddylad's in the most ancient version of Gwynn ap Nudd's and Gwythyr's combat for her:

> Blessed be the judgement and he who gave it! There are three trees that are good of their kind, holly and ivy and yew, which keep their leaves as long as they live. I am Trystan's as long as he lives.[49]

The circumstances of Tristan's birth are similar in nearly every respect with Culhwch's, for Tristan's mother runs mad.

But while *she* is called Blanchfleur in most medieval versions, *Culhwch's mother*'s name is derived from Essylt's companion of the Welsh Tristan story. Goleuddydd means 'bright day'; Essylt's companion is called Golwg Hafddydd, 'shining summer's day'. The coincidences are too consistent for mere accidental transmission of one story into another.

It is even possible to see connections between Custennin's wife and the roles played by both Iseult's mother and Brangwain in the later Tristan stories: all three are wise-women, foster-mothers to the young Flower-Bride who is wed to a man whose attributes make him every much as restrictive as Yspaddaden to his daughter. All three are willing to smooth the bride's way with magic or with a potent cup of desire which will extinguish the differences of age.

But while these charming medieval excursions are of interest we must look for another ancestor in Culhwch's genealogy – the god Lugh of the Shining Spear, for the correspondences between Culhwch and Lugh are manifestly apparent. It is almost possible to see the invisible join between *Culhwch* and *Math* when we look at the Irish text of *The Second Battle of Mag Tured* in which Lugh is the champion of the Tuatha de Danaan and defeats his enemy and grandfather, Balor, of the Fomorians. As we have stated, the Tuatha de Danaan and the Children of Don are the same lineage; although Irish and Welsh traditions give different family members, a number are recognisably the same person, e.g. Lugh and Llew, Goibniu and Gofannon.

At the beginning of the story the king of the Tuatha de Danaan, Nuadu, loses his hand in battle and so his kingship is forfeit under the rules of Celtic kingship which state that no blemished man should reign. The kingship is passed to Bres – the son of a Tuatha woman and a Fomorian man. The Fomorians gain the ascendancy and put the Tuatha to servile tasks. The great god, the Dagda, has to build the Fomorian's fort and suffers many iniquities.

When the oppression is at its height, a stranger comes to the hall of Nuadu. He seeks entrance in the exact exchange which Culhwch and Glewlwyd mark at the gate. He is Lugh, the son of Ethniu, the daughter of Balor, the Fomorian, and of Cian, son of Diancecht of the Tuatha. The porter will allow no man to enter unless he is a man of skill. Lugh vouchsafes himself to be not only a wright, but a smith, a champion, a harper, a hero, a poet, a historian, a sorcerer, a healer, a cupbearer and a fire-maker. Although Nuadu has men possessed of these abilities, Lugh is let in because he combines them all, for he is *Samildanach* or many-gifted. After a test of his various skills, Nuadu cedes place to him and goes to consult with his council for a year.

The result of this council is an assembly of men each of whom will perform some particularly wonderful deed by which the Fomorians can be defeated: the druid, Mathgen, says he will cast the twelve principal mountains of Ireland on their enemies' heads. The cupbearer will withhold water from the Fomor men. A great battle is prepared, but Lugh is restrained from entering it by the Tuatha who fear his early death, since he is clearly gifted by the gods. However, he escapes his guardians and encounters his grandfather Balor whose evil eye he pierces with a sling-stone. The battle is won, but Nuadu is slain. Lugh then takes up his place.[28]

While Lugh is here possessed of many special skills, he nevertheless draws on a great host of other specially equipped men, just as Culhwch does. The court of Nuadu, like that of Arthur, is in retirement – in a semi-Otherworld place. The Dagda is so like Custennin in description, and is put in so exactly a servile position as guardian and builder of what was once his own property, that it is not hard to make the connection.

Although Culhwch seems to have acquired a more subsidiary role, the qualities of Lugh are still visible in his make-up: he is a satirist, a hero, he is nephew to a great king and he is the one who wounds Yspaddaden in the eye with a spear. The other qualities of Lugh are discernible in other characters within *Culhwch*: Goreu and Mabon share the role of wondrous youth; Taliesin is the harper and poet; Cacamri is the fire-maker.

Further, there is another interesting connection. In the legend of the Black Pig's Dike, the enchanted pig was once a druid called Cian Mac Cainte (Hound Son of Speech). Lugh's father is Cian Mac Diancecht (Hound Son of ? – the Tuatha's healer). Do we discern here a reason for the transposition of Lugh's narrative to Culhwch? The Irish pronunciation of Lugh is

Looch: it is identical to the Welsh pronunciation of the last syllable of *Culhwch*'s name. The prefix *cu* means hound, in Irish. Is Culhwch then possessed of two hidden names? Is he both Cul-Hwch or Pig-Sty, as well as Cu-Lhwch, the Hound of Lugh? Here are two singularly appropriate names for the hero who gains the Flower-Bride by his great prowess in hunting the boar, and who wounds the giant in his baleful eye.

What does all this signify? To find the answer we must plunge ever deeper to the confines of Annwn to find the treasures that we seek.

3   THE SPOILS OF ANNWN

The hunting of Twrch Trwyth, the shaving and death of Yspaddaden and the Harrowing of Annwn are three closely interrelated themes central to the Mysteries of Britain. The first two themes are clearly stated in the text of Culhwch, yet the last is only implicit. We read that Arthur sent Menw into Ireland 'to see if the treasures were between the ears of Twrch Trwyth' and that he then sailed to Ireland in his ship *Prydwen* in order to fetch the cauldron of Diwrnach. From the list of thirteen treasures of Britain, we know that this cauldron would not boil the meat of a coward, but only a hero (p.51). The finding of the cauldron occupies three paragraphs of the text, where it is slotted in as only one of many *anoethu*, yet it is crucial to our understanding of *Culhwch*.

The importance of this episode would remain unclear if we did not have the evidence of an early Welsh poem, the *Preiddeu Annwn* – the Spoils of Annwn – in which Arthur goes to Annwn to rescue a prisoner and to gain certain of the Hallows, notably the cauldron of Annwn. The version which follows is my own translation. Welsh scholars universally attest to its extreme obscurity and ambiguity; my translation should not be considered definitive. Interested readers are directed to consult both Welsh original and English translation in R.S. Loomis's *Wales and the Arthurian Legend*.[64] The poem is attributed to Taliesin – one of the survivors of this expedition, and the only competent poet to record the exploits of Arthur in the confines of Annwn.

PREIDDEU ANNWN

Perfect was the captivity of Gweir in Caer Sidi,
According to the tale of Pwyll and Pryderi.
None before him was sent into it
Into the heavy blue chain which bound the youth.
5 From before the reeving of Annwn he has groaned,
Until the ending of the world this prayer of poets:
Three shipburdens of Prydwen entered the Spiral City
Except seven, none returned from Caer Sidi.

Is not my song worthily to be heard
10 In the four-square Caer, four times revolving!
I draw my knowledge from the famous cauldron,
The breath of nine muses keeps it boiling.
Is not the Head of Annwn's cauldron so shaped:
Ridged with enamel, rimmed with pearl?
15 It will not boil the cowardly traitor's portion.
The sword of Lluch Lleawc flashed before it
And in the hand of Lleminawc was it wielded.
Before hell's gate the lights were lifted
When with Arthur we went to the harrowing –
20 Except seven none returned from Caer Veddwit.

Is not my song fit recital for kings
In the four-square Caer, in the Island of the Strong Door
Where noon and night made half-light,
Where bright wine is brought before the host?
25 Three shipburdens of Prydwen took to sea:
Except seven none returned from Caer Rigor.

I sing not for those exiled of tradition
Who beyond Caer Wydyr saw not Arthur's valour.
Six thousand men there stood upon the wall,
30 Hard it was to parley with their sentinel.
Three shipburdens of Prydwen we went with Arthur:
Except seven none returned from Caer Goludd.

I sing not for bards on cowardly circuit
Who know not day nor hour nor causation
35 Nor when the glorious Son of Light appears,

Nor who prevents his journey to Defwy.
They know not whose the brindled, harnessed ox
With seven score notches on his collar.
When we went with Arthur on difficult errand;
40   Except seven none returned from Caer Vandwy.

I sing not for those not of our companions,
Who know not on what day the chief was born,
Who do not know the hour of his kingship,
Nor of the silver-headed beast they guard for him.
45   When we went with Arthur of mournful mien:
Except seven, none returned from Caer Ochren.

The complexities of this poem deserve a longer commentary
than can be given here. The first stanza refers specifically to the
role of the prisoner of Annwn, here named as Gweir, which is
one of Mabon's aliases. The fate of this prisoner will be
discussed in Chapter 9. Seven Caers or castles are named, and
these are the gates of Annwn, as Arthur sails deeper into the
Underworld. Lines 11-15 refer to the very cauldron Arthur goes
in search of in *Culhwch*. Lines 16-17 refer to the hero whose
sword of light enables Arthur's men to snatch up the cauldron.
In *Culhwch* the sword is identified as Caledfwlch, Arthur's
Excalibur, which Llenlleawg the Irishman wields as Arthur's
champion.

Who is this hero? None other than Lugh of the Shining Spear
himself, transposed from the Irish texts to become the
champion of Arthur. Lugh is the one who also slays Balor, of
course: the killing of which giant is an integral feature in
winning the treasures of Annwn. And as with Bran and his
companions, only seven return with Arthur, as the mournful
chorus sings. The wielder of the Sword of Light in *Culhwch* is
not Culhwch himself, but Goreu, Custennin's son; it is he who
leaps across three courtyards and who beheads Yspaddaden. It
would seem that in the Welsh story, both Goreu and Culhwch
perform the function of King's champion which Lugh performs
for Nuadu in the Irish story.

The intricate weaving of the *Preiddeu Annwn* with *Culhwch*
can best be appreciated if we see Culhwch's progress in the
story as a series of levels at which stand certain protagonists as

porters at the gates, as shown in Figure 6.2. Only by a descent through the levels of Annwn can Culhwch gain Olwen. This descent is marked by encounters which give Culhwch the maturity and experience necessary, and which incidentally help both Arthur and Mabon to take their rightful place in the Succession of the Pendragons.

Level	Porter/Encounter	Caer		Experience
1	Glewlwyd	Veddwit		Culhwch gains recognition as a man and status of kingly heir
2	Custennin	Ochren		Kinship with Custennin's wife; cousin Goreu is disclosed; Olwen meets Culhwch
3	Yspaddaden	Goludd	THE PATH OF GOREU	The impossible tasks are set
4	Wrnach's porter	Rigor		The Sword of Light is won; Goreu is named
5	The Oldest Animals	Sidi		Culhwch meets the totem beasts who are the remembrancers of the prisoner. Mabon is released
6	The boars Ysgithrwyn Twrch Trwyth	Vandwy		The giant's death implements are won
7	Pen Annwn	Pedryfan		Pen Annwn's cauldron and the other hallows are achieved

Figure 6.2: *The Gates of Annwn*

The ascriptions of the Caers to each of the seven levels of the descent to Annwn may seem arbitrary, but they can be successfully applied with reference to the poem and their meanings. Caer Veddwit is the Castle of Carousal, where Arthur and his men feast. Caer Ochren has no translation, but the stanza it appears in deals with the destiny of the Son of Light, the hero or champion who will come. Caer Goludd is the Castle of Frustration where Yspaddaden lays down his

anoethu on Culhwch's shoulders. Caer Rigor has no translation. Caer Sidi and Caer Wydyr are the same – the Tower of
Glass, the Spiral Castle of the Otherworld where the dead are
imprisoned, according to mortal opinion, but where they learn
the wisdom of the initiating Goddess according to esoteric lore
(cf. Chapter 7). Caer Vandwy is untranslated. The reference to
the ox in this stanza is not explained in Welsh tradition, but
possibly refers to another reeving of an Underworld beast
which is lost to us; I have applied it to the two boars. Caer
Pedryfan is the Four-Square or Four-Cornered Castle where the
hallows are housed. It is the sacred and innermost chamber of
Annwn, where only initiates dare brave the perils.

The straight path to the depths of Annwn is taken by Goreu
who wields the sword of light as Arthur's champion. He it is
who acts as a rescuer to Arthur himself, as we will see in
Chapter 9. (Readers may wish to compare 'The Path of Goreu'
with R.J. Stewart's 'Path of the Thief' in his *Underworld
Initiation*.)[98] A hint of this path is given in the episode in
Culhwch where Goreu crosses three courtyards.

We turn at last to the Succession of the Pendragons, which
has its fullest manifestation within *Culhwch and Olwen*. We
will recall that the pattern of roles for the Succession is
comprised of three positions: those of Mabon, Pendragon and
Pen Annwn (cf. p.164). At the beginning of *Culhwch* the pattern
is as follows:

Position/Role	Role-Player
MABON	Culhwch
PENDRAGON	Arthur
PEN ANNWN	Yspaddaden

But this pattern soon changes radically and we begin to see the
Succession in action. Culhwch passes from being a child and
becomes Arthur's champion; his destiny is bound up with that
of the Twrch Trwyth which makes waste the land of Britain in
its rampage through the country. Arthur is Pendragon, the ruler
of his land, but the unbalanced forces of the Underworld are
abroad and threaten his reign. In the *Second Battle of Mag
Tured*, Nuadu is the Wounded King, to whose court Lugh
comes. Lugh takes Nuadu's place on the throne and in battle,

eventually succeeding to his place permanently. Arthur's case is similar. In Culhwch, he is past his prime, his men strive to prevent him exposing his person to combat. Traditionally, he passes to the Otherworldly realm of Avalon where his wounds are healed, and he becomes an Innerworld guardian. Arthur's Avalon has been frequently fused with the Underworld.

Lastly, Yspaddaden himself is a restrictive Underworld King in the mould of Cronos. In fact, if we superimpose the myth of Cronos and Rhea upon him and Custennin's wife, much of the story becomes clear. Custennin's wife bears twenty-four sons, twenty-three of whom are slain by Yspaddaden. She hides the last, Goreu, whose Zeus-like task is to kill his oppressor – which he indeed fulfils, as well as helping the prisoners of Annwn escape (cf. p.53).

Yspaddaden is called Pencawr or Chief Giant: Twrch Trwyth and Ysgithrwyn seem to be the totemistic doubles of the giant: the latter boar is termed Chief Boar. It is the 'treasures' which these boars have which bring about Yspaddaden's death. From the evidence of folkstory, the giant cannot be killed until his daughter marries or until his heart or soul are discovered. The hiding place of the heart/soul is often guarded by fierce animals and impossible tasks which the suitor-champion has to master.

We have noted the similarities and resonances between Lugh and Culhwch. With regard to Yspaddaden we see that he is analogous to Balor, whom Lugh slays. Culhwch, although he is not the giant's grandson, but only his son-in-law, nevertheless casts a spear through the giant's eye, just as Lugh does.

The new pattern in the Succession of the Pendragons at the conclusion of Culhwch is subtly altered:

Position/Role	Role Player
MABON	Mabon (who is released from the toils of Annwn)
PENDRAGON	Culhwch (who frees the land and gains the Sovereignty of Olwen)
PEN ANNWN	Arthur (who harrows Annwn and gains its treasures)

Each character becomes the guardian of the state which he has mastered. Mabon passes from baby to kingly champion;

Culhwch passes from childhood to champion to Pendragon, if we follow the parallel story of Lugh; Arthur passes from being King of Britain to being King of the Underworld, the inner guardian of the Hallows, which he guards for the next Pendragon when he shall come. Yspaddaden, at the end of his term of office, is disestablished. Although it is not stated in the story, the giant is responsible for the imprisonment of Mabon, and prolongs the duration of the cycle beyond its limits. He therefore loses his place in the Succession, and gives way to Mabon (cf. Chapters 9 and 10).

In *Culhwch and Olwen*, Mabon earns the name Goreu, although he has other names in other stories.

If we need further evidence of this Succession, we may recall that one of Arthur's ancient titles is the Boar of Cornwall – a name which confers its own honour:

> because this was the Day
> of the Passion of the Men of Britain
> when they hunted the Hog
> life for life.[118]

CHAPTER 7
Taliesin

The Radiant Brow

Who was Taliesin? I did not ask, but Pryderi breathed the answer:
'Mabon'.
I should have known. This was indeed the Glorious Youth.

JOHN JAMES
Not for All the Gold in Ireland

GWION: He who would seek the Muse, he who would seek
        To marry himself to any kind of sovereignty,
        Must make the descent down to the earth's centre,
        To face his utmost fears, and his most secret
        anxieties.

JOHN HEATH-STUBBS
Artorius

1   THE LUCK OF THE WEIR

In this non-canonical story, we encounter the Wondrous Youth, Taliesin, the poet-seer and rescuer of his patron, Elphin. As his story is not found in either the *Red Book of Hergist* nor the *White Book of Rhydderch* (the manuscripts from which the rest of the *Mabinogion* were derived), many translations of the *Mabinogion* omit *Hanes Taliesin*, which is a great shame as few readers have the opportunity of studying it for themselves unless they possess the Lady Charlotte Guest edition,[4] or the more recent translation by Patrick K. Ford.[2] (Professor Ford is, at the time of writing, at work on a comprehensive analysis of the Taliesin texts.) The manuscripts which contain versions of *Taliesin* are generally late copies and there is much dispute about authenticity and order of presentation. I have drawn upon both the editions mentioned above.

Taliesin Ben Beirdd, Chief Poet, was one of the *cynfeirdd* or first poets of Wales; a historical character who was poet to Urien Rheged in the sixth century. Fragments of his poetry turn up at all levels of Welsh literature, but his main work is found in the thirteenth-century manuscript, *The Book of Taliesin*. The poetry shows strongly the nature of ancient poetic discipline and inner knowledge of the mysteries; unfortunately it also shows the hands of an 'improver' who has unhelpfully recast much of the original verse. There is also the problem of false ascription; many lesser poets' work has been ascribed to Taliesin.

These problems aside, we are at the root of the poet's initiatory quest in the story of Taliesin. His escape from Ceridwen reveals to us the mystery of the Turning of the Totems (cf. Chapter 8); his concern with Elphin's freedom is a resonance of Mabon's release; while his utterances about the elemental changes of the initiate put us in touch with the primal mysteries of creation of which Ceridwen is the mistress and chief-alchemist.

1   In the days of Arthur there lived a man called Tegid Foel and his wife Ceridwen. 2   Their daughter, Creirwy, was the most beautiful maiden, but their son Morfran (Great Crow) was so ugly that he was

nicknamed Afagddu (Utter Darkness). In order to compensate for his appearance, Ceridwen prepared a 3   cauldron of inspiration so that he might be possessed of prophetic insight and secret knowledge. This was distilled from numerous herbs and plants, and the cauldron was to be kept boiling for a year and a day. 4   She set Gwion Bach, son of Gwreang of Llanfair in Powys, to stir it and an old man, Morda, to tend the fire under it. 5   Near the end of the year, three drops flew out of the boiling cauldron and fell on Gwion's finger. To cool the scald, he put his fingers in his mouth and so received the inspiration intended for Morfran. 6   The cauldron burst in two, since the remainder of its contents were poisonous; the liquor flowed into a stream, and so the horses of Gwyddno Garanhir were poisoned.

7   Perceiving Ceridwen's wrath, Gwion fled in the shape of a hare, but Ceridwen followed as a greyhound. He became a fish, she an otter. He turned into a bird, she changed into a hawk; finally he fell from the sky into a pile of wheat, becoming a grain himself, but Ceridwen became a hen and swallowed him. 8   He was born of her womb nine months later. So great was his beauty that she did not kill him, but set him adrift in a coracle on 29 April.

9   Gwyddno's son, Elphin, was a spendthrift courtier in the service of King Maelgwn. His luck and fortunes were so bad that his father allowed him to go and catch the salmon which were annually caught in the weir on May Eve: their value was £100. He saw nothing but a coracle. Opening its leather wrappings, he exclaimed, 'Behold the radiant brow' (*tal-iesin*) – and so the child was named. The child sang to Elphin, consoling him for the loss of the salmon, and prophesying that what he had found would be worth far more. 10   When asked who he was, Taliesin sang of his transformations. Elphin's fortunes improved, and the child was given to his wife to nurse.

11   Thirteen years passed. Elphin went to his uncle Maelgwn's Christmas court. Maelgwn's twenty-four poets praised the king and his possessions above all others, but Elphin was moved to boast that his wife was as chaste as the Queen and his poet better than the King's. He was instantly imprisoned until a test could be made of this. 12   Rhun, a notorious lecher, was despatched to debauch Elphin's wife, but Taliesin, who knew everything, had her change shape with a kitchen maid. Rhun made the maid drunk and cut off her finger, on which was Elphin's ring: this was produced as proof positive of his wife's disgrace. However, Elphin refuted it on three points: the finger was too large for his wife's; its nails had not been cut for a month unlike his wife's usual custom; and it had been kneading dough, something his wife had never done. Elphin was put

back in prison until his last boast could be proved.

13   With a satire on his tongue dispraising Rhun and Maelgwn, Taliesin set out for the court to refute the poets. He sat in a corner playing blerwm, blerwm on his lips with a finger. When the poets came to sing before Maelgwn, they did likewise, to their confusion. Maelgwn had the chief-poet struck for impudence, but he blamed his behaviour on Taliesin. 14   Maelgwn enquired who he was and where he came from. In a lengthy poem, Taliesin explained in prophetic and analeptic verse his true nature: he had been existent since the creation of the world, present at all its works; he knew all knowledge; he should be until the end of the world. The poets could make no reply. 15   Taliesin then asked for the release of Elphin from his chains. He challenged the poets to answer riddles impossible to them. He then sang the wind and other elements so that Maelgwn speedily had Elphin released. Since the poets could not answer him, Taliesin satirised the poets, while upholding the princeliness of true poetry.

16   He then bade Elphin wager Maelgwn that his horse was the better. A race was arranged at Morfa Rhiannedd, the King having twenty-four horses in the race. Taliesin gave Elphin's jockey twenty-four holly sticks with their ends blackened, and told him to strike each of Maelgwn's mounts as he overtook them, and then to throw down his cap at the point where his horse finished. At this place, men were set to dig and they discovered a cauldron full of gold which Taliesin gave to Elphin in recompense for his barren night at the weir.

17   Taliesin was then brought before Maelgwn to sing of the creation. He sang of Adam and Eve, of the Fall, the mystery of Christ's sacrifice. He sang of the fate of Troy's descendants, the invasion of the Saxons, the servitude of the Britons, and of their final liberation.

1   Tegid the Bald makes no further appearance in this story. His name survives in the Welsh lake, Llyn Tegid: a typical 'cauldron lake' such as Llassar Llaesgyfnewid and his wife emerge from, in *Branwen*. In this instance, the cauldron belongs to Ceridwen, one of the titanic aspects of the Goddess. The mythology of Ceridwen is scant, but it can be related directly to that of the Mountain Mothers of Scottish and Irish tradition,[71] the Cailleachs who drop stones from their apron to form mountain ranges and who play an important role in the annual chase of the God of Youth by the Old Hag (cf. p.126).

2 Creirwy is named in Triad 78 as one of the fairest maidens of Britain. She stands in the place of Kore to Ceridwen's Demeter. Morfran, the ugly son, we have already encountered in *Culhwch*, where he appears as one who was not slain at Camlann because all who saw him believed him to be a devil, not a man. But though the cauldron is prepared for his benefit, it is Gwion who becomes a seer-poet and, incidentally, Ceridwen's child.

3 The text invests Ceridwen with the mantle of a medieval alchemist, consulting her planetary hours and culling herbs under the phases of the moon. She is said to prepare the brew according to the books of the Fferyllt. This word has often been translated as 'the Faeries', but in Welsh it has the connotation of chemist, alchemist or magician. Notably Virgil, who in medieval mythology became associated less with his poetic achievements and more with the magical arts, is called Fferyll in Welsh. It is interesting to compare this cauldron with the one which nine muses cool with their breath in the *Preiddeu Annwn* (cf. p.107). Both are cauldrons of Underworld deities, both are vessels of poetic or prophetic inspiration. The vessel is kept boiling for a year and a day just as the spear which slays Llew is forged for the same duration. There is a reference to a similarly prepared cauldron in the *Second Battle of Mag Tuired* (cf. p.45), but more generally in Celtic myth the food which bestows knowledge is the salmon. As we will see, this theme is not absent from *Taliesin*.

4 Gwion the Small and blind Morda tend the cauldron: extreme youth and extreme age. Ceridwen beats Morda so hard when the cauldron's contents are lost that he loses an eye – a feature of Balor's story where he loses the sight of one eye from spying on a similar cauldron. Instead of receiving wisdom, however, Balor is poisoned by the steam of the vessel.[28]

Gwion is fated to become Taliesin, the seer-poet. Throughout this story it is necessary to look below the levels of the text because more than the surface meaning is present. As with many another Wondrous Youth, Taliesin has his childhood name. The sense of creative continuity which motivates his verse makes it impossible to see the poet and Gwion as two different people: they share the same identity.

5   The cooling of the burnt finger is_a universal folk theme, but one central to all Celtic traditions. We will discuss the Thumb of Knowledge in relation to other texts in the next section.

6   Gwyddno Garanhir, Elphin's father, appears in many Welsh texts and is often associated with the Kingdom of Rheged – which court gave the historical Taliesin his patronage. Gwyddno is associated also with an inundation of land in Cardigan Bay; folk tradition speaks of a lost *cantref* and makes him the ruler over it. He also seems to have had trouble with Gwynn ap Nudd, according to an early dialogue poem.[5] Both these events may be hinted at in the poisoning of his horses episode, whereby his lands are lost or made barren by an Underworld deity.

    Most importantly we must note that he appears in the list of the Thirteen Treasures of Britain as the possesser of a miraculous hamper into which food for one could be put, but from which food for a hundred could be extracted.[5]

7   The transformations which Gwion and Ceridwen undergo are part of an initiatory sequence. Other shape-changes are hinted at in the songs which Taliesin sings at Maelgwn's court. These changes correspond to certain levels of poetic training during which the initiate is given deeper and deeper insights into the nature of creation. And although on one level Ceridwen appears as his aggressor, she is in fact his initiator, forcing him to deeper levels of understanding until he reaches the primal essence of life itself, here symbolised by a grain of wheat (cf. p.126 and Chapter 8).

8   This mysterious rebirth of the initiate as a weak and helpless baby is connected to the incubation period during which the mysteries are learned. His mother does not name her child, but he is put into a womb-shaped coracle and left to the mercy of the waves. He is on his own. The Ford text says, 'He had been floating in the pouch from the beginning of Arthur's time until about the beginning of Maelgwn's time.'[2] This is reckoned at forty years. In many mythologies children who have a hard destiny are often cast adrift on the sea in a form of ark, like Moses, to find their own luck.

9   Elphin is known as the unfortunate youth in all the stories. His luck seems to be at an even lower ebb when instead of a draught of salmon he finds a baby-poet floating in the weir. But he is destined to better fortune yet. The Ford text says that this annual draught of salmon was caught at Samhain eve, All Hallows, whereas Guest has Elphin come to the weir at May Eve, Beltaine. But whether the salmon are on their upstream mating run or their downstream return to the Gulf Stream does not matter. Elphin goes expecting salmon and catches the Salmon of Wisdom himself. This is Taliesin's own totem and one of the essential identities of all seer-poets. He gains his name in much the same way as Pryderi, Llew or Goreu do.

10   The many poems which occur in the text of the story appear in different manuscripts. The Guest translation has often interspersed these poems in a random way. In any case, like the obscure *Preiddeu Annwn*, Taliesin's verse is only translatable by analeptic means and by one whose knowledge of early Welsh surpasses any scholar now alive. So much of their inner meaning is lost in translation that it is doubtful whether we will ever fully comprehend the esoteric references and internal puns. Taliesin's inspired utterances are as far beyond poetry as ordinary poetry is beyond prose. Because he shares the nature of the Blessed Ones, he is able, while still a baby, to reveal his transformations:

> In the court of Ceridwen I have done penance . . .
> I have fled as a chain,
> I have fled as a roe into an entangled thicket;
>
>   . . .
>
> I have fled as a fierce bull bitterly fighting,
> I have fled as a bristling boar seen in a ravine,
> I have fled as a white grain of pure wheat,
> On the skirt of a hempen sheet entangled,
> That seemed of the size of a mare's foal,
> That is filling like a ship on the waters. . . . [4]

These references are clearly not to be understood as rational statements; indeed, in the last three lines, we may discern a faint reference to another child who is reeved of his mother in a another shape (cf. Chapter 2).

11 King Maelgwn was a historical character; according to the *Annales Cambriae*, he died of the Yellow Plague in 547.[94] In one of his satires, Taliesin proclaims:

> And I will tell your king what will befall him,
> A most strange creature will come from the sea marsh of Rhianedd
> As a punishment of iniquity on Maelgwn Gwynedd;
> His hair, his teeth, and his eyes being as gold. . . . [4]

Elphin's boast is curiously like that of Crunnchu mac Agnoman in the *Debility of the Ulstermen* story (cf. p.31). It certainly draws down disaster on his head, since Elphin is imprisoned and chained – but with silver chains because of his nobility – by Maelgwn who has a kingly reputation to uphold.

12 The chastity test is exactly that which Shakespeare uses in his strangely haunting retelling of one of our national stories, *Cymbeline*. Here Iachimo secretes himself in Imogen's chamber and steals a bracelet. The Elphin of this story is Posthumus; only here Imogen, his wife, is his liberator. She takes the name Fidele and, dressed as a boy, rescues her husband and brothers from imprisonment and death. (This theme is followed closely in Beethoven's working of the female liberator, Fidelio, who releases all the prisoners imprisoned with her husband. This is a very potent motif when compared with the release of Mabon.) In *Cymbeline*, the king of the title is in the place of Tegid, while his queen is Ceridwen. Her loathsome son, Cloten, is analogous to Afagddu.

Elphin vindicates his wife by a piece of neat detective work. But, as Elphin once freed Taliesin from the leather bag, now it is up to Taliesin to release him.

13 The thirteen-year-old seer-poet now pits his considerable wits against Maelgwn's twenty-four poets, starting by the use of some sympathetic magic. Idiot-like he plays on his lips with his finger and Maelgwn's poets make the same unpoetic utterances before their kingly patron! This passage is part of the manifestation of Mabon (cf. Chapter 9), where the Wondrous Youth confronts his elders and betters and confounds

their combined wits. This pattern is observable in the lives of Christ and of Merlin who both, while still youths, confound the elders in the Temple and the magicians of Vortigern, respectively.

14   The parallels with Merlin are extremely close, as Taliesin himself attests in his reply to Maelgwn's ill-placed enquiry about his antecedents:

> Primary chief bard am I to Elphin,
> And my original country in the region of the summer stars;
> Idno and Heinin called me Merlin,
> At length every king will call me Taliesin.[4]

This statement is curiously like that of Christ to his disciples: 'Who do people say the Son of Man is?' The disciples say, 'Some say he is John the Baptist, some Elijah, and others Jeremiah or one of the prophets.' (Matt. 16,14.) It is also suspiciously like the words which Wisdom utters in Proverbs and the other Wisdom texts of the Bible and Apocrypha. However, we need not suspect the hand of a clerical improver necessarily. Taliesin's boasts, his 'I have beens', are a prophetic sequence relating to his initiation and participation in the whole of creation. He has been to no less than the highest heavens as well as through the gates of Annwn. He has companioned Christ, the prophets and Mary Magdalene, as well as in the court of Don, the prison of Arianrhod and on the White Hill with the head of Bran. Maelgwn should have known better than to ask!

15   The freeing of Elphin is accomplished. This episode bears comparison again with the freeing of Gweir from Annwn in the *Preiddeu Annwn* (see p.107); for there 'a heavy blue chain bound the youth', whereas Elphin is 'released from the golden fetter'. The magical nature of Celtic poetry lives solely in Taliesin. The original poet was part-shaman, one whose word was manifest. The 'puny bards' of Maelgwn's court can only offer barren words which have no effect, whereas Taliesin is able to raise the elements to do his bidding.

16   In the succeeding race this feature is upheld once more. Taliesin instructs Elphin's jockey to overtake the other horses

by striking them with twenty-four blackened holly staves. Without resorting to the semantic word-games of Robert Graves's *White Goddess*, might these staves be engraved oghams – wooden billets enscribed with the alphabet?[41] Taliesin wins by the power of speech. He overcomes twenty-four poets with his eloquence. He then overcomes twenty-four horses. Holly is the wood sacred to the Green Man of Knowledge – a folk character appearing in Celtic folkstory, analogous to both the Green Knight of the Gawaine cycle and to the seer-poet of earlier Celtic story. We shall perhaps never fully comprehend the complexity of levels within this story. The cauldron of gold is the guerdon of poets – the poet's fee, but instead of Elphin giving it to Taliesin, the poet gives it to his master. Taliesin has, after all, drunk of an Otherworldly cauldron. Elphin is not an initiate, and so his reward is a more earthly one.

17   Taliesin's last poem bears comparison with the prophecies of Merlin, which it much resembles.[96,97] It starts with the creation of humanity. Adam and Eve are outcast and made to break the earth for bread. The lines following relate the mystical levels on which the grain of wheat can be understood, from the stark bread of toil and disobedience to the mysterious transubstantiation of the host on the altar of the cross. The poem then relates the descent of esoteric knowledge through to the race of Troy, of which remnant Taliesin can be seen as the prophet. The final victory of the Britons over their invaders is hinted at, and the restored sovereignty is implied.

This poem and Merlin's prophecies are the nearest native parallel to the *Revelations of St John*; apocalyptic and full of mystery, they tell of a world before this and of a time which comes after our own.

2   THE THUMB OF KNOWLEDGE

In Taliesin we see one of the last great seer-poets, the remnant of a mighty professional class whose utterances were of magical origin, not merely a product of the intellectual faculty. The roots of seer-poet and shaman are very close. Throughout the High Classical period of Irish history (c. 450-900) it is possible to see the progressive disuetude of the seer-poet in action. (We are forced to turn to Irish texts as they give us the laws and customs of poets in great detail: Welsh manuscripts have either been lost or perhaps their parallel customs were unrecorded.) The once great class of poets who were able to effect outside circumstance – by healing the sick, foretelling destinies and shape-shifting – are gradually stripped of their powers until the greatest thing they can accomplish is the blighting of a reluctant patron with a satire. Fear of the satire, which could raise blotches on the victim's face or drive him insane, was the cause of the famous assembly in 574 at which kings and nobles determined to have the whole order of poets suppressed: St Columba represented the poets and saved the day, but their power was considerably lessened.

Taliesin seems to leap from the depths of the ancestral past, for not only can he satirise his opponents, but he has 'birds' knowledge'. He shows such complete accord with the whole of creation that he can identify with it with poetic omniscience. The three drops which fall upon his finger are echoed in a parallel Irish tradition which is recounted in *The Boyhood Deeds of Finn*. Finn Mac Cumhall lives in Irish tradition, much as Arthur does in British tradition – a mighty war-leader with his band of champions, troubled with an unfaithful wife. However, the boyhood of Finn is particularly relevant to the story of Taliesin.

Finn was secretly raised by two women-warriors and a druidess. His boyhood name was Demne and he had to be hidden because the sons of Morna, his hereditary enemies and the slayers of his father, would have killed him; so he was kept ignorant of his ancestors. During a hurling match he overcame many noble youths and the chief of that place called him a shapely fair youth, whence he was called Finn, which means fair. His identity was revealed and Finn caught up with the enemy who had killed his father and taken his treasure-bag.

He then went to Finneces to be taught poetry. The poet watched the salmon of Fec's Pool on the Boyne for seven years because it had been prophesied that he would eat of it and know everything. The salmon was found and Finn was set to cook it, but he burned his thumb, and though warned to eat none of the fish, he put the thumb under his tongue to cool it.

Finneces then willingly gave Finn the salmon to eat, since he was indeed the one destined to its knowledge. He thereby learned the three things which make a poet, the techniques of *teinm laida*, *imbas forosna* and *dichetul dichennaib*.[28]

The story further tells how Finn captured a faery woman (Ban Sidi) who gave him 'a vessel full of gold, of glorious silver', which he distributed among his *fian* (war-band).[93]

The Salmon of Wisdom which swims in the Fountain of Nine Hazels is, of course, the source of all wisdom in Celtic tradition. It is one of the oldest beasts, having the richest store of wisdom and is often the prime totem of the seer-poet who seeks its wisdom. The person who watches for it and who often catches it is rarely the one who acquires the knowledge. Just as Ceridwen and Finneces – both seers of considerable power – prepare the brew or salmon only to have it tasted by an apprentice, so too Elphin loses his valuable draught of salmon. The cauldron of Ceridwen is analogous to the Fountain of Nine Hazels, a drink of which gives memory of the past and knowledge of the future. It is also clear, from the subtext of our story, that Taliesin *is* the Salmon of Wisdom. He himself states: 'it is not known whether my body is flesh or fish'.

We have little direct knowledge of the poet's training, but this is hinted at in Finn's story. Much ink has been spilt over the true meanings of the three techniques which he acquires.[80,93] *The Ancient Laws of Ireland* state that all three are necessary for an *ollamh* poet (a doctor of poetry). They may be summarised as follows:

1 *Teinm Laida* = the cracking open of the bones or the chewing of the marrow. Finn, in order to have access to his gift, has to chew upon his thumb (by putting it under his wisdom tooth?). This method gives access to intuitive or inherent wisdom.

2 *Imbas Forosna* = the inspiration of the masters. *Cormac's Glossary* tells us that this was achieved by chewing on the flesh of an animal, and by certain ritual invocations, after which the poet would set himself into an incubation of meditative sleep. This method gives access to the wisdom of ancestors and the totems.

3 *Dichetul Dichennaib* = extemporary incantation. This is

described variously as 'composing on one's fingers' ends' or 'on the ends of one's bones'. All these techniques were outlawed in Ireland after the time of St Patrick, but formerly the texts tell of the poet spontaneously composing a poem upon meeting a person and touching him with his staff, or of picking up an object and telling of its history by a process akin to psychometry. This method gives access to analeptic wisdom – discovering that which cannot be known by rational means.

I have detailed these techniques in order to show the parallels within Taliesin's own poetic methods. It is known that throughout the Celtic countries until the eighteenth and nineteenth centuries, poets still followed a curious incubation, such as *Imbas Forosna*. They would lie in a darkened room, with a mantle over their heads – sometimes after imbibing certain special foods or drinks – in order to compose a poem.[100] Taliesin's period of incubation is 'three periods in the prison of Arianrhod' – the three times three months which he spent in the womb of Ceridwen (of whom Arianrhod is an Otherworldly aspect). The variant texts say also that his coracle floated for forty years: long enough perhaps to learn the wisdom of the totems and that of the masters of wisdom? Prior to his great 'I have been' boast, he plays blerwm, blerwm on his lips with his fingers' ends, as in *Teinm Laida*: here he reveals his true inherent identity. And by means of *Dichetul Dichennaib*, analeptic wisdom, he tells of future events as well as relating the nature of creation.

By such techniques the seer-poet can answer impossible questions and see into the heart of things, relating their history and destiny. He is enabled to change shape and to travel between the worlds, for their thresholds are open to him. In a variant story we are told how Finn trapped his finger in a Faery Mound and this became his source of wisdom: forever afterwards he chewed upon this finger to stimulate knowledge and so could learn the necessary resonances between this world and that. Finn's name is also associated with the oghams – the inscribed alphabet of Irish poets. Tree Ogham, as popularised in Graves's *The White Goddess*, is only one way of many.[41] The *Scholar's Primer* gives many alternative ogham alphabets, such as Bird Ogham, King Ogham or Sow Ogham. Among the many methods of inscribing these are three: Finn's window – a circular ogham formation, Finn's ladder, and the Tooth Ogham of Finn where each character is shaped like a tooth.[22]

Yet while these word-games are interesting, these are merely the tools of the poet. It is poetic omniscience which alone discerns the truth, and this cannot be learned by intellectual means. It is received by those who have been through the mill of the Goddess and who have drunk of her life-giving cauldron.

3 THE HAG AND THE POET

The pursuit of the youthful god by the hag is a perennial theme in Celtic tradition. The interrelation of their roles and the subtle polarities which affect them have often been wilfully misunderstood by both feminist and psychoanalytic schools of thought. It is plain to all initiates that the Hag or Cailleach, typified by Ceridwen, is the Mother of Creation whose role is that of opposer and initiator of the candidate. The Son of Wisdom, typified by Gwion, is pursued throughout all his transformations, just as a tutor pushes a student through harder and more varied forms of learning until a synthesis of knowledge is acquired. Only then does the Hag rest and send the newly-born seer-poet out into the world.

Ceridwen's cauldron is both the Fountain of Wisdom and the womb of life. It also has its place in the native scheme of alchemy, as a vessel of transformation. Here we see the katabolic action of the Hag-aspect of the Goddess, whereby everything she encounters is broken down to its essential constituents. The pursuit of Gwion through many shape-changings is not a retributive one but an initiatory sequence which we can call the Turning of the Totems. Each one of the beasts which Gwion becomes represents a deeper level of experience, as we shall see in the next chapter. Many further shape-changings and related experiences are detailed in his own poetry.

> Unless a grain of wheat falls on the ground and dies,
> it remains only a single grain;
> but if it dies,
> it yields a rich harvest (John 12,₂₄)

is a mystery saying common to many cultures. In his final transformation, Gwion becomes such a grain of wheat and is fermented, with many other elements, to become the drink of initiates. In his last poem, Taliesin speaks lyrically of Christ's formation from such a brew:

> From wheat of true privilege,
> From red wine generous and privileged
> Is made the finely molded body
> Of Christ son of Alpha.
>
> From the wafer is the flesh,
> From the wine is the flow of blood
> And the words of the Trinity
> Consecrated him.[2]

These verses are not a later Christian interpolation, but true understandings of the initiatory state of the seer-poet. Non-initiates die only once at their physical death. Initiates die twice: once to the flesh and once to the world, being reborn as the Blessed Ones. Taliesin is such a being, and subtly refers to his own state within this poem. As Christ is the living bread who must be consumed for initiates of his cult to be reborn to the heavenly state, so Taliesin is the living fish, the salmon of wisdom, who must also be consumed by the next seer-poet at his initiation.

We have seen how the Succession of the Pendragons can be applied to the Kingship. A similar pattern is also discernible among the poet-kind. This is the Poet's Wheel which the candidate seer-poet undergoes. There are such close resonances between the two cycles that it is perhaps unnecessary to distinguish but roughly between them. The Kingly cycle affects the king's champion, the king and the inner guardian of the hallows. The pattern of poets, or Poet's Wheel, is as follows:

Position	Held By
MABON	the apprentice-poet, Gwion; the Wondrous Youth as typified by Mabon or Emrys, the young Merlin
SEER-POET	Taliesin or Merlin

| OTHERWORLDLY GUARDIAN
OF KNOWLEDGE | The Salmon of Wisdom, the oldest of the Totems; Fintan, the oldest guardian (cf. Chapter 8). The withdrawn Merlin and Taliesin. |

Corresponding with this pattern is a complex set of polarities which are filled by the representatives of the Goddess. For the Taliesin story these may be seen as:

Position	Held By	Companioning Initiating
KATABOLIC HAG/MOTHER	CERIDWEN	GWION
MAIDEN MUSE	CREIRWY	TALIESIN
OTHERWORLDLY QUEEN CONSORT	ARIANRHOD	THE WITHDRAWN TALIESIN

Both the Succession of the Pendragons and the Poet's Wheel start with a Mabon position because Mabon has dual roles of hunter and harper. The female pattern works in a similar way within the Succession of the Pendragons as we will see in Chapter 9. Ceridwen is the transforming Hag, changing to her Maiden-aspect in the shape of daughter, Creirwy, the most beautiful maiden; finally she becomes Arianrhod, the queen of the Otherworldly Caer Sidi – itself a Faery Kingdom where the riches of knowledge are guarded by her king-consort, the Salmon of Wisdom. It will be seen that Ceridwen is not a needlessly Cruel Mother; she merely sends away her initiated son 'to learn his gramerie' in another world, receiving him back as her consort when he at last 'dies to the world' and is born once again on the Inner, in the Otherworld.

The final mystery story of Gwion Bach may be summarised as follows:

Set to stir the Cauldron of Inspiration, Gwion licks the three drops from his oracular finger. He undergoes the initiation of the Turning of the Totems, until finally becoming the Salmon of Wisdom – the totem of all knowledge. He swims into the Cauldron of Rebirth, into the fountain of knowledge which is the womb of Ceridwen herself, the great creator. He flows forth on the birth-waters into the sea, still in his caul of incubation, and so into the realms of manifestation, whence he is taken by Elphin, his patron. He comes to set prisoners free from ignorance, pride and despair. He comes to succour the unfortunate and to chastise the unworthy. He knows all wisdom. He was from the beginning of the world the child of the Goddess, the Modron. He will be until the end of time, the liberator of the lost. No more a Wondrous Child or a Seer-Poet, he swims in the Fountain of Knowledge waiting for a worthy successor to attain to his store of knowledge.

CHAPTER 8
The Totem Beasts of Britain

The Wild Herdsman

Through my voice the Son of the Morning speaks ...
Cronos is his name ... and my animals and my birds
and my fishes hear his voice and rejoice.

J.C. POWYS
Porius

He became a silvan man just as though devoted to the
woods. For a whole summer after this, hidden like a wild
animal, he remained buried in the woods, found by no one
and forgetful of himself and of his kindred.

GEOFFREY OF MONMOUTH
Vita Merlini

1   MABON AND THE OLDEST ANIMALS

Armed with the evidence of Taliesin's transformations we can begin to view Mabon's story in some detail, particularly in relation to the Totems. What is a totem beast? It is an animal emblematic of a tribe or person which has its reality and draws its power from the Otherworld. A tribe might acquire a totem by virtue of a famous ancestor's exploits or through some inherent affinity with a beast. Such a totem would appear as a standard in battle and play an important role in the tribal mysteries. In later ages, when heraldry took over the old formulas of the tribal genealogist, the animal found its way on to the arms and livery of a family; different families were therefore distinguishable in battle and assembly by their totemic sign. Modern armorials portray mythical and realistic beasts along with their motto or device embodying the virtue of that animal, e.g. 'touch not the cat but a glaive', of Scottish Clan Chattan, whose emblem is a wild cat.

Within the *Mabinogion*, totems have a deeper mystery significance. The totem beast is an Otherworldly helper whose resonance is with the ancestral source of wisdom: the adoption of such a totem is a powerful link with the Otherworld, conveying not only the virtues and qualities of that beast to the person under its aegis but also contact with ancestral levels. The totem beast is not to be confused with an animal of the same species which can be hunted or eaten for food: it is a beast of the Platonic realms, having archetypal reality. The appearance of talking beasts in folkstory denotes a shift of emphasis to a deeper level of awareness; such beasts are not anthropomorphic animals, but archetypal forms. They may mask enchanted human beings but more often they are the ancestral resonances or even aliases for the characters within that story.

The freeing of Mabon, told in *Culhwch and Olwen*, is brought about by a chain of such totems. It may be summarised as follows.

The 26th *anoethu* which Yspaddaden set Culhwch was this:

'There is no huntsman who can hunt with that dog (i.e. Drudwyn, the whelp of Greid ap Eri), but Mabon son of Modron. He was taken from his mother when three nights old, and it is not known where he now is, nor whether he is living or dead.'

Four men are appointed to search for Mabon: Eidoel ap Aer, Mabon's kinsman, who had first to be released from his own imprisonment in the Castle of Glini; Gwrhyr Gwastas Ieithoedd, who knew the language of birds and beasts; and Cai and Bedwyr.

They seek first the Blackbird of Cilgwri (Gwri's Retreat): 'tell me if thou knowest aught of Mabon the son of Modron, who was taken when three nights old from between his mother and the wall?' is the ritual question asked of all the beasts by Gwrhyr. The Blackbird replies that she has been in that place since a smith's anvil was there, and this she has worn away by the pecking of her beak, but she has never heard of Mabon. She directs them to an older race of beasts, to the Stag of Rhedynfr (Fernbrake Hill). He has roamed the plain since a single oak sapling first grew to be an oak of a hundred branches. Now nothing remains but the withered stump, and he has never heard of Mabon. But he directs them to the Owl of Cawlwyd (the Wood of Caw the Grey).

The Owl has flown the wood since a wooded glen had been uprooted twice and grown a third forest, yet never heard of Mabon. She directs the seekers to the Eagle of Gwern Abwy (Alder Swamp) as the most travelled and the oldest bird in the world. The Eagle has pecked the stars from a high rock every night, but now the rock is a span high. In seeking for food he attacked a salmon which drew him to the deep. After a long contention they made peace. He directs the seekers to the Salmon of Llyn Llyw (Lake of the Leader). The Salmon has heard cries coming from the walls of the castle at Gloucester, and takes Cai and Gwrhyr on his shoulders. Gwrhyr asks, 'Who is it that laments in this house of stone?' He is answered: 'It is Mabon, the son of Modron, who is here imprisoned; and no imprisonment was ever so grievous as mine, neither that of Lludd Llaw Ereint, nor that of Greid ap Eri.' (Cf. Chapter 9.)

Mabon cannot be released by the payment of ransom, but only by fighting. Accordingly, the company return to fetch Arthur and his warriors who attack the castle while Cai goes on the Salmon's back, breaking through the dungeon walls and bringing Mabon out on his back. Mabon subsequently leads the hunt for Twrch Trwyth and obtains the razor from between his ears.

Throughout the story, no one, neither man nor beast, can tell where Mabon is, nor whether he is indeed still alive. The reason for this is clear from the context of the story: *no one is old enough to remember*. It follows that Mabon is the Eldest, the first-born of creation, of his mother Modron; and because he was stolen when a new-born child, he is also the Youngest. Only the Salmon is able to locate Mabon, although the chain of Totems leads the seekers to him. As we have seen, the Salmon of Wisdom is one of the totemic identities of the Inner Guardian in the Poet's Wheel sequence.

The loss of Mabon dates from such an early time that even the most ancient memory is out of its reckoning. Here we may perceive the Celtic and native pre-Celtic legend of paradise. Not a myth concerned with lust for power, but one where knowledge is immortality based on reverence for memory. In this paradise, beasts have understanding, memory and knowledge; and the sweet singer of dawn – Mabon, Orpheus, Christ, Apollo – sings in the garden very early. Before humankind, there were animals; before animals, trees and rocks. The reckoning of time's continuity is by means of generations of successive men, animals and elements.

We have already seen that the totems represent successively deeper levels of understanding in the Taliesin story. This can be seen more clearly if we look at some of the methods of reckoning time. One of the earliest of these is recorded in Plutarch's *Moralia*:

> Nine generations long is the life of the crow and his cawing,
> Nine generations of vigorous men. Lives of four crows together
> Equal the life of a stag, and three stags the old age of a raven.
> Nine of the lives of the raven the life of the Phoenix doth equal:
> Ten of the Phoenix we Nymphs, fair daughters of Zeus of the aegis.[84]

Within native tradition, a similar pattern is found:

> Three ages of a dog, the age of a horse.

Three ages of a horse, the age of a man.
Three ages of man, the age of a deer.
Three ages of a deer, the age of an eagle.
Three ages of an eagle, the age of an oak tree.[36]

This Scottish Gaelic saying takes us back at least 2800 years.
But closest to the totems of the Mabon sequence is this
reckoning from the Irish *Book of Lismore*[50]:

Three life-times of the Stag for the Blackbird;
three life-times of the Blackbird for the Eagle;
three life-times of the Eagle for the Salmon;
three life-times of the Salmon for the Yew.

Interestingly, in folk tradition, Christ is crucified on the yew-
tree, thus aligning himself with the Guardian who has passed
beyond the Totems, as both Mabon and Taliesin do.

Triad 92 relates that the three elders of the world are the
Owl of Cwm Cowlwyd, the Eagle of Gwernabwy, and the
Blackbird of Celli Gardarn (Strong Wood): this omits both the
Stag and the Salmon of Mabon's liberation. But it is clear to see
that the Totem Beasts have a unique place in ancestral memory.

What is the significance of these ages of time? They predate
numeracy on one level; on another, they connect us with the
roots of memory. The reckoning of successive ages had little to
do with linear time as we understand it. If a person was not
immortalised in story or song, then he or she was forgotten
after three generations, which must have been the extent of
human memory; hence the importance for learning genealogies.
Poets boasted that their praise-songs kept memory alive, for:
'no man can be famous without an *ollamh* (poet)'.[54] Beyond
human memory lay ages uncounted. The longest-living animals
drew their memory from their own kind and within them,
genetically encoded, were even older species; the remembrance
of times past could be garnered from some part of creation.
The earth remembers, even if we do not.

The proto-story which relates the great memory of the oldest
animals is found in an Irish folkstory, *The Hawk of Achill*:
numerous variants are found across the Celtic world.

The coldest night in the history of the world was one Beltane
Eve. Hundreds of years later there came another severe night

when the Hawk of Achill took shelter in an eagle's nest, killing the fledging. The mother eagle returned and thinking that the hawk was her chick, she fed it. She complained about the night's coldness. The Hawk replied that he remembered a yet colder night. 'How is that possible, since you were only hatched from the egg a month ago?' For answer, the Hawk bade her go to the blackbird of the forge for confirmation. The blackbird (ghobha-dhu: Irish for blacksmith also) had rubbed an iron bar near in two, but couldn't remember a colder night. The eagle flew on to the bull or stag who had lived 4,000 years and whose horns/antlers had gone to make a fence for a one-acre field. He sent her to the Blind Salmon of Assaroe who remembered a colder night. He had been frozen into the ice of the pool and the Hawk of Achill had pecked out his eye. 'By which reckoning, that fledgling of yours is none other than the Hawk of Achill.' The eagle flew back to her nest, but the Hawk was gone.[33]

In another variant it is said that this salmon was none other than Fintan, the great ancestor, who had lived through all the ages of Ireland. Yet another tells that the hawk and salmon are younger still than the Cailleach Beare to whom they award the branch of victory because she is as old 'as the old grandmother long ago who ate the apples'.[50] Each story pushes back the memory to the beginning of time, when time was not.

These ancient stories form part of the native mystery tradition, giving us keys to deeper levels of the Otherworld and its knowledge. Taliesin's own transformations bring him through the Turning of the Totems, through successive ages where wisdom is stored, until he emerges apprised of ultimate knowledge. As a seer-poet he stands in unique relation to the source of life. Mabon's case is slightly different in that he stands at the foundation of a chain of totems, by whose means he is found and liberated. He is, in fact, in the position of the Inner Guardian, unable to leave the Otherworld and assume his position of Wondrous Youth and champion to the Pendragon.

His association with the animals is a very subtle one: he is guarded by them, and yet he is also their guardian and brother. This will be clearer in the next chapter where the Mabon theme is shown to parallel that of other *Mabinogion* heroes whose birth and death days are shared with a totem beast.

Yet the initiate who has passed through the Totems is enabled to become initiator and instructor, in his turn, for he or she has the power of the Totems, and the knowledge of every age. This power is only granted to one who is willing to acknowledge the Totems, as we can witness in folkstories worldwide. The two elder brothers or sisters who will not aid animals in distress are rejected by the animals in *their* hour of need. Only the youngest brother or sister is successful on their quest because they have given their last crust or sup of water to an animal in need. There is nothing anthropomorphic or Disney-like in this revelation. It is a fundamental law of the Otherworld that when a mortal helps a totem beast, then that Totem is bound, by obligation, to aid the mortal. To find and associate with one's ancestral totem is therefore of great importance;[71] it is one step down a personal ladder of successive totems who lead to the initiator – the great ancestor who can be male or female, and who controls the Totems.

The role of the ancestors both in traditional lore and in modern life has been discussed at length by Bob Stewart,[98] and the reader is directed to consult this seminal work if any practical work with the ancestors is attempted. Each person living has many thousand ancestors: among them may be persons famous and infamous, as well as those who are forgotten. The great ancestor of which we speak here is the Inner Guardian from whom we learn; one whose reality is within the Otherworld, but whose teachings are available to us by means of meditative resonance. This Guardian will be one who passed through the Turning of the Totems, and who is willing to instruct others. It is possible to find one's own Inner Guardian by means of the Clan Totem exercise given in *Western Way I*,[71] or one may prefer to use a known archetype. One such is Merlin.

T.H. White's youthful Arthur is turned by his teacher, Merlin, into many different kinds of animal in order to understand the nature of the kingdom he is to govern, and in order to gain a deeper knowledge than the mere acquaintance of mankind can give him.[128] He learns the nature of the beasts, the foolishness of man-made rules and boundaries, and finds the resources of courage, caution and love which he will need to survive. The only defence he does not learn is how to cope with betrayal from his own kind. Nevertheless, this is a real initiation into the Totems and it is administered by the great Inner Guardian himself, Merlin, behind whom stands an array of mighty ancestral powers, each of whom is a powerful guardian of the Totems.

2 GUARDIAN OF THE BEASTS

Within the *Mabinogion* we are given a clear picture of this Guardian, in both *Culhwch* and in the later romance of *The Lady of the Fountain*. We have already met Custennin, the monstrous herdsman who sits outside Yspaddaden's fort, and who warns all comers of their imminent danger. His role is not very clearly defined within the context of the story, and we need to look at the romance to understand just what he represents.

In *The Lady of the Fountain*, Owain and Cynan each make an Otherworld journey in search of adventures beyond the ordinary. Each man is directed to a crossroad within a wood.

> Thou wilt see a black man of great stature on the top of the mound. He is not smaller in size than two of the men of this world. He has but one foot; and one eye in the middle of his forehead. And he has a club of iron . . . he is the woodward of that wood.

Each man finds this Wild Herdsman in turn and is dumbfounded at his stature and strength. He will only speak in answer to questions, and so Cynan enquires what power he has over the thousands of animals grazing near him. He replies:

> 'I will show thee, little man.' . . . And he took his club in his hand, and with it he struck a stag a great blow so that he brayed vehemently, and at his braying the animals came together, as numerous as the stars in the sky. . . . There were serpents, and dragons, and divers sorts of animals. And he looked at them, and bade them go and feed; and they bowed their heads, and they did homage as vassals to their lord. Then the black man said to me, 'Seest thou now, little man, what power I hold over these animals?'[4]

He is the Guardian of the Totems, a powerful figure who instructs adventurers what paths to follow, urging them on to more daring feats and dangerous enterprises. Because he is rough and primitive in appearance he is a figure many might pass by with a shudder, yet he holds many important keys to initiation within the Otherworld.

The Wild Herdsman is indeed an ancient archetype. He can be seen depicted on the Gundestrup Cauldron in Denmark as an antlered god with the torc of sovereignty in his left hand and a serpent in his right, while nearby sport many animals, including the stag and the boar. He is identifiable as the Irish Dagda, with his grotesquely short tunic which reveals his genitals, and who carries a giant's club. He is likewise discernible as Custernnin, the herdsman of Yspaddaden. Lastly, Merlin shares the archetype.

While popular imagination has retained Merlin as an aged sorcerer, it has mainly forgotten Merlin Emrys, the Wondrous Youth, who refutes Vortigern's wizards. It has barely heard of the poet-seer who runs mad after a catastrophic battle into the lonely forest of Celyddon. The Merlin of Celtic tradition is a man of the woods, a shaman, nearer in type to the medieval legend of the wild-man, an Adamic guardian of beasts and tree-herd.[104] Merlin's association with the Wild Herdsman can be seen in the *Vita Merlini*. His former wife is going to remarry, since Merlin is now deranged. When he hears the news, Merlin:

> Went all about the woods and groves and collected a herd
> of stags in a single line, and the deer and she-goats
> likewise, and he himself mounted a stag.[104]

Driving the other animals before him, he rides to where his former wife and her suitor are. He wrenches the antlers from his mount, flings them at the suitor and kills him.

The complexities of this text have been untangled by Bob Stewart,[96] to whom the reader is referred. The role of Wild Herdsman is often associated with temporary madness or displacement from society and is a phase which many heroes undergo. Merlin's madness is related to that of Lailokan of Scottish tradition and of Suibhne Gelt of Irish story.[103] Even Lancelot undergoes a temporary madness after the shock of sleeping with Elaine whom he had thought to be really

Guinevere in the Arthurian legend. Custennin's own herdsman-
ship is onerously placed upon him after Yspaddaden has
stripped him of his property. We are forcibly reminded of the
role of Powerful Swineherd which Pryderi and Tristan assume
(Triad 26; cf. Chapters 4 and 6). But what seems to be a phase
of madness or temporary servitude is in fact an initiation in
which the candidate is forced to face the totems and become
responsible for himself in the Otherworld. This removal from
the world of men is a sabbatical for the purpose of intense
tuition in Otherworldly ways. Only such a sequestration is able
to heal trauma inflicted by the world. It is seldom a gentle
healing, but it is wholesome and invigorating.

Yet the role of Wild Herdsman is only held by one who has
passed through the totems and who has great knowledge. This
is why this figure is one of the Great Ancestors. His role of
instructor is more clearly seen in the story of *Fintan mac
Bochra*. This extraordinarily rich story, garnered from many
sources, relates an entire sequence of ages, shows the relationship between the worlds and hints at the relationship between
oldest man and the oldest animals.

Bith, the granddaughter of Noah, fled to Ireland before the
Deluge, but she and her companions were all drowned except
her son, Fintan. He survived alone, in many animal shapes,
until he finally became a salmon. He was known as Goll of
Assaroe (The Blind One), since a night when the Hawk of
Achill plucked out his eye, when he was stuck in the ice during
the coldest winter since the beginning of the world.

In the times of men, when he was once more in human
shape, he was called upon to judge how Ireland should be
divided. He began to relate his own history until someone cast
doubt upon his memory. In order to show the length of his life
he told this story. He had once picked up a yew-berry which he
plated. It grew into a tree big enough to shelter a hundred
warriors under its branches. When it at last grew old, he made
vessels and barrels out of the wood until at length the iron
hoops fell off. Of the remaining wood he made smaller and
smaller vessels until there was nothing left of the original tree.

He was asked how he acquired his great wisdom and
memory. He told how he had once been present at a great
assembly at which a great hero appeared:

he was high as wood . . . the sky and the sun visible
between his legs . . . a shining crystal veil about him . . .
sandals upon his feet . . . golden-yellow hair . . . falling to
the level of his thighs. . . . Stone tablets in his left hand, a
branch with three fruits in his right hand . . . nuts, apples
and acorns.[14]

The hero's name was Trefuilngid Tre-eochair (T. of the Three
Keys or Saplings). His role was to cause the rising and setting
of the sun. Since the sun had not risen that day over the
Paradise of Adam (the East) he had travelled to the furthest
West to find what kept it from rising. It had been revealed to
him that on that day a man had been tortured and crucified.
Tre-eochair wished to know about the antecedents and
ancestors of that assembly and demanded that chroniclers be
brought.
    'And they answered, "We have no old seanachies . . . to
whom we could entrust the chronicles till thou didst come to
us." Tre-eochair undertook to instruct them, "for I am a
learned witness who explains to all everything unknown".'
Fintan was entrusted with remembering and was given some
berries from Tre-eochair's branch. From these, the greatest
trees of Ireland were sprung, including the yew-tree.
    Satisfied with this answer, Fintan was allowed to relate all
the stories of Ireland to the people of his race until the trees
themselves decayed. He ended his life with the affirmation:

> I am Fintan, I have lived long,
> I am an ancient seanachie of the noble hosts.
> Neither wisdom nor brilliant deeds repressed me
> until age came upon me and decay.

It was asserted that his mortal body was taken to be with Elijah
and Enoch in the secret paradise to await the resurrection of
the world.[14]
    Here then is a complete cycle of one of the oldest ancestors
whose wisdom comes from his own passing through the
totems, and from an Otherworldly instructor who gives him a
branch of the great Tree of Tradition, the axial tree which
interpenetrates both the ancestral wisdom and that of the stars.
After instructing others in his wisdom, Fintan is withdrawn to

the 'secret paradise' of the Otherworld. He does not die or suffer further translation.

Logically, Fintan has the salmon for his prime totem, for he is the receptacle of memory and knowledge. He has undergone the transformations and, like Odin, he loses an eye in his search for wisdom. He joins the Wild Herdsman in his guardianship of the deep native memory.

What then is the nature and function of the Wild Herdsman? This is sometimes hard to seek, since whenever this archetype appears in later stories he is classed with devils, demons and ancestral horrors who have power to scathe good Christian souls. In *Peredur* he appears under many guises, but chiefly as the Black Man; in *The Lady of the Fountain* he turns up as the Black Oppressor; in later Arthurian story he appears frequently as the ubiquitous Black Knight at the ford. But although he has a black skin and an uncouth appearance, his aid is wholesome and real at the deepest levels. Like Tom Bombadil of Tolkien's *Lord of the Rings* – a much scaled-down archetype – he is partly an Adamic man, one of the first created beings who holds all beasts in his stewardship. He is the guardian of the totems and the repository of memory.

We have already remarked on his role as obstructor of the seeker. But 'hostility . . . is often a camouflage for real goodwill on the part of supernatural beings'.[63] This is not an evil but a helpful function. We must view it as we would a master-class teacher who elicits all that the apprentice knows in order to push him to greater heights. He throws back criticism which is not intended to be destructive, but which roots out bad habits and mental apathy which obstruct the path of progress. He cannot be avoided, only challenged. This is clear from every text in which the archetype appears, for he answers all questions put to him in a clear and unambiguous manner. Those who are afraid to ask get to know nothing.

This ancient teaching model can be observed in many stories and songs. *The False Knight Upon the Road*[26] is a typical challenge song in which a child responds with quick-thinking answers to the challenge of the knight. It is the dialogue of master and apprentice. The dialogue between Custennin and the seekers for Olwen is of this nature: and on one level it can be seen that he actually initiates Culhwch into the correct course of action to gain Olwen, as well as enabling his wife's child, Goreu, to revenge his brothers and his father's disgrace. In this regard, the Wild Herdsman is also the Knight of the Riddles[24]: the master-enchanter with all the answers whose delight is, at the last, to be bested by his pupil. The meaning is clear: the seeker cannot succeed on his or her quest without a worthy challenger. Because the quest is a serious one, requiring professional knowledge and precise technique, the Guardian of the Beasts is remorseless in his challenges and in his manipulation of the totems which the seeker encounters on his way. This has led to the Wild Herdsman's reputation as the Black Oppressor: a Saturnine guardian with horns, whom later cultures have incorporated into their dark pantheons of fear.

His real nature is not uncompassionate: he is the Wild Herdsman, perhaps, but he is still a *buachaill* – a herder of flocks – whose first thought is for his beasts. His nature is to draw out the seeker's ability to be truthful, courageous and resourceful in the face of challenge. After all, he is always looking for his successor among his apprentices, for one who will surpass him.

In an oral Irish tale, *Spioras na H-Aoise*,[82] a boy sets out to serve an Old Man who has caused the disappearance of his sister and brothers. After his term of service is over and the boy has visited the many regions of the Otherworld without shrinking from his duty of herding the Old Man's vigorous cow, he demands that the Old Man release his siblings from enchantment. The Old Man, who is none other than a Guardian of great power, replies:

> Under enchantment! What is enchantment? The cunning device of the crafty, the foolish excuse of the timorous. What is enchantment? – the bugbear of fools, a cause of dread to the fainthearted – a thing that was not and that is not and shall not be. *Against the dutiful and the upright there is no magic nor device.*

The boy is sent home with his sister, but his worthless brothers who have failed to serve the Old Man, are made to roam the world as wanderers. The boy asks him, curiously, who he is. 'I am the Oldest,' he replied. 'The blessing of Age be on your journeying and on your going.' The Wild Herdsman is after all the chieftain of the totems who will not deceive the determined seeker, but one who will lead the way with his herdsman's club.

3   THE INITIATION OF THE TOTEMS

When totem beasts make their appearance in the *Mabinogion*, they usually signify a change of consciousness from everyday to Otherworldly reality. If we have been alert to these changes while reading the stories we will have discovered many such instances.

The Wild Herdsman is revealed as the Lord of the Underworld in *Pwyll* and *Manawyddan*, when he sends his White Stag and White Boar to fetch Pwyll and Pryderi into the Otherworld. In the course of the chase neither father nor son realise that they have entered a different state of being until it is too late to retreat. The way through the tangled forest is difficult without the guidance of the totems. Fortunately, the characters within the *Mabinogion* each have their own totemic resonances whereby they can call upon Otherworldly aid in times of stress.

Bran's totem is the raven; although his story is forgotten by visitors to the White Tower of London, his ravens are still there, emblematic of his guardianship of the land. Branwen sends a starling to warn her brother of her treatment, having imbued the bird with her personality by tending and teaching it. Llew becomes an eagle while his erstwhile wife is condemned to owlhood for her treachery. Only Gwydion – himself a master of the totems – can coax the eagle from its perch because he is a poet who speaks the language of the birds. Traditionally, to 'speak the language of the birds' was to be possessed of prophecy and inner knowledge. *The Colloquy or Battle of the Birds* is a strong motif in Celtic lore,[24,50] and we have already seen how the hawk, crow, raven or eagle was one of the oldest birds.

The oldest and most oracular beast among the totems is the salmon. It is in this guise that both Taliesin and Fintan appear; it is the beast who knows the beginnings of the world, who conveys wisdom and who, at length, leads the way to Mabon's prison.

Running through the *Mabinogion*, famed for its ferocity,

greed and cunning, is the boar or pig. Although pork was the staple diet of the Celts, this did not make the totem boar any less mysterious. It came from the Underworld, the gift of Arawn himself. As Twrch Trwyth, it ravaged countrysides, swept its devastating path across Wales, Ireland and Cornwall before vanishing into the sea. It was also a chthonic beast and, when it appeared in the shape of a sow, was a messenger of the Dark Earth Mother herself, the feeder-on-carrion: Llew suffered her attentions until released from his totemic shape by Gwydion.

The totem of the parent is sometimes also that of the child, as is the case with Pryderi who is foal to his mare-mother, Rhiannon. The appearance of pigs causes Goleuddydd to give birth to her son who is then called Culhwch or Pig-Sty. Where we are given such direct evidence of personal totems, it is easier to estimate the effect of the Otherworld upon the characters of the *Mabinogion*, for deeper levels of the story are revealed and we are enabled to glimpse the potency of the native mysteries of Britain.

What then is the connection between the totems and the Wild Herdsman? In what manner are the totems significant of an initiatory pattern? The Otherworldly provenance of the totems is our key. As Bob Stewart has observed, 'the Ancestors of the land are at one': they form a deep matrix of awareness which the totems embody, so that when they make their appearance in a story, the totems 'speak with the unified voice of the Ancestors and the land'.[98] Whoever encounters the Guardian of the Beasts meets one of the mighty ancestral guardians of memory and knowledge. In order to have this knowledge, which is the fruit of memory, the initiate – whether poet, hero or heroine – must suffer the transformation of the totems in his or her own person.

The Wild Herdsman is only one of many possible initiators and instructors. His female counterpart is the Dark Woman of Knowledge, who appears in many guises as the Loathly Lady, the Hag or Cailleach and who is, ultimately, the Sovereignty of the Land itself. We are exceedingly fortunate in our possession of the Taliesin story which clearly illustrates the pattern of female initiator and male initiate:

Taliesin Becomes	Ceridwen Pursues As
hare	greyhound
fish (salmon?)	otter
bird	hawk
wheat	hen

Here Ceridwen shows herself as the Mistress of Beasts, like the Black Artemis or Ephesian Diana, whose many-breasted shape is attended by numerous animals: she is Goddess of the Chase and a wise initiator. She gives birth to her pupil, after his many transformations through the totems.

We do not have a surviving parallel story which gives the polarised pattern of male initiator and female initiate within the *Mabinogion* itself, but we can reconstruct this from an extant folk song of venerable tradition. *The Two Magicians* (Child no.44) is a version of widely-distributed song in which a blacksmith woos a maiden who refuses to give up her maidenhead without a fight. In this song the pattern is as follows:

Maiden Becomes	Blacksmith Pursues As
duck	water-dog
hare	greyhound
eel	trout
mare	saddle
plaid sheet	green coverlid

The final pair of transformations sees the maiden's defeat (or assimilation) and the song is roundly enjoyed for its frank sexual connotations. Its title, *The Two Magicians*, suggests that the protagonists are indeed seasoned shape-shifters engaged in a totemic initiation. Remnants of this tradition were still apparent in the Old Religion of Britain, which retained the following song, *The Fith-Fath Song*, in its initiatory rituals:

> I will go as a wren in Spring,
> With sorrow and sighing on silent wing
> And I will go in our Lady's name,
> Aye, till I come home again.

We will follow as falcons grey
And hunt thee cruelly for our prey.
And we will go in the Good God's name,
Aye, to fetch thee home again.

I will go as a mouse in May,
In fields by night, in cellars by day.
And I will go in our Lady's name,
Aye, till I come home again.

We will follow as black tom cats
And hunt thee through the corn and vats.
And we will go in the Good God's name,
Aye, to fetch thee home again.

'I will go as an Autumn hare,
With sorrow and sighing and mickle care.
And I will go in our Lady's name,
Aye, till I come home again.

We will follow as swift greyhounds,
And dog thy tracks by leaps and bounds.
And we will go in the Good God's name,
Aye, to fetch thee home again.

I will go as a Winter trout
With sorrow and sighing and mickle doubt
And I will go in Our Lady's name,
Aye, till I come home again.

We will follow as otters swift
And snare thee fast ere thou canst shift
And we will go in the Good God's name,
Aye, to fetch thee home again.

This traditional initiatory Craft song has hidden its true nature by the use of 'Our Lady's name' and 'the Good God's name'. In this instance, the initiate puts him or herself under the protection of the Dark Woman of Knowledge, the Goddess herself, while the initiators pursue in the name of the Wild

Herdsman. The pattern in all instances is remarkably consistent, whether the initiator be male or female.

While both Ceridwen and the Blacksmith of the *Two Magicians* appear as predators to modern eyes, in the totemic initiation they are the initiators. Traditionally, the blacksmith was a man of magical powers, whose ability to work metals was a godlike skill; it put him in direct contact with Otherworldly forces and often enabled him to act in a priest-like capacity. Ceridwen is also an alchemist in the transformatory process with her cauldron of herbs culled in the correct planetary hours which boils for a year. They are both fosterers and teachers.

The turning of the totems does not imply a fleshly shape-shifting of the initiate, but an encounter and understanding of the totems in the manner of a ritual challenge. The polarity implied in this process is one of a ritual tension, not of mundane sexual congress. This meeting is asexual for the transformation of the initiate makes him as the newly-born: both innocent and full of knowledge, like Mabon and Taliesin. Both have climbed down the Tree of Tradition, pursuing the totems ever deeper until they find their true selves and oneness with the Ancestors. The totems are symbolic of the initiatory changes which are wrought within the subject.

The pattern of initiator and initiate is consistent within the *Mabinogion*, as well as within other Celtic texts. The following table gives some of the main correspondences for further study. We have lost Mabon's own initiator from his story but Apollo, upon whom the Gaulish Maponus was modelled, may supply the deficit. Apollo – hunter, singer and herdsman – had Cheiron – half-man and half-horse – for the tutor of his son, Aristaios. We may see him as a type of the Wild Herdsman who shares the nature of the totems in his great power.

Teacher Initiator	Initiate Pupil	Totemic Experience
Cheiron	Aristaios	taught the art of herding
Custennin	Culhwch/Goreu	meets the Guardian totems of Mabon
Math	Gwydion	is changed into stag, sow and wolf
Gwydion	Llew	is changed into an eagle
Manawyddan	Pryderi	Otherworld servitude as a foal/horse

To this list may be, apocryphally, added the transformation of Arthur by Merlin into many shapes, which T.H. White fortuitously stumbled upon.[128] Of these initiate-pupils, Aristaios and Pryderi both serve a term as a herdsman; while Culhwch, Llew and Arthur all marry Flower-Brides in the respective shapes of Olwen, Blodeuwedd and Gwenhwyfar.

The patterns and characters are converging rapidly into a final pattern and subject. With the help of the totems and the initiator we may have Otherworldly knowledge and skill enough to release Mabon at last.

CHAPTER 9
Mabon, Son of Modron

The Release of Mabon

'the beginning of the *Mabinogi* of the Maban the Pantocrator, the true and eternal Maponus, and of Rhiannon . . . Matrona of the Calumniations, seven winters at the horse-block telling her own *mabinogi* of detractions.
DAVID JONES
Anathemata

Golden, gold-skinned, I shall deck myself in riches,
And I shall be in luxury because of the prophecy of Virgil.
TALIESIN
Cad Goddeu

1   PERPETUAL PRISONER AND INNER SOVEREIGN

The mystery of Mabon is hard to disentangle and restore. We have already uncovered much of the information concerning Mabon and Modron within the *Mabinogion* itself, but it remains to compare our store of facts. What information do we have which directly relates to Youth, son of the Mother?

The main textual source appears in *Culhwch and Olwen*, as we have seen, yet we also have assorted triads which refer to Mabon as well as medieval texts from the Arthurian corpus in which he develops into another sort of character. Where textual evidence is meagre it is possible to assume further facts about Mabon from his many aliases who appear as heroes within the *Mabinogion* and related literature, although we must be circumspect when drawing from secondary sources.

Yet texts alone do not give us a full picture. We have only to look at the archaeological evidence to understand that Mabon was a living god among the tribes of Britain. The cult of the Divine Youth, Maponus, was localised in both Gaul and Northern Britain. Two place names survive: Lochmaben, a village, and Clochmabenstane, a prehistoric stone, both in Dumfriesshire. The stone was a tribal assembly point and stands only 1½ miles away from Gretna where runaway lovers had their marriages solemnised by a blacksmith.[92] The extent of the cult cannot be judged prior to the Roman occupation except in the most general terms. After the Roman invasion, Maponus's cult spread swiftly along the length of Hadrian's Wall where it enjoyed great popularity among the legions stationed on the most northerly frontier of Pax Romana. A great fusion of deities, both Roman and British, occurs at this time so that it is hard to say which gained the upper hand. The Romans swiftly identified many native deities as aspects of their own, as well as recognising the *genii loci* of the land in their own right. Maponus was soon identified as a type of Apollo – a Greek aspect which the Romans retained, although they renamed his sister Artemis as Diana.

Apollo had long associations with the British Isles which, in Pythagorean tradition, were the home of Hyperborean Apollo. Abaris, a priest of these mysteries, had travelled to

Greece to meet with Pythagoras, riding on the god's own golden arrow, according to legend. In Greek tradition, the name of Apollo, or Apple-Man, recalled the hidden youth of Britain whose mysteries were celebrated within a circular temple, and whose cult was associated with music and the paradisal Otherworld.[39,40] Apollo became more closely associated with the sun by the Romans, while retaining his functions as god of healing and prophecy. To the legionaries stationed on the Wall, men drawn from as far away as North Africa, Bulgaria and the Rhine, the cold, gloomy Northern winter must have seemed intolerable. Maponus/Apollo was a god of the sun, of music and hunting: it is not hard to understand his popularity.

Several heads, identified as Maponus, have been discovered along the Wall. Although worn and weathered, the faces are ritually blank – the face of a youth who has suffered or studied over-long. The formation of the features is comparable to those of the saints and of Christ in the *Book of Kells*. There is also a relief, much worn, showing Maponus in a helmet or cap, flanked on either side by two niches in which Apollo and Diana can be identified by their attributes of sun and moon disks.[90] Apollo Citharoedus, Apollo the Harper, has been identified closely with Maponus,[92] just as Orpheus has adopted the attributes of Apollo in Classical legend.

Although there are no similar dedications to Modron, there are numerous inscriptions and reliefs dedicated to the Matres, the Mothers – a triplicity of goddesses peculiar to the Celts, representing the threefold power and transformatory aspects of the Great Mother herself. We must ever remember that Mabon and Modron are merely titles, not names. They are honorifics, in much the same way as Demeter and Kore merely signify The Mother and The Maiden. Initiates of a particular cult always spoke of their gods in such a guarded manner, while preserving the secret names and inner titles from the profane.

From the archaeological evidence we can see Maponus as a native god who has acquired Classical attributes. But such is the subtle power of Celtic symbolism and magical polarity that though he seems to acquire his musical ability from Apollo, his harp is that of a Celtic poet; while he seems to be a hunter under the protection of Diana, he is the champion of the

Matres, swift and eager to avenge, gentle and loving with animals or women.

The hidden mystery of Mabon, son of Modron is that of the Youth, Son of the Mother – a universal archetypal pattern of which all peoples have some knowledge, but which has particular native variants depending on the culture and time-scale involved. Within British tradition, 'Mabon is not only the Great Prisoner, he is also the Immemorial Prisoner, the Great Son who has been lost for aeons and is at last found.'[44] And if he is without a personal name, what might that name be?

The great *Mabinogion* scholar, W.G. Gruffydd, suggested that the Four Branches represent the birth, exploits, imprisonment and death of Pryderi, son of Rhiannon – that they form, in effect, a *Vita Pryderi*. To prove this theory, Gruffydd engaged in some factual contortions which have not proved acceptable to other scholars.[46] The author, while grateful to many of his insights, cannot follow his thesis to the letter. However, a more exciting realisation arises from consideration of his argument: that there is an archetypal mystery pattern underlying the *Mabinogion* in which many of its heroes can be seen as *types of Mabon*. This theory seems less far-fetched when we consider the evidence presented from the *Mabinogion* itself, especially if this is set side by side with a very important textual source: Triad 52.

> Three Exalted Prisoners of the Island of Britain:
> Llyr Half-Speech, who was imprisoned by Euroswydd,
> and second, Mabon son of Modron,
> and third, Gwair, son of Geirioedd.
> And one [prisoner] who was more exalted than the three of them, was three nights in prison in Caer Oeth and Anoeth, and three nights imprisoned by Gwen Pendragon, and three nights in an enchanted prison under the Stone of Echymeint. This Exalted Prisoner was Arthur. And it was the same lad who released him from each of these three prisons – Goreu, son of Custennin, his cousin.[5]

Within the Mabon sequence in *Culhwch*, Mabon says: 'It is Mabon son of Modron who is here imprisoned; and no imprisonment was ever so grievous as mine, neither that of

Llydd Llaw Ereint, nor that of Greid the son of Eri.' This seems very close to the triad above. Nothing can be told about Llyr's imprisonment; however, he has been equated by Rachel Bromwich with Lludd Llaw Ereint, Lludd of the Silver Arm, about whom we know much more. We have already encountered Nuadu of the Silver Arm, his Irish equivalent (p.110) in the *Second Battle of Mag Tured* story; Nuadu lost his hand in battle and had to resign his kingship until a silver arm was made for him. During his retirement, Llew became his champion and eventually his successor.

Nuadu and Llydd are the focus of power behind the Romano-British god, Nodens, whose temple at Lydney in Gloucestershire is in tempting proximity both to the site of Mabon's imprisonment at Caer Loyw (Gloucester) and to the place of Pryderi's own boyhood seclusion in Gwent-is-Coed. The totemic symbol of Llydd/Nodens is the salmon, while the temple at Lydney seems to have been used for the purposes of temple-sleep, whereby clients slept within the temple precincts to have their dreams interpreted under the aegis of the god. Mabon's own totem is the salmon, of course, it being the totem of wisdom. The method of dream incubation is very similar to the manner in which poets received their poetry. Yet there is little of the youth about Llydd/Nodens, that we can associate him with Mabon: he is one of the Innerworld guardians, from an earlier level of belief. Yet those who have the salmon for their totem have the means of transformation as Gwion/Taliesin discovered.

What of the third prisoner of the triad? We have already seen how Pryderi is closely associated with Mabon's own pattern from the *Preiddeu Annwn* poem:

> Perfect was the captivity of Gweir in Caer Sidi
> According to the tale of Pwyll and Pryderi.

In Chapter 4 we saw how Gweir means hay, and just how this name is fitting for Pryderi who with his mother undergoes the penance of the Hay-Collar and the Door-Knocker. Pryderi is such a prisoner as Mabon: one who stands in a long line of prisoners, since his own father has already endured a year in Annwn before assuming the title of honours of that place.

Yet what of Mabon's words concerning the imprisonment of

Greid ap Eri; is there another identification clue here? Gruffydd has ingeniously suggested that Greid ap Eri may be a corruption of Pryderi, by means of the elision of P into G, i.e. Gr(e)id (ap) Eri or Pryderi. If this seems far-fetched, stranger copyists' errors have been known.[46] Pryderi is textually linked with Mabon son of Mellt (which may be another epithet for our Mabon) as Gware Gwallt Euryn – a corruption of his child-hood name, Gwri Wallt Euryn. It is also not without significance that the search for Mabon begins with the Blackbird of Cilgwri. Gwri is Pryderi's fosterage name; Cilgwri means the Retreat of Gwri – the place of his fostering. And who else is the Blackbird but one of Rhiannon's own totemic birds who sing the way between the worlds?

Gwri, Gwair or Gwion, a definite tradition of famous prisoners cross-tracks the Mabon pattern. Yet, we are told, there is a yet more famous prisoner. We are fortunate that the lode-bearing evidence of the Arthurian corpus has such perennial power to move and delight. Whatever is told of lesser heroes becomes lodged into the legend of Arthur, so that long-dead traditions live through him.

If we look again at the Triad we will see that Arthur spends three sets of three nights in different captivities. These may be seen as parallel imprisonments to those endured by Taliesin in the prsion of Arianrhod. The places of captivity are as follows:

(a)   Caer Oeth and Anoeth
(b)   imprisonment by Gwen Pendragon
(c)   in an enchanted prison under the Stone of Echymeint.

In *Culhwch*, we will recall that Arthur's porter Glewlwyd enumerates the many places he has accompanied his king:

> I was once in Caer Oeth and Anoeth,
> in Caer Nefenhir of the Nine Natures.

Anoeth means both 'difficult' and 'a wonder'. These Caers are indeed the Castles of Ease and Hardship, for those who travel in the Underworld, as Arthur does to claim the Cauldron and other Hallows of Sovereignty from Annwn, are given the choice of the hard, the easy or the middle way to their destination.[98] In this captivity the Pendragon goes down to fetch the wisdom of the ancestors and to become Pen Annwn.

The imprisonment by Gwen Pendragon is impossible to solve as it stands. No such character appears anywhere in Arthurian legend. Gwen, as an adjective, merely means 'white'. Some scholars have considered the possibility of Uther as a possible answer since in two Irish Arthurian romances Uther is rendered 'Uighir Finndraeguin' or White Dragon.[5] However, this seems an unlikely explanation since in British symbolism the white dragon is understood to be emblematic of the Saxons – Britain's enemy.[37,97]

Lastly there is the enchanted prison under the Stone of Echymeint. This has never been identified. Within immediate parallel tradition two such imprisoning stones are known: the stone under which Lunet is trapped in *The Lady of the Fountain*, and the rock or tower which encloses Merlin. These three prisons of Arthur are a challenge for the serious student of the British Mysteries. They represent part of a lost tradition which, like many of the triads and fragmentary poems of Taliesin, remain partially uncovered. We can only pass on, with many a backward glance at the clues which tease our understanding. For the purposes of practical research, each captivity may be considered as part of an initiatory cycle of 'imprisonments' within the Otherworld where Hell is Harrowed, and where Arthur joins the Succession of the Pendragons, becoming in turn the guardian or porter on the threshold of the worlds.

Let us turn to the final sentence of the triad: 'and it was the same lad who released him from each of these three prisons – Goreu, son of Custennin'. If we turn to the genealogy on p.96 we will see how Goreu, Culhwch and Arthur are cousins. We will remember how Goreu is hidden, by his mother, in a cupboard, for fear of Yspaddaden who has slain twenty-three of her sons, until Cai comes and makes him a companion and page. During the attainment of Wrnach's sword, the boy fights his way across three courtyards and gains entrance. For this feat the hitherto unnamed boy is called Goreu, or 'the Best'.

Goreu is uniquely suited to act in the role of liberator of Arthur because he combines the qualities of prisoner and champion. To summarise: Goreu is a yellow-haired boy (like Gwri); he is himself imprisoned by his own mother for his own safety (like Mabon); he is the cousin of Arthur and wielder of the Sword of Light which illumines the way in Annwn for Arthur; he avenges the wrongs endured by his family by slaying the giant who oppresses them (like Llew). Goreu plays an important part in the Succession of the Pendragons in that he cuts through the restrictive layers of custom, releasing all three role-bearers to succeed to their next role, releasing them from former cycles of responsibility and initiating them into the next. The Path of Goreu (cf. p.109) leaps through difficulties and across cyclic barriers in order to empower the next Pendragon. We may see then that the role of Mabon is a dual one: he bears responsibilities and burdens, and releases others from them: he is both prisoner and champion.

The wielder of the Sword of Light in the *Preiddeu Annwn* is Llwch Lleminiawg whom we have identified with Llew Llaw Gyffes and the Irish Lugh (cf. p.108). There is a further fragment which shows the correspondence between the prisoner and the champion:

> The grave in the upland of Nantlleu,
> Nobody knows its properties:
> It is Mabon's, the swift son of Modron.[88]

Nantlleu is the place where Llew perched while in his totemic shape as an eagle. But as for a grave for Mabon? Perhaps such a consideration should be as strange to us as a grave for Arthur – an unchancy thought! Let those who come after us find graves for gods. If Mabon and Arthur should ever leave us, their rest will be an Otherworldly one where they pass within to become guardians. All who have negotiated the Path of Goreu become immortal and the dust does not claim them. Maponus the avenging hunter still rides the Northern hills; Maponus the harper still sings under them.

2   THE LADY'S CHAMPION

The Celtic sources for Mabon were sufficiently strong to project the archetype of the prisoner/champion into the Arthurian literature of the Middle Ages where Mabon lived on under other guises as Mabuz and Mabonograin. And while

Modron is noticeably absent from the early Celtic narratives which survive, her role is more clearly defined in the medieval texts where she appears in the guise of many Otherworldly women, including Arthur's half-sister, Morgan.

Mabon reappears as the evil knight, Mabuz, in *Lanzelet*, an Arthurian text in Middle High German by Ulrich von Zatzikhoven, a Swiss priest who reworked this story from a French original. In this text Lancelot is brought up in seclusion by a Water-Fay on an island where he is taught skill at arms and where he plays prisoner's base. In all respects, the narrative transfers all the qualities of an imprisoned champion to Lancelot. Mabuz's mother is none other than Lancelot's foster-mother. But Mabuz himself is a cowardly knight inhabiting the Castle of Death: 'Whoever he captured was led into a vast prison, where lay . . . a hundred knights or more. They were all filled with sorrow, perpetually in fear of death. Whenever Mabuz was angry . . . he ordered a man killed.'[105]

It is almost as though the term 'Mabon's prison' has suffered a radical misunderstanding. Instead of it meaning 'the place where Mabon was imprisoned', it has become 'the prison guarded by Mabon'. Yet, though our Mabon has suffered alteration in this text, it is interesting to note that the story is still true to its archetypal themes: he is still a species of Otherworldly guardian, though nearer to the Pen Annwn than to the Mabon archetype. The description of the Otherworldly island where Lancelot is fostered is clearly a proto-Avalon where Modron rules as queen, with her maiden attendants.

This text is already at a remove of secondary translation and too corrupt for it to be of much use to us. Is there something nearer home which will serve? Luckily there is, in the shape of the related stories stemming from the British tale, *Gereint and Enid*. This romance appears in most editions of the *Mabinogion*, though it is much later in date than the Four Branches and the other tales covered in the present work. There has been much dispute as to whether *Gereint and Enid* or Chrétien de Troyes's version, *Erec and Enid*, was the original. It is evident that both versions draw from a common source, whatever the facts of the matter, and that either can be drawn upon confidently as part of the authentic tradition of Mabon's lineage.

In the British story, Gereint, after many adventures, arrives at the castle of Owain and hears about some enchanted games. Knowing nothing about them, Gereint is determined to try his skill, whatever the cost. We take up the story in Chrétien's version which is fuller. Here Gereint becomes Erec and Owain is Yvain; instead of enchanted games, they are called 'The Joy of the Court' – a strange adventure from which knights do not return. Erec approaches a garden in which this dangerous adventure lies. The garden is bordered solely by air, yet this is impassable save through one narrow entrance. Inside fruit grows all year round, and he is told that though it is safe to eat the fruit inside the garden, whoever attempts to carry it out at once becomes sealed forever in that place, unable to find the exit. Bewitched by this paradisal garden, Erec strives to recall the mysterious Joy which he has come to seek. He sees a stake which he is told is intended for his head, should he be unsuccessful. (In the British version, the whole garden is surrounded by heads on stakes, in true Celtic fashion.) He sees also the horn which no one has been able to blow: he who does so will be renowned throughout the land.

Under a canopy beneath a tree sits a beautiful maiden. When he approaches her, a red knight of great stature challenges him. They fight, and Erec overcomes him. Erec reveals his name to his defeated opponent and demands to know his own name and what the Joy of the Court entails. The red knight reveals that he knows Erec's father, King Lac, and was knighted at his court. He has been detained in this garden because of love and service to the maiden under the canopy who made him swear never to leave the garden until a knight should conquer him by force of arms. Being bound by his oath he has, perforce, defeated and killed many knights who have come to the garden. He continues:

> You have given great joy to the court of my uncle [Brandigan] and my friends; for now I shall be released from here; and because all those who are at court will have joy of it, therefore those who awaited the joy called it 'Joy of the Court'. They have awaited it so long that now it will be granted them by you who have won it by your fight. . . . Now it is right that I tell you my name, if you would know it, I am called Mabonograin; but I am not

remembered by that name in any land where I have been, save only in this region; for never, when I was a squire, did I tell or make known my name.[62]

Erec is then asked to blow the horn which will signal the commencement of the Joy.

Here is a flowering of Mabon's story! Yet in a German variant text the amazing similarities between Mabonograin, Mabon and Pryderi are further reinforced. Mabonograin says:

> Today my troubles are over. . . . Your coming was truly a great blessing for this court, because it lost all its merriment with me and was stripped of its pleasures. There have been no festivals of any kind since I left, because for all my youth and noble birth, I was buried alive – and the Joy of the Court entirely disappeared. But now they shall begin them again, because they have their favourite back. Your brave arm has freed this troubled land from great sorrow and led it back to happiness.[105]

The garden is an Otherworldly paradise with its *genia*, who acts as the representative of the Goddess. Yet the red knight is trapped there and cannot assume his role as the bringer of joy: he cannot, in fact, succeed to the next appointed role in the cycle. His uncle Brandigan is an echo of Bran, the great Innerworld guardian – the Pen Annwn who cannot become the Mabon until the Pendragon comes. Just as Mabon's name is unknown, so the red knight's name is unknown and perhaps forgotten. His release can only be brought about by combat with a worthy opponent, just as Mabon can only be released by fighting. And just as Mabon has been imprisoned from the beginning of the world, so Mabonograin has been bound to the garden so long that its paradisal bliss has become a living hell: only his return can usher in a new reign of pleasure. The name Mabonograin can be interpreted as Son of the Sun: Mabon (son, Welsh) Grian (sun, Irish).

Gereint (or Erec) wins great renown for this deed, far beyond the rationale of the story. But if we place him in the line of the great liberators of Otherworldly prisoners, with Goreu, Culhwch and Llew, then this fame seems well earned. Those who take the Path of Goreu become candidates in the Succession of the Pendragons.

Despite Chrétien's ignorance of the inner mysteries under-lying this story, some remarkable features emerge. The impending threat of the stake set ready for the loser's head reminds us of Bran's own sacrifice of kingship: it is the action whereby he transfers his power to the Underworld kingdom and becomes a Pen Annwn. Mabonograin, in Chrétien, has passed from being a young saviour of an earlier time cycle, a bringer of joy – a role consistent with the Divine Youth, Mabon – into an oppressor of the most restrictive Cronos model. Mabon the youth has become Mabon the Titan.

The horn which hangs ready to signal the joy of Mabonograin's return to the world is an important instrument in the lore of recalling the spent Pendragons who spend their next cycle renewing their strength in sleep in the Hollow Hills. It is the horn of legend which the shepherd, stumbling into a tumulus, ignores, though he sees Arthur and his court sleeping with a horde of treasure. Disturbed from his rest Arthur berates the unprepared seeker:

> O woe betide that evil day
> On which this witless wight was born.
> Who drew the sword – the garter cut,
> But never blew the bugle-horn![35]

This legend comes from Sewingshields, Northumberland on the Wall, in Mabon's country. The Pendragon can only pass from his long rest when the horn is blown, so that he can walk the land once more.

Chrétien does not fully understand the role of the Lady in the garden, she is a mere cipher of romance, chaining her champion with bonds of love and oaths of loyalty. Beneath this one-dimensional character stands an Otherworldly woman, perhaps Modron herself, in the role of Avalonian queen. The clues to this realisation lie in the close association of Owain, under whose aegis these games are held, with Modron. This association is underscored in *The Lady of the Fountain*, one of the late romances from the *Mabinogion*, where Owain becomes the champion of an Otherworldly mistress. But his true relationship with Modron is best understood from a reading of Triad 70 which speaks of 'the Three Fair Womb Burdens of the Island of Britain'; the second of which is 'Owain, son of Urien, and Morfudd his sister, who were carried together *in the womb of Modron, Ferch Afallach*'.[5]

Do we have here a vital clue to Mabon's identity? Our long search is almost done, but first we must take ship for the Otherworld and find the Lady.

3   THE ROYAL VIRGIN OF AVALON

Let us hear an old story which preserves the bloodline of the mystery:

> In Denbighshire there is a parish which is called Llanferres, and is a Rhyd a Gyfartha [Ford of Barking]. In the old days the hounds of the countryside used to come together to the side of that ford to bark and nobody dared to go to find out what was there until Urien Rheged came. And when he came to the side of the ford he saw nothing there except a woman washing. And then the hounds ceased barking, and Urien seized the woman and had his will of her; and then she said, 'God's blessing on the feet which brought thee here.' 'Why?' 'Because I have been fated to wash here until I should conceive a son by a Christian. And I am the daughter to the King of Annwn, and come thou here at the end of the year and then thou shalt receive the boy.' And so he came and he received there a boy and a girl: this is Owein, son of Urien, and Morfydd, daughter of Urien.[5]

The woman washing at the Ford of Barking is none other than Modron – or, we should be careful to note, *a woman who bears the title 'Modron'*. After the fashion of women in this role, she bears twins. Owain, like Pryderi, is the child of an Otherworldly and mortal liaison; his mother, like Rhiannon, is the daughter of the King of the Underworld or, according to the foregoing Triad, the daughter of the King of Avalon.

In Celtic legend the woman who washes at the ford is invariably a representative of the Dark Goddess or Cailleach – the Hecate of Celtic tradition: she who men fear to encounter since she usually washes the bloody garments of those destined to fall in battle. In this story, Modron appears with her totem

Underworld hounds at a ford, just as in Classical legend Hecate appears at a crossroads with her dogs who bay the moon. Her purpose at the ford is solely to conceive a child who will be a saviour to her people. In the light of this realisation, Rhiannon's appearance at the Mound of Arberth, and forthright demand of Pwyll that he marry her, can be seen in a more ritual light than before. Both Modron and Rhiannon purposely loiter at the local way-between-the-worlds in order to conceive a son. Modron bears Owain and Morfydd: this twin birth is a factor which we have already seen as significant to the story of Epona, Rhiannon and Macha, as well as the Black Demeter story of Phygalia (cf. Chapter 2).

We must not be put off the scent by Triad 70's use of the title Modron as the mother of Urien's children. We know from both Welsh genealogy and Arthurian legend that Owain's mother, Urien's wife, is none other than Morgan, half-sister to Arthur. The same Morgan who is elsewhere described as daughter to the Rex Avallonis.[5]

The name Morgan is derived from the same root as the Irish Morrighan, the Cailleach aspect of the Goddess, whose totem is the crow. Morgan means 'of the sea', and she is associated with Avalon in a very special way. Both Morgan and Modron are associated with the aspect of the Goddess who guards the apple orchard of the Otherworld. (Modron's name survives in this context in the place name Garth Madrun, Talgarth, Brecon.) Modron's realm seems also to be bordered by the sea if we follow the clues supplied by Rhiannon and the Water-Fay of *Lanzelet*.

We are indeed fortunate that so many texts attest to the role of Modron as she appears in the guise of Morgan, for these help us at last to reconstruct the polarised pattern of Female Correspondences which connect with the Succession of the Pendragons. Morgan is not only the sister of Arthur but the Royal Virgin of Avalon, according to both the *Vita Merlini* (c.1150) and the *Gesta Regnum Britanniae* (c.1235); a mighty queen, attended by her nine maidens, living in Otherworldly state and bliss. Let the *Gesta* tell us about that place:

This wondrous island is girdled by the ocean; it lacks no good things; no thief, reiver nor enemy lurks in ambush there. No snow falls; neither summer nor winter rages uncontrollably, but unbroken peace and harmony and the gentle warmth of eternal spring. Not a flower is lacking, neither lilies, rose nor violet; the apple-tree bears flowers and fruit together on one bough. Youth and maiden live together in that place without blot of shame. Old age is unknown; there is neither sickness nor suffering – everything is full of joy. No one selfishly keeps anything to himself; here everything is shared.

A royal virgin is the guardian of this place and everything in it: a nymph of surpassing beauty, attended by the fairest maidens, graceful of feature, sprung of noble ancestors, potent of counsel, renowned for her healing skills.

At that same time when Arthur bequeathed the diadem of royalty and set another king in his place, it was she who brought him over there in the five hundred and forty-second year after the Word became incarnate without the seed of human father. Wounded beyond measure, Arthur took the way to the court of the King of Avalon, where the royal virgin, tending his wound, keeps his healed body for her very own and they live together – if it is lawful to believe this.

Despite that suspicion of doubt from the cleric who transcribed this sequence, we may indeed believe that we have at last found the key which helps turn the Cycle of the Pendragons. Morgan, the Royal Virgin of Avalon, is the Otherworld mistress of Arthur: he goes thither and becomes her consort and champion. Whatever aspect Modron assumes, she remains the innerworld focus for her hero and champion, as he succeeds to the next role, as shown in Figure 9.1.

The *Gesta* clearly indicates that Arthur relinquishes his kingship to another voluntarily, and 'sets another king in his place', but he does not lose the guiding influence of Modron, the Great Goddess. The Mother who bore him, the woman of Sovereignty who upheld his Pendragonship, becomes at last his Otherworld consort and healer.

Perhaps now we can see that the imprisonment of Mabon is of another kind to what we had supposed. In the Succession of

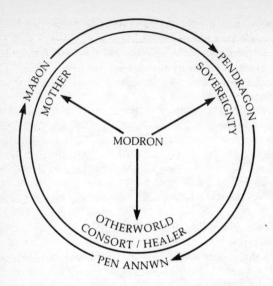

Figure 9.1: *The Succession of the Pendragons*

the Pendragons, the hero who descends to the Underworld becomes the guardian of the Otherworldly Hallows in the paradise of Avalon. Those who have eaten of the fruit of the apple which grows there can only return as the reborn Mabon, the son of Modron, because that fruit bestows eternal youth with potent restoration of spent strength. Cronos is chained in the middle of his island paradise as Gweir is chained in Annwn; Merlin does not return from the embraces of Niniane in *Le Val Sans Retour* of Breton legend; Mabonograin is bound to serve his mistress; Mabon is hidden by his mother in a secret place, like Goreu. Endlessly the imprisonment theme is retold and always the storytellers miss the cause: they blame a beguiling woman, an enchantress or old hag. And even though Taliesin boasts of his initiatory service with the Goddess: 'I have been three periods in the prison of Arianrhod', they still cannot see the pattern.

The further back we penetrate into the roots of the native mysteries, the clearer it becomes that the hero's imprisonment is a willing one. Merlin is not beguiled by Niniane, but goes willingly with her to the abode of bliss at the end of his appointed cycle to become the arbiter and Master of Wisdom at the side of the Lady of the Hollow Hills, who is the Queen of Faery, the Dark Woman of Knowledge herself.

In the Succession of the Pendragons, the series of captivities becomes clear to us:

Nature of Captivity	Position	Exemplified By
initiatory	Mabon	Goreu and Mabon
sacrificial	Pendragon	Arthur and Bran
redemptive	Pen Annwn	Bran and Merlin

Set against this is the pattern of Modron, the Great Goddess:

Aspects	Exemplified By
Initiating Mother	Ceridwen, Rhiannon
Lady of Sovereignty	Branwen, the Flower Bride in all her guises
Otherworldly Consort	Arianrhod, Morgan

Modron is the enabling and empowering Goddess who controls the cycle, but, because she is the daughter of Pen Annwn or Rex Avallonis, she has to fight in order to keep the cycle revolving. Whoever becomes her consort automatically defeats her father; and if her consort fails then she uses him to engender a son who will grow up and defeat his grandfather. Modron must use all her power to defeat the Titanic strength of her father, which is why she has to resort to mortal men who are likely to be worthy champions. Nowhere is there a clearer template for this theme than in the story of Cronos, Rhea and Zeus (cf. Chapter 3). Beside the orthodox legend, let us set this Akkadian story, recorded by Pausanius:

> When Rhea gave birth to Poseidon she left him in a sheepfold to live with the lambs. . . . She told Cronos her baby was a horse and gave him a foal to swallow instead of her son, just as later on she gave him a stone to swallow wrapped in baby-clothes in place of Zeus.[40]

And so Zeus defeats Cronos, as Gwri, the son of another

Modron, defeats his father's ancient enemy from Annwn.
Mabon defeats the Pen Annwn and there is an exchange of
attributes. But Pen Annwn grows ever younger in the
Otherworld and is again reborn as Mabon, just as Cronos puts
away his oppressive rule to become the king of the paradisal
island.

Modron, whether she is Rhea or Rhiannon, triumphs
through her sons who are as countless as the blossom blowing
from the bough in Avalon, ever fruiting and flowering into
eternity.

4   THE LOST FIFTH BRANCH

The patient reader may well wonder whether there is indeed a
lost Fifth Branch to discover since this tree has more branches
than can be counted at one blink; not to speak of innumerable
roots to be tripped over. We have seen the consistency and
cohesion of the themes which link the Four Branches with
Culhwch and *Taliesin*; we have descended with Arthur to
Annwn, met the totems and their guardian and sailed to Avalon
to meet the Goddess. Where else can we go but home?

An amalgamation or conflation of the stories in which
Mabon's mysteries can be found would make for a very
confusing narrative. All that is possible is to establish a pattern,
applicable on many levels of storytelling to many protagonists
who stand in the place of Mabon. Mabon is 'the birth that has
never been born, and never will be',[30] his titles and names are
many, but he is recognisably the same, just as the colour blue is
universally understood no matter what language one speaks.

The following table of correspondences, showing the different
types of Mabon and Modron, is in no wise a full list – other
names will occur to the reader from other traditions.

Modron	*Mabon*	*Unknown or Doubtful Father*
Rhiannon	Gwri/Pryderi	Pwyll/Arawn
Custennin's Wife	Goreu	Custennin/Yspaddaden
?	Gwair	Llwch Lleminawg/Llew
Arianrhod	Llew	Gwydion/Math
Morgan	Owain	Urien
Lady of the Lake	Lancelot	Afallach

Igrayne	Arthur	Uther/Gorlois
Rhea	Zeus	Cronos
Leto	Apollo	Zeus
Cyrene	Aristios	Apollo
Mary	Jesus	Holy Spirit/Joseph

The inclusion of the last triplicity of names is not intended blasphemously, but only in order to show the true universality of this salvific story which has not despised the vehicle of folkstory, mythology or scripture. If the mystery of Mabon and Modron is truly the lost Fifth Branch, then it is a remarkably ill-hidden mystery, since it lodges in any likely crevice of traditional story. The kernel of the mystery story always follows this pattern:

The boy is conceived by a virgin, of an unknown or Otherworldly father: which of the two is often uncertain. The virgin's father or tribe reject her because of a prophecy which will endanger the tribal order of things if she bears a son. She gives birth to her child in great difficulty, friendless but for beasts or simple people. The child is in great danger and is hidden among animals or poor people, who also rear and foster him. The qualities of the child soon reveal him to a person of wisdom who agrees to foster him and teach him his knowledge or skills. The boy is then brought to court, among his own kindred, where he astounds royalty and wisemen by his precocity. His mother, who has lost her child or put him from her, receives him again secretly and gives him a name and destiny, arming him with weapons or magical powers.

He becomes either a great hero of deep wisdom and daring, or else a seer-poet. He changes the old order of things, threatens all which is entrenched and overturns evil customs. His opponents challenge, but are unable to overcome him: this can only be achieved when he voluntarily accepts his destiny. Before the final test he has, in the order of things, slept with a virgin unknown to him, who will give birth to the next Mabon in the new cosmic sequence.

He accepts his destiny, encountering all his geise at once. If his life-pattern has been as an earthly ruler or Pendragon, then he submits to his destiny as Lord of the Underworld. If he has been a seer-poet, he passes within to become an Otherworldly guardian and mentor to future seekers.

Modron's theme is similar. She is a virgin of the royal or holy bloodline which will act as the vehicle for Mabon's manifestation. She suffers disgrace and exile from her tribe to give birth to her son. She prepares suitable foster-parents for his early rearing, and later supplies a tutor of her choosing. She then prepares a suitable mate for her son, instructing her in the rites of engendering a Mabon. Lastly, she oversees and conducts him through the final change of the passing-within.

The sequence of successive Mabons is not necessarily one which occurs within each earthly generation: it may miss several generations and reoccur as the thresholds of the Aeons, or when the cosmic tides permit.

There is always an imminent Mabon: there is always an appointed Guardian.

If there is only one story at the heart of the mystery, then this is it. Ultimately it is for you, the reader, to find out who your Mabon and Modron are and to become initiates of their mysteries. In the next chapter, the challenge passes into your hands. All theories stop here and must be transmuted into practice if the mystery of Mabon and Modron is to be given to the succeeding generations.

> For Modron's son they do me call
> And Mabon is my name.
> Who does me find shall blessing have,
> Who frees me shall have fame.
> *Mabon's Hunt*

CHAPTER 10
The Lyre of Mabon

The Harp of Mabon

Be hushed, ye that hear, at the song to Apollo . . . Apollo is in the choir; I hear the lyre.

CALLIMACHUS

Time is already big by sacred commerce with the Timeless courses. Fore-chose and lode-bright, here is the maiden, Equity! The chthonic Old Sower restores the wastelands. The First-Begotten, of the *caer* of heaven . . . would bring his new orient down for our alignment.

DAVID JONES
Anathemata

169

1 THE RETURN OF SATURN

Now that we have understood how the hidden line of Pendragons sustains the inner guardianship of the land, it is time to ask the mystery question:

'WHO SHALL BE PENDRAGON IN THE TIME WHEN SATURN SHALL DESCEND FROM HIS SPHERE?'

In other words, how shall these mysteries find their continuance in our own times?[120]

This question is the very same one which Merlin asks Ransom in C.S. Lewis's *That Hideous Strength*, and it is a crucial one which all who work with the *Mabinogion* must attempt to answer; it underlies the nature of esoteric commitment to the Great Work of Remaking, which every generation must work towards. We live in the time when the prophecy is to be accomplished concerning Saturn's return to earth and the reinstitution of a Golden Age; another such prophecy concerns the return of the Goddess, Justice, to earth.

We must be cautious in attempting to realise these prophecies within our lives in a literal or political light, still less should we view the coming millennium in a   clear manner. The Golden Age has long been recognised as the metaphorical glyph of the Blessed Otherworld, wherein the sacred harmonies are maintained in balance. In primal Otherworld tradition, no redemption which erases the earth and its memories is envisaged.

In Classical times the king of the Golden Age was Saturn or Cronos who, as we have read, is imprisoned in the Blessed Isles by his son Zeus, there to rule over the heroes at the Westernmost edge of the world.[85] The reign of Saturn/Cronos is the *Saturnia Regna*. It is also the reign of Pen Annwn, of Bran and Afallach who, as Lord of the Underworld, Guardian of the Land and as King of Avalon, respectively, are actively present on each level of the Otherworld. When Saturn/Cronos descends from his sphere, his post is vacant, necessitating a new officeholder; when he descends, the Golden Age – understood as a resonance of the Otherworld – is operative on earth.

This understanding is inextricably tied up with the prophetic writings of Virgil, particularly with the *Fourth Eclogue*, wherein we hear about the return of the Golden Age in connection with a Wondrous Child:

> Now has the last great age begun,
> by Cumae's seer foretold;
> new born the mighty cycles run
> their course, and quit the old.
> 5 Now too, the Virgin reappears,
> and Saturn re-controls the spheres.
>
> Now is a new race on the way
> from heaven; do thou befriend
> the Infant, all but born, whose day
> 10 the iron brood shall end
> and with the golden fill the earth.
> O chaste Lucina, speed his birth.
>
> Thy own Apollo now is king. . . . [102]

Line 2 refers to the oracle at Cumae whose Sibyl was under the aegis of Apollo; she was the compiler of the *Sibylline Books* which were consulted by the augurs – Roman priests – at times of national calamity. Line 5 refers to the return of the Goddess Justice, called also Dicte or Astraea, to the earth: Astraea left the earth for the stars at the end of the Golden Age, becoming associated with the constellation of Virgo.[10,132] Lucina, line 12, is one of Juno's titles, in her role as goddess of childbirth: her festival, the *Matronalia*, was celebrated in March, corresponding to our Lady Day, 25 March. (Matrona was also one of the titles of Modron.)

The prophesied child is to be a type of Apollo, although many early Christian commentators read it as a reference to the Messianic coming of Christ. Both the return of the Goddess and the reign of an Apollonian child are indicated in this poem.

The myth of the Golden Age exercised the Classical imagination a good deal: it was the Otherworldly reality made manifest for them, analogous to the Celtic vision of Avalon, complete with Arthur and his court, returning to the earth. This theme, translated into the Kingdom of Heaven, was also a potent hope for successive ages in the West. If we trace the descent of Saturn through the traditions of the West, we notice that, like T.H. White's Merlin, he 'youthens'.[128]

> Saturn/Kronos, he whom his own Zeus dethroned by throwing him off his chariot, and banished in chains to a blissful island, where he dwells in sleep, for being immortal he cannot die, but is thought to live a life-in-death wrapped in funerary linen, until his time, say some, shall come to awaken again, and he will be reborn to us as a child.[31]

The child is Mabon, the transformed Pen Annwn, whose star rises once again. What kind of imprisonment and release can be endured and effected by a mere child? To answer this question we must broaden our vision beyond the particularities of one native tradition, and embrace a more cosmic pattern of archetypal occurrence. Mabon's story is a template for other stories: he shows forth the archetype of the Puer Eternus whose youth and strength is polarised against the Titan of Age and rigidity. Or, to look at this from a spiritual standpoint, it is the battle to release all prisoners of the planet from the sterility of outworn tradition in which they lie bound, into a new cycle of enlightened strength.

Each mystery tradition, from pre-Classical times onwards, has worked from this central premise: a young and vital saviour is, of his or her own free will, made prisoner of an older cycle of spiritual bondage; by breaking the pattern – usually by means of a simple affirmation of belief or by a redemptive offering – he or she establishes a new pattern of responsibility, which can then be taught to initiates of that cult. This process of redemption is unfortunately often misunderstood by those who have only experienced its application in a narrow religious context. To revalue the process of redemption – which only means to 'buy back' or ransom from prison that which has been improperly aligned or diverted from its prime purpose – we need to observe the recurrent patterns of cyclic renewal in many traditions. The redeemer or ransomer, who can be male or female, stands in the place of Mabon, whose task is to share the common lot of the prisoner, the unredeemed, for the sole purpose of ending all imprisonment; in order to realign creation and its creatures with their primal directive.

The task of redemption occurs on all levels of existence, not only in cosmic or Innerworld alignment. Anyone who has succeeded to a post of responsibility is aware of the challenge to maintain the pure archetype of service, whether it be to promote justice, peace, beauty, wholeness or whatever: a welter of lethargy, stale custom and corruption of practice stands between the maintenance of duty and its actual performance. This is why many positions of public power are formally conferred by the administration of a solemn oath, binding the individual to uphold only the purest ideals.

Within our native British tradition, the model of service is the Pendragon and his court. An examination of the Arthurian legends will reveal that this is an ideal not always successfully maintained, since even at the centre of the Round Table lurk all the human failings which flesh is heir to. And yet, it is possible to see how 'the old story of the breeding and birth of the infant, his seclusion and foster-training, and his final claim to the rightful throne, may be successfully applied as an analogy of the inner development of any man or woman'.[98]

The most crucial oath which the Pendragon makes is that by which the sovereign is wedded to the land: this is a promise which is both literal and figurative. In order to rule a land, the monarch must first of all respect the land: on the inner levels, the king joins with Lady Sovereignty, who personifies the land itself. Further to his coronation oath, the king must guard the treasures and traditions of the land – often represented by the Hallows, which are the regalia bestowing Innerworld power. These are not freely given nor thoughtlessly bestowed. Since these Hallows reside in the possession of the ancestral guardians, the Pendragon must venture into the Underworld in order to fetch them. And here the king makes a commitment to the Otherworld also: for whoever ventures there to fetch the Hallows, becomes the candidate for Innerworld Guardianship.

Bob Stewart has given ample evidence of such figures who have 'passed-within', or who have attuned to an Otherworldly resonance, in order to become guardians of tradition.[98] Their names are familiar to us from folkstory and history alike: the Reverend Robert Kirk, Michael Scot and Thomas the Rhymer all entered Faery, as the Otherworld was latterly perceived. Some say they strayed there; others that their going had a purpose. Such people pass within the Otherworld in order to exemplify the Son of Light, the Redeemer or Mabon.

Just as human beings may enter the Otherworld and become effective therein, so also do Innerworld archetypes enter the outer world and become manifest here. The New or Aquarian Age is upon us: we are entering into the sign of the Water-Carrier in the cosmic succession of the world's horoscope. Contemporary prophets have already made their auguries concerning its unfolding: these are alternatively full of unrealistic hope or apocalyptic destruction. The Aquarian Age cannot be predicted or coloured by such prophets since its patterns are already laid down according to the laws of cosmic harmony. It is our duty to perceive and work with the harmonics of this new tide, whose ripples already lap at our feet. The precession of the equinoxes, which causes the cosmic tide-change, must be seen not as part of linear time, but as a series of harmonies which resonate in a special way as earlier occurrence overlies later event.

This is a time of great re-ordering and vital change in which the Innerworld ushers in the Aeon with a vibratory force which causes ripples on the outer world. These harmonics are perceived by means of symbols, archetypes and cosmic patterns by all who are attuned to their vibration. The archetype of Mabon is such a harmonic. A saviour is born on the new tide, and a fresh impulse is made available at the intersection of linear by cosmic time, where Outerworld and Otherworld meet.

Although Mabon brings a powerful impulse for change, he does not come as a physical child. This 'second coming' is of a different nature to the one expected. Although it shares a resonance with the coming of Christ, the Messianic hope of the Jews, as well as of other expected figures, it does not imply any apocalyptic ending. Rather, it resonates with the foundations of the earth, of primal creation and the note of remaking.

In order to effect such a change, Mabon is a virgin – that is, one of unadulterated power and purpose in all his phases. As child, youth or sage, he brings the gift of creation intact from the wells of life. He is Blake's Albion, the 'Glad Day' breaking on the hillside; he is Apollo, the singer of morning; he is Merlin appearing in Arthur's dream as a young child. Deep dreams bring creation's weave into our hands; we are bespelled and quietened, forgetful of our mundane problems as we listen to the song of creation which Mabon sings.

As Vortigern sought to entomb Merlin Emrys in the foundations of his tower, so too is Mabon destined to become the prisoner of the planet for the false purposes of our will, unless we discern our motives. For he comes as a virgin to reconcile differences, to bestow the peace of the shepherd upon the flocks of the perplexed who wander into the self-made toils of the world. He comes into manifestation by means of the rainbow bridge of light – a bridge between the worlds which is opened to all seekers of reconciliation. He himself is a ray of sunlight across the waters, down which the influence of the Otherworld is shed, and by which we may cross over. 'Who would be chief, let him be a bridge.'

The answer to the mystery question is a mystery answer: Mabon shall be Pendragon, he who is child of the Modron, daughter of Afallach, ruler of the Blessed Isles.

New times need new guardians. The insights of native spirituality combine with those of Classical and Christian modes to form a full-voiced choir of response in us. None of these Otherworldly visions may be jettisoned without loss of harmony, since each has been grafted on to our traditional mysteries.

The role of mystery guardian today is open to whoever is willing to take up the story of the loss and finding, of the helping animals, of the royal succession of Mabon; it is a story which can be told anywhere to anyone, using the most appropriate name in that system of correspondences. It is a story which *you* can tell.

But remember: those who go in search of the treasures of tradition become candidates for the role of Innerworld guardian. And if that is so, how then shall the mystery question be answered in our own age? Mabon comes in many guises, through many exemplars. . . .

2 INTO THE EYE OF THE AEON

Those who have heard Mabon's lyre become enchanted and inspired; they become rememberers and guardians of the notes which sang creation. When these notes are sounded harmoniously throughout the world, the octave of creation will usher in the Age of Blessedness when the Otherworldly gates will open and many will be enabled to pass to and fro between the worlds once more. It may be asked whether such a traffic is desirable, by those who have no experience of the Otherworld reality either through dreams or through meditation. If these things move you, then the chances are you have already found the door between the worlds, and already know what benefits such a traffic affords.

Within the last thirty years or so, it has been possible to discern a rising interest in the Western Mysteries – as opposed to Eastern methods of spiritual progress.[71] This movement has been affected by people in many Western countries studying their own native mystery traditions. Within Britain, the *Mabinogion* is but one means of revitalising the native mysteries, but is a very effective one because its ancient resonance is in tune with the present need. The prime movers in this valuable work realise that for such a revitalisation to be effective, it must spring from the very source of the Otherworld tradition which is timelessly current. Only in this way will it be regenerated. Any attempt to live in the past or indulge in obsessive nationalism is to be avoided, since the native mysteries must be operative in our own time, not drawing off a vein of atavistic homesickness. The work must go forward under the aegis of Mabon, not of the restrictive Cronos aspect.

Who are these people who are rediscovering the ancient mysteries? They are those successors of the seer-poet, the shaman and storyteller who retell the old stories, setting them into relevant contexts for today; those who reenact the mysteries as a sacred anamnesis; those who mediate the life-giving strength of the Otherworld through to our own world. Drawing on many different traditions, they nevertheless have a family likeness: at the deepest levels, all traditions stem from a common source. Such people drink from the primal wells of the Otherworld. As artists, singers and writers their work is imbued with an archetypal force and beauty. As mystics, prophets and rememberers, their sayings are wise and profoundly moving. As ordinary people who dream extraordinary dreams, their eyes are bright and their hearts compassionate.

How is their work accomplished? They turn their faces to the Otherworld, profoundly meditating on its living symbols to find their meaning for our world; they then synthesise their realisations into their own lives. If the Mysteries of Britain – or of any land – cannot be applied in such a way, then those mysteries are redundant and deserve to be forgotten indeed.

Anyone wishing to follow this work will find practical meditation and group-visualisation a very effective means of mediating their own native mysteries. Only ten years ago, such methods were inaccessible to the seeker, being the secret methods of esoteric fraternities and schools of spiritual wisdom. Today, meditation is practised by many people; it is known as a valuable key to discovering one's own inner life. The reader is directed to volumes one and two of *The Western Way*[71] which give many practical hints for those who have never meditated before.

This book has presented original sources and parallel texts for the reader to study and compare for him or herself: it remains for the reader to make something of this work in a practical way. There follow two practical exercises which may enable the reader to earth the realisations arising from this book. For those who are outside Britain or who have valid traditions of their own, the first exercise is offered as a basis for experiment: it can be adapted to most traditions, as I have indicated on p.166.

We have already mentioned the many Innerworld beings who have been working to establish the new note of the Aeon among us. These Otherworld beings are the inner guardians, the Innerworld resonance of the poets, singers and storytellers of our own world. They can be visualised as a double chorus of sibyls and prophets whose song weaves the weft across the warp strings of the Cosmic Lyre of Mabon. Within native understanding, these sibyls and prophets can be seen as the faery women and poet-seers of Celtic tradition. In Classical tradition, they may be seen as Ocean's daughters, the Oceanides, and the Winds, sons of Night and Morning. The basis for this group-visualisation is the meditational glyph, shown in Figure 10.1, which can form the basis for a ritual enactment.

The warp of the strings on the Cosmic Lyre is strung between

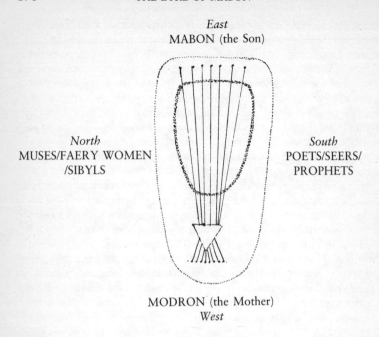

East
MABON (the Son)

North
MUSES/FAERY WOMEN
/SIBYLS

South
POETS/SEERS/
PROPHETS

MODRON (the Mother)
West

Figure 10.1: *The Cosmic Lyre*

Mabon, in the East and Modron in the West. The weft of melody is exchanged between the Muses in the North and the Poets in the South. Their antiphonal song interweaves the many levels of the worlds. The muses are chthonically situated, in the underearth and the poets are celestially situated, in the stars. The interpenetration of their song is vitally important. We can hear it on many levels: with our physical ears, as music; with our instincts, as earth's rhythmic harmony; and with our intuition as the music of the spheres. Modron and Mabon form the joint constants between which the fabric of the new Aeon is stretched.

Before attempting the ritual enactment, participants should meditate on the significance of this glyph, contemplating each character separately until a measure of understanding and facility is gained.

For the enactment, at least four operators are needed: two

men and two women. The two principal officers stand in the place of Mabon and Modron; the other woman stands in the place of the muses, and the second man in the place of the poets. If more operators are available, then these can help make up a full complement of muses and poets – to the number of nine men and nine women. The operators are positioned as in Figure 10.1: if there are a number of muses and poets, these stand along the northern and southern sides of the working area, respectively.

The ritual enactment which follows is fragmentary, to allow for personal preference in practical working. Mabon and Modron are equivalent to X and Y in algebra; they denote the Son and the Mother, and so groups may choose to substitute other native archetypes, Classical deities or figures drawn from other spiritual traditions, as preferred.

This working begins with the Making Sacred. The officers Son and Mother mark out the area of working, which can be an outdoor or indoor location. This may be done in the usual manner by calling upon the Four Elemental Guardians of the cardinal points; by saining the area with salt, water and incense, which are carried clockwise round the area; or the Mother can present the Son with a basket in which is sufficient red cording to demark the area – the Mother holds the basket, walking backwards, while the Son, starting in the east, unwinds the cord to surround the area. If the working is outdoors, the area can be denoted by drawing a line in the earth with a rod.

SON (Stands in the east throughout): THE LYRE IS FORMED
MOTHER (Stands in the west throughout): LET IT NOW BE STRUNG
(The Son then sings an ascending scale of seven notes, each note of which the Mother repeats. The scale can be the one most aurally acceptable to Western ears – C major or E major – but some countries still retain their own native modes. Use a scale which is suitable for the working and the group's abilities.)

The officer in the place of Mabon, or any suitable person, reads the following, while the others close their eyes and listen.

SON: WE ARE MET TO ACTIVATE THE WAY BETWEEN THE

WORLDS, TO SOUND THE LYRE OF THE AEON. LISTEN THEN AND BUILD THE IMAGES WHICH I DESCRIBE IN OUR ACTIVE IMAGIN-ATION. IT IS NIGHT AND WE STAND IN A LONELY PLACE, ON A LEVEL PLAIN. ABOVE US THE SKY IS FULL OF STARS. (Here the reader gives details of specific constellations appearing at that time and in those latitudes, which are usual for the time of year.) BENEATH US IS THE EARTH, OUR HOME. (Here the reader describes terrain usual to that country and season.) THIS PLACE IS SACRED TO (THE MOTHER) AND (THE SON). (Here the reader substitutes the mystery names of whatever system of correspon-dences worked by that group. The list given on p.166 gives some parallels which may be suitable; the only important thing to observe is that the mysteries worked parallel to the Mabon and Modron archetype, and that they tell a redemptive story which hearers can meditate upon deeply and mediate effectively to their generation.) IN THIS PLACE WE RECALL THEIR MYSTERIES WHEREIN ... (Here the reader enumerates the main themes of the story in a few short lines in order to establish the native resonance or specific spiritual harmonic of the group. Frequent pauses for mediation should be allowed.)

SON: WHO GATHERS THE STRINGS OF THE LYRE?

MOTHER: I (THE MOTHER) GATHER THE STRINGS INTO MY HANDS. I STAND IN THE WEST, THE PLACE OF THE SETTING SUN. I RECEIVE THE DEAD AND GIVE THEM LIFE. WHO CAUSES THE LYRE TO BE TUNED?

SON: I (THE SON) TUNE THE STRINGS OF THE LYRE. I STAND IN THE EAST, IN THE PLACE OF THE RISING SUN. I AM THE BRINGER OF MORNING AND THE DAWN OF HOPE.

MOTHER: WHOSE VOICES BRIGHTEN ITS STRINGS?

POET/S: MY/OUR VOICE BRINGS THE SINGING OF STARS. I/WE STAND IN THE PLACE OF THE SOUTH.* I/WE ARE THE SONS OF KNOWLEDGE

MUSE/S: MY/OUR VOICE BRINGS THE SONG OF THE EARTH. I/WE ARE THE DAUGHTERS OF MEMORY

SON: LET EARTH'S VOICE SOUND

---

*Readers in the Southern Hemisphere should alter the compass directions in accordance with their location. North and South will be reversed, as the place of greatest darkness and cold, corresponding to the earth position, is the South Pole for them.

(The Muse/s stamp or clap out a rhythm of four beats, repeated as necessary; the stress comes on the first beat, i.e. d́ d d d, d́ d d d. If stamping is impractical, then a small drum – not a tambourine – can be struck.)

MOTHER: LET THE STARRY VOICES BE HEARD

(The Poet/s whistle, sing or intone a rhythmic tone of eight beats on one note. In this way the Poets will be sounding two beats of their note to one of the Muse's stamps. These joint rhythms continue while the group visualise the joint forces of stars and earth.)

SON: IS THE EARTH PREPARED?

MOTHER: IT IS. THE VOICES OF THE WATERS UNDER THE EARTH ARE RUSHING, THE ROOTS OF THE MOUNTAINS ARE AWAKE. DO THE STARS ANSWER?

SON: THEY DO. THE CONSTELLATIONS CIRCLE, THE STARWAYS ARE REVEALED

MUSE/S: (resuming their rhythm with this chant)

THIS IS THE PLACE OF (THE MOTHER)

HER VOICE IS HEARD IN OUR LAND.

POET/S: (resuming their rhythm in double time)

THIS IS THE PLACE OF (THE SON)

THIS IS THE PLACE WHERE SHE LAID HIM.

LET ALL WHO ENTER THIS DWELLING

HEAR NOW THE SONG OF HIS BLESSING.

(This double chant can be performed simultaneously, north and south. Alternatively, the group can write its own chant, in which further stanzas can be improvised turn and turn about. The words should reflect the nature of the mysteries being worked. See *Mabon's Hunt*, p.189, as an example of this kind of chant.) The chanting should speed up towards the end: each person should be mediating the earth or star forces of their relevant positions, while the officers of east and west hold their own archetypes strongly in mind. The conclusion of this part of the ceremony may be resolved by the assembled group breaking out into exultant ululation or, if there is space and sufficient people, a double circle dance can be performed – the inner circle of women moving anti-clockwise, while the outer circle of men moves clockwise, after the manner of a Greek komos. The Son or Mother should signal the finish of this section by a loud call or prearranged signal which is clear to the group. The company then sit, on chairs or on the floor, to meditate.

SON: BENEATH US THE EARTH CIRCLES

MOTHER: ABOVE US THE STARS WHEEL

SON AND MOTHER: IN OUR HEARTS WE ARE CENTRED AND STILL.

(There follows a full exposition of the mysteries being worked. This can be read by the Son and the Mother, or by other designated officers. If a large company is present, each person can contribute to the telling, starting in the east and working round clockwise. The mysteries should unfold just like a folkstory. If a small number of people who have experience of these mysteries are present, then they may extemporise the story between them, which is a more powerful and immediate method. At the conclusion of this section, everyone should be powerfully aware of the images, archetypes and symbols of these mysteries. The Son and Mother may ritually show the physical tokens which the group uses at this time; these may be processed about the area. If one present is skilled as a singer or musician, then a specific piece of ritual music may be played, or a mystery song, such as those on p.187, sung.)

SON: AS THE HEAVENS ARE OVER THE EARTH

MOTHER: AND THE EARTH BENEATH THE HEAVENS

BOTH: SO ARE OUR MYSTERIES MAINTAINED FROM THE ENDLESS AGES

SON: SO IS OUR LAND BLESSED

MOTHER: SO ARE OUR HEARTS OPENED

BOTH: AND THE WAY BETWEEN THE WORLDS MADE PLAIN

SON: THANKS TO THE DAUGHTERS OF MEMORY

MOTHER: THANKS TO THE SONS OF KNOWLEDGE

SON: THE PEACE OF (THE SON)

MOTHER: THE PEACE OF (THE MOTHER)

BOTH: ON ALL HERE
         IN THIS WORLD AND THAT WORLD
         IN THE WORLDS BETWEEN THE WORLDS
         UPON THOSE WHO ARE AND WHO HAVE BEEN AND
         WHO ARE YET TO BE.

SON: LET THE LYRE BE UNSTRUNG

MOTHER: AND LET THE NOTE OF REMAKING BE SOUNDED.

(The Son sings, as before, an ascending scale of seven notes which is echoed by the Mother. The octave note is then gently hummed by all present, accompanied by the visualisation of the Lyre rising to take its place in the heavens. The octave note is sung by men and women in their own vocal register.)

SON: WE HAVE OPENED THE WAY BETWEEN THE WORLDS

MOTHER: AND HEARD THE MUSIC OF THE SPHERES

(The Son or designated officer then thanks the Elemental Guardians for attending, or walks anti-clockwise around the area to indicate it is no longer made sacred, or takes up the red cording anti-clockwise, passing it into the Mother's basket. The company then depart, share a meal and any realisations.)

Such a ritual enactment is very effective for small groups who are studying the mysteries, but what of those individuals who are working alone? The following meditation, *Opening the Eye of the Aeon*, is particularly suited to lone workers and can be adapted, like the Cosmic Lyre exercise, to any tradition.

The Vesica Pisces is the symbol denoting the overlapping ages of Pisces and Aquarius, under whose joint influence we now live in this present time. In the meditational glyph shown in Figure 10.2, the native, trilithon – the traditional gateway between our world and the Otherworld – has the Vesica Pisces or the Eye of the Aeon, superimposed upon it, to make an Aquarian gateway for the joint influences of Mabon and Modron. The starry gateway superimposed upon the gate of the Otherworld becomes the entrance for the Son of Light, the Mabon, in all his aspects. While the mandorla, formed by the overlapping ages, forms the womb of the Virgin Goddess, Justice, whose return to earth is prophesied by Virgil and others. It is also the womb of Modron. (It will be noted that in some icons of the Anastasis – the Harrowing of Hell – Christ appears from just such a mandorla of stars, in order to visit the peoples of the past and bring them to the light of rebirth.) It will be seen that this image makes a powerful meditational symbol in which both Underworld and Overworld are united in a timeless dimension of reality – in the Otherworldly 'now' which is eternal.

To meditate actively upon this symbol, sit in a quiet place. Close your eyes and breathe evenly in an upright posture, free from strain. Demark your area of working, if you wish, and set up your intention by formulating: 'In the names of Mabon and

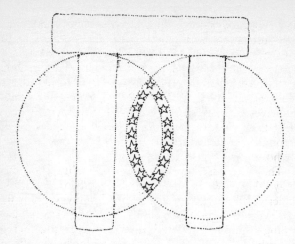

Figure 10.2: *The Eye of the Aeon*

Modron, I open the Eye of the Aeon' (or similar). If meditation is unfamiliar to you, then perform this exercise in three parts; otherwise, it can be worked as a straightforward sequence.

(a) Visualise the gateway of the Underworld trilithon. See it as a gateway of rough stone about twice your height. Feel the texture of the rock, see the plants which grow about it. Through and beyond the gateway lie the Places of Peace. Step through the gateway and see around you a countryside of green hills and trees. Before you, beneath a tree, is the Golden Child, the Son of Light or Mabon. He may appear in any shape from a swaddled baby or little boy to a mature youth with implements of hunting or with his lyre. As you look upon him, know that this is the liberated Mabon. You may converse, or not. You may also be aware of numerous faery women or muses attendant upon him, who dance or sing to his lyre. These are the Daughters of Memory and may be seven or nine in number.

(b) Visualise the overlapping circles of the ages, forming their mandorla-shaped gateway rimmed with stars. Around you are the blue heavens. Beyond the gateway, through which silver light shines, like that of the moon, lies the Place of Light. You do not attempt to enter this gate, but wait until the figure of the

Goddess appears. Glory shines around her and the light becomes surcharged with gold. This is the Goddess of Justice, the Lady of Wisdom or Modron. She may appear as a young maiden, as a mother or as a mature woman. If as the latter, do not be alarmed if her aspect seems severe; trust her and accept her as she is. She may bear different implements or symbols: a distaff, scales of justice or riding whip – these indicate which aspect of the Goddess is operating. She may speak to you or not. Around her, like a chorus of stars, you may see the seer-poets who are the Sons of Knowledge.

(c)   The last phase superimposes one reality upon another. This may take a few sessions to achieve, so be patient. Visualise the Underworld gateway rising up to a midway point in your field of vision, simultaneously seeing the Starry gateway descending. Mabon and Modron will appear together in the centre of the two gateways. Meditate upon the significance of this and mediate its influence in your own way. This part of the meditation may be accompanied by a sense of physical displacement or disorientation. If this occurs, allow the images to fade, breathe evenly, place both hands over your solar plexus and become aware of the real earth under your feet and the chair you are sitting on. To seal off completely, take a light meal and hot beverage.

The purpose of this meditation is to 'earth' the joint influences of Mabon and Modron. No esoteric work can take place in a vacuum otherwise it becomes the private fantasy of the operator and serves no regenerative purpose whatever. It is necessary to 'bring ideas into consciousness' by first training oneself in meditative techniques such as these, and then by earthing them in one's life.

Mabon and Modron are the guardians of the gateways between the worlds and between the aeons – true constants who act as intermediaries of masculine and feminine polarity. Because the Aquarian Age is in its infancy, the masculine archetype governing its mode is a child or young man. As the age progresses, so the youth will grow and the archetype will subtly change, though not in the lifetime of those who read this book. Because the coming age is as yet immature, it has the archetype of the Mother as its guardian and protector. The Passion of Modron has been a long one, but her Child has been restored to her at last. The many imbalances between the sexes will become less evident when the archetypal energies which govern our Age are understood. This meditation should activate a healthier polarity between men and women in our own world, as well as bringing in a realisation of the Aquarian Age through the ancient skills of the storyteller. If people about the world perform this meditation, substituting the names of the Son and Mother relevant to their own mysteries or of some tradition which is spiritually vital in their land, then the transition between the two aeons will be more harmonious.

It is a long way from the Mysteries of Britain to the new Aeon, or so it seems. There are more themes within the *Mabinogion*, which the enterprising reader can find and work with, than I have dealt with in this book. There are many native traditions which await the first explorers.

The times are at their end and their beginning. The millennial horn is already blowing. Like the Titan, encrusted with the growths of old strength, this age must become young and fresh again. The Succession of the Pendragons awaits our capable and daring initiates: only those who know the inner name of the land may set out on this quest. And not only the name of our own land, but of its mother, the Earth herself.

Our collective vocation is to bring about change, to guard the land – our earth – to install an inner guardian, and to look for Mabon's influence in the darkest of prisons.

APPENDIX:
Three Mystery Songs to Mabon

The Totem Beasts

I THE SONG OF MABON
a mystery sequence (for voice and harp)

CHORUS: Oh do you know, or have you heard
                 Of Mabon, Modron's son?
                 Who from his mother's womb was reived
                 When time was first begun?

1   Go ask the ousel on the green if beast or bird on earth
      Knows aught of Mabon, Modron's son, who vanished
         at his birth.

(Blackbird) 2   When first I came into this place, a mighty anvil stood;
      But I have pecked it all away, right down unto
      the wood.

187

3   A race of beasts more ancient yet there lives
    upon the earth.
    Go ask the stag upon the plain if he can
    help you search.

CHORUS

(Stag) 4   When first I came into the plain, a lone oak
           sapling grew,
           Became a tree of many tines, now branches it has few.

5   Though I have roved the plains so wide, of Mabon
    I've seen none;
    Go ask the owl of the wood, if he knows
    Modron's son.

CHORUS

(Owl) 6   When first I came, a valley bare raised upon
          a wooded glen,
          But twice it was uprooted by hordes of greedy men.

7   Though I have flown this valley wide, since day was
    birthed with dawn,
    I never met with Modron's son, though thin my wings
    have worn.

8   A race of birds more ancient yet still wings upon
    the air,
    Go ask the eagle of the heights if he knows
    Mabon's lair.

CHORUS

(Eagle) 9   When first I came I pecked the stars each evening
            from this height;
            But now it is a bare span tall, and hungry is the night.

10   I stuck my talons in a fish: he drew me to the deep;
     We made a peace the two between – go see
     the salmon leap.

CHORUS

(Salmon) 11 With every tide I heard a cry, in every stream a moan;
 I swam to Gloucester's walls so high, and found
 a wicked wrong.

 12 Upon my back I shall you bear, upon my
 shoulders strong,
 And we shall find who is it groans within
 these walls alone.

 13 Oh tell us who is it laments within a house of stone:
 But Mabon, born of Modron's womb, within these
 walls alone.

(Mabon) 14 Now I have dwelt within this house before the birth
 of time;
 Three hours from my mother's womb, and what was
 then my crime?

 15 Go back beyond the birth of time and see the
 giant stand.
 He swallowed me up and snatched me from
 my own sweet mother's hand.

 16 For Modron's son they do me call and Mabon
 is my name;
 Who does me find shall blessing have, who frees me
 shall have fame.

Caitlín Matthews, 4 December 1983

II MABON'S HUNT
(to be chanted with drum and horse-brasses)

1 Seek for the Mabon;
He shall be found.
Son of the Modron,
Lord of the Hound.

2 Seek for the Modron,
Under the hill.
Seek for the salmon,
Swimming there still.

3 Seek for the Modron
In the wood;
There she sorrowed
And there she stood.

4 Animals come
At break of day.
To wash the stain
Of the blood away.

5 Seek for the Mabon;
He shall be found
Near the smithy,
Beneath the ground.

6 Seek for the Mabon,
Under the hill.
There he waits
Till she eats her fill.

7 Seek for the Modron
Cantering by;
The hill her manger,
Her stall the sky

8 Animals bow
As she rides past;
Modron first
And Modron last.

9 Seek for the Mabon;
Call his name.
He shall enter
And join our game.

10 Mabon dances
Like the sun;
Mabon's hounds
And hunters run.

11 How they canter
And how they cry:
Modron's daughters
Stand on high.

12 Seven bright shiners
Hold the glass,
Watching their brother
Hurrying past.

13 When sun and moon
Stand in one sky:
Mabon and Modron!
We shall cry.

Caitlín Matthews, 31 December 1984

III MABON'S JOURNEY
(song for two voices)

MODRON 1 Where are you going to, Mabon, my son?
Where are you going to, my pretty one?
MABON I'm bound on a journey, Mother, he said,
To the lands of the living, the lands of the dead.

MODRON 2 Where is that country, Mabon, my son?
Who is its ruler, my pretty one?
MABON Where the cold winds cease blowing, where snows
never fall,
To the place where the Sleeping Lord sits in his hall.

MODRON 3 How will you journey, Mabon, my son?
What will you fetch there, my pretty one?

MABON   On the ship that is silent, by the cold river deep,
          And I'll bring back the cauldron from the Lord locked
            in sleep.

MODRON   4 When will I see you, Mabon, my son?
          When will I kiss you, my pretty one?
MABON   When the ages turn round at the brink of the sun,
          When the birds at the wellhead have ended their song.

MODRON   5 How shall I find you, Mabon, my son?
          How shall I know you, my pretty one?
MABON   By leaf, flower and feather, by ways high and low.
          By the brand of the cauldron, the radiant brow.

                          Caitlín Matthews, 11 November 1985

BIBLIOGRAPHY

The Signs on the Stone

TEXTUAL SOURCES IN TRANSLATION

(1) *Mabinogion*, trans. T.P. Ellis and J. Lloyd, London, Oxford University Press, 1929.
(2) *The Mabinogi and Other Medieval Welsh Tales*, trans. P.K. Ford, Berkeley, University of California Press, 1977.
(3) *Mabinogion*, trans. J. Gantz, Harmondsworth, Penguin, 1976.
(4) *Mabinogion*, trans. Lady C. Guest, London, Ballantyne Press, 1910.
(5) *Trioedd Ynys Prydein*, trans. R. Bromwich, Cardiff, University of Wales Press, 1961.

GENERAL

(6)   Allen, R.H., *Star Names, Their Lore and Meaning*, New York, Dover Publications, 1963.

(7)   Anwyl, E., *Value of the Mabinogion for the Study of Celtic Religion*, vol. 2 of Transactions of the 3rd International Congress for History of Religion, pp.234-44, London, Oxford University Press, 1908.

(8)   Apollodorous, *The Library*, vols I and II, London, Heinemann, 1963, 1976.

(9)   Apuleius, *The Golden Ass*, Harmondsworth, Penguin, 1950.

(10) Aratus, *Phaenomena*, London, Heinemann, 1921.

(11) Ashe, G., *Camelot and the Vision of Albion*, London, Heinemann, 1971.

(12) Bailey, A., *Treatise on White Magic*, London, Lucis Trust, 1934.

(13) Barber, C., *Mysterious Wales*, London, Paladin, 1982.

(14) Best, R.I., 'Settling of the Manor of Tara', *Eriu*, vol. 4, part 2, n.d.

(15) Birley, E., *Maponus: The Epigraphical Evidence*, Dumfriesshire and Galloway National History and Antiquarian Society Transactions, 1954, vol. 31, pp.39-42.

(16   Blake, W., *Poetry and Prose*, London, Nonesuch Press, 1975.

(17) Brewer, E., *From Cuchulainn to Gawaine*, Cambridge, D.S. Brewer, 1973.

(18) Brown, A.C.L., 'Barinthus', *Revue Celtique XXII*, pp.339-44, n.d.

(19) Brown, A.C.L., *The Origin of the Grail Legend*, Cambridge, Mass., Harvard University Press, 1943.

(20) Bryant, N., *High Book of the Grail (Perlesvaus)*, Cambridge, D.S. Brewer, 1978.

(21) Byrne, F.J., *The Irish Kings and High Kings*, London, Batsford, 1973.

(22) Calder, G., *Auraicept na N'Éces* (Scholar's Primer), Edinburgh, John Grant, 1917.

(23) Callimachus, *Hymns and Epigrams*, London, Heinemann, 1921.

(24) Campbell, J.F., *Popular Tales of the West Highlands* (4 vols), London, Wildwood Press, 1983-4.

(25) Chadwick, N.K., *Poetry and Prophecy*, Cambridge, 1942.

(26) Child, F.J., *English and Scottish Popular Ballads* (5 vols), New York, Dover Publications, 1963.

(27) Cornford, F.M., *Principium Sapientiae*, Cambridge, Cambridge University Press, 1952.

(28) Cross, T.P. and Slover, C.H., *Ancient Irish Tales*, Dublin, Figgis, 1936.

(29) Crossley-Holland, K., *Norse Myths*, London, Andre Deutsch, 1980.

(30) Curtin, J., *Hero Tales of Ireland*, London, Macmillan, 1894.

(31) De Santillana, G. and Von Dechend, H., *Hamlet's Mill*, London, Macmillan, 1969.

(32) Dillon, M., *Cycles of the Irish Kings*, London, Geoffrey Cumberlege/Oxford University Press, 1946.

(33) Dorson, R.M., *Folk Tales Told Round the World*, Chicago, University of Chicago Press, 1975.

(34) Embleton, R., *Hadrian's Wall*, Newcastle-upon-Tyne, Frank Graham, 1984.

(35) Fontenrose, J., *Python: A Study of the Delphic Myth and its Origins*, Berkeley, University of California Press, 1959.

(36) Forbes, A.R., *Gaelic Names of Beasts, Birds, Fishes, Insects, Reptiles etc.*, Edinburgh, Oliver & Boyd, 1905.

(37) Geoffrey of Monmouth, *History of the Kings of Britain*, Harmondsworth, Penguin, 1966.

(38) Glob, P.V., *The Bog People*, London, Paladin, 1971.

(39) Gorman, P., *Pythagoras*, London, Routledge & Kegan Paul, 1979.

(40) Graves, R., *The Greek Myths*, London, Cassell, 1958.

(41) Graves, R., *The White Goddess*, London, Faber, 1961.

(42) Green, M.J., *The Gods of Roman Britain*, Aylesbury, Shire Archaeology, 1983.

(43) Gruffydd, W.J., *Folklore and Myth in the Mabinogion*, Cardiff, University of Wales Press, 1955.

(44) Gruffydd, W.J., *Mabon and Modron*, W.J. Gruffydd Collection, University of Wales.

(45) Gruffydd, W.J., *Math vab Mathonwy*, London, Humphrey Milford/Oxford University Press, 1928.

(46) Gruffydd, W.J., *Rhiannon*, Cardiff, University of Wales Press, 1953.

(47) Hall, L.B., *Knightly Tales of Sir Gawaine*, Chicago, Nelson-Hall, 1976.

(48) Hayward, R., *Border Foray*, London, Arthur Barker, 1957.

(49) Hill, J., *The Tristan Legend*, Leeds, University of Leeds Press, 1977.

(50) Hull, E., 'The Hawk of Achill', from *Folklore*, vol. 43, 1932, pp.376-409.

(51) Humphrey, E., *The Taliesin Tradition*, London, Black Raven Press, 1983.

(52) Hyde, D., 'Adventures of Leithin', from *Celtic Review 10* (1914-16), pp.116-43.

(53) Jackson, K.H., *International Popular Tale and Early Welsh Tradition*, Cardiff, University of Wales Press, 1961.

(54) Jarman, A.O.H., *A Guide to Welsh Literature*, vol. I, Swansea, Christopher Davis, 1976.

(55) John, I.B., *The Mabinogion*, London, David Nutt, 1901.

(56) Jones, G., *Kings, Beasts and Heroes*, London, Oxford University Press, 1972.

(57) Kerenyi, C., *Gods of the Greeks*, London, Thames & Hudson, 1951.

(58) Kitteridge, G.L., *A Study of Gawaine and the Green Knight*, Gloucester, Mass., Peter Smith, 1960.

(59) Lethbridge, T.C., *Witches*, London, Routledge & Kegan Paul, 1962.

(60) Levi, P., *A History of Greek Literature*, London, Viking, 1985.

(61) Lewis, C.B., *Classical Mythology and Arthurian Romance*, London, Oxford University Press, 1932.

(62) Loomis, R.S., *Arthurian Tradition and Chrétien de Troyes*, New York, Columbia University Press, 1949.

(63) Loomis, R.S., *Celtic Myth and Arthurian Legend*, New York, Haskell House Pubs, 1967.

(64) Loomis, R.S., *Wales and the Arthurian Legend*, London, Folcroft Library Editions, 1977.

(65) MacCana, P., *Branwen, Daughter of Llyr*, Cardiff, University of Wales Press, 1958.

(66) MacCana, P., *The Mabinogi*, Cardiff, University of Wales Press, 1977.

(67) MacQueen, J., *Maponus in Medieval Tradition*, from Dumfriesshire and Galloway Natural History and Antiquarian Society Transactions 1954, vol. 31, pp.43-57.

(68) Magnen, R., *Epona: Déesse Gauloise des Chevaux*, Paris, Delmas, 1953.

(69) Matthews, C., 'The Rosicrucian Vault as Sepulchre and Wedding Chamber', in *Underworld Initiation* by Bob Stewart, Wellingborough, Aquarian Press, 1985.

(70) Matthews, C., 'Sophia as Companion on the Quest', in *At the Table of the Grail*, ed. J. Matthews, Routledge & Kegan Paul, 1981.

(71) Matthews, C. and Matthews, J., *The Western Way*, vols I and II, London, Arkana, 1985, 1986.

(72) Matthews, J., *The Grail: Quest for the Eternal*, London, Thames & Hudson, 1981.

(73) Matthews, J. and Stewart, B., *Warriors of Arthur*, Poole, Blandford Press, 1987.

(74) Morris, J., *The Matter of Wales*, London, Oxford University Press, 1985.

(75) Newstead, H., *Bran the Blessed*, New York, Columbia University Press, 1939.

(76) North, F.J., *Sunken Cities*, Cardiff, University of Wales Press, 1957.

(77) Nutt, A., 'Branwen, Daughter of Llyr', in *Folklore Record*, vol. V, 1882, pp.1-32.

(78) O'Flaherty, W.D., *Women, Androgynes and Other Mythical Beasts*, Chicago, University of Chicago Press, 1980.

(79) Oosten, J.G., *War of the Gods*, London, Routledge & Kegan Paul, 1985.

(80) O'Rahilly, T.F., *Early Irish History and Mythology*, Dublin, Dublin Institute for Advanced Studies, 1976.

(81) Ovazza, M., 'D'Apollon – Maponos à Mabonograin', in *Actes du 14ème Congrès International Arthurian*, Rennes, Presses Universitaires, 1984.

(82) Parker, W., *Gaelic Fairy Tales*, Glasgow, Archibald Sinclair, 1908.

(83) Pearce, S.M. 'Cornish Elements in the Arthurian Tradition', in *Folklore*, vol. 85, pp.145-63.

(84) Plutarch, *Moralia V*, London, Heinemann, 1947.

(85) Plutarch, *Moralia XII*, London, Heinemann, 1958.

(86) Powys, J.C., *Obstinate Cymric*, London, Village Press, 1973.

(87) Rees, A. and Rees, B., *Celtic Heritage*, London, Thames & Hudson, 1961.

(88) Rhys, J., *The Hibbert Lectures*, London, Williams & Norgate, 1888.

(89) Rhys, J., *Studies in the Arthurian Legend*, London, Oxford at the Clarendon Press, 1891.

(90) Richmond, I.A., 'Two Celtic Heads in Stone from Corbridge, Northumberland', in *Dark Age Britain*, ed. D.B. Harden, London, Methuen, 1956.

(91) Ross, A., *Pagan Celtic Britain*, London, Routledge & Kegan Paul, 1967.

(92) Ross, A., *A Traveller's Guide to Celtic Britain*, London, Routledge & Kegan Paul, 1985.

(93) Scott, R.D., *Thumb of Knowledge*, New York, Columbia University Press, 1930.

(94) Senior, M., *Myths of Britain*, London, Orbis, 1979.
(95) Skeels, D., *Romance of Perceval in Prose (Didot Perceval)*, Seattle, University of Washington Press, 1966.
(96) Stewart, R.J., *Mystic Life of Merlin*, London, Arkana, 1986.
(97) Stewart, R.J., *The Prophetic Vision of Merlin*, London, Arkana, 1985.
(98) Stewart, R.J., *The Underworld Initiation*, Wellingborough, Aquarian, 1985.
(99) Stewart, R.J., *The Waters of the Gap*, Bath, Bath City Council, 1981.
(100) Sutherland, E., *Ravens and Black Rain*, London, Constable, 1983.
(101) *Tain Bo Cuailnge*, trans. T. Kinsella, Dublin, Dolmen Press, 1970.
(102) Todd, J. and Todd, J.M., *Voices from the Past*, London, Reader's Union, 1956.
(103) Tolstoy, N., *The Quest for Merlin*, London, Hamish Hamilton, 1985.
(104) *Vita Merlini*, ed. and trans. J.J. Parry, Illinois, University of Illinois Press, 1925.
(105) von Zatzikhovan, U., *Lanzelet*, New York, Columbia University Press, 1951.
(106) Williams, G.A., *When Was Wales?*, Harmondsworth, Penguin, 1985.
(107) Wood, J., 'The Elphin Section of the Hanes Taliesin', Paris, *Etudes Celtiques*, 1981, vol. 18, pp.229-44.

THE MABINOGION AND THE MYSTERIES OF BRITAIN IN LITERATURE (SELECT LIST)
(F = Fiction, D = Drama, P = Poetry)

(108) Arden, J. and D'Arcy, M., *The Island of the Mighty*, London, Eyre Methuen, 1973.(D)
(109) Ashe, G., *The Finger and the Moon*, London, Heinemann, 1973.(F)
(110) Garner, A., *The Owl Service*, London, Collins, 1967.(F)
(111) Herbert, K., *The Ghost in the Sunlight*, London, Bodley Head, 1986.(F)
(112) Herbert, K., *Lady of the Fountain*, Frome, Bran's Head Books, 1982.(F)
(113) Herbert, K., *Queen of the Lightening*, London, Bodley Head, 1984.(F)

(114) James, J., *Not for All the Gold in Ireland*, London, Cassell, 1968.

(115) Jones, A.R., *Presenting Saunders Lewis*, Cardiff, University of Wales Press, 1973.(D)

(116) Jones, D., *Anathemata*, London, Faber, 1952.(P)

(117) Jones, D., *In Parenthesis*, London, Faber, 1937.(P)

(118) Jones, D., *The Sleeping Lord*, London, Faber, 1974.(P)

(119) Kipling, R., *Puck of Pook's Hill*, London, Macmillan, 1983.(F)

(120) Lewis, C.S., *That Hideous Strength*, London, Bodley Head, 1945.(F)

(121) Morris, K., *The Fates of the Princes of Dyfed*, North Hollywood, Newcastle Publishing Company, 1978.(F)

(122) Powys, J.C., *Porius*, London, Village Press, 1974.(F)

(123) Walton, E., *Children of Llyr*, New York, Ballantyne, 1971.(F)

(124) Walton, E., *Island of the Mighty*, New York, Ballantyne, 1964.(F)

(125) Walton, E., *Prince of Annwn*, New York, Ballantyne, 1974.(F)

(126) Walton, E., *The Song of Rhiannon*, New York, Ballantyne, 1982.(F)

(127) Watkins, V., *Ballad of the Mari Lwyd*, London, Faber, 1946.(P)

(128) White, T.H., *The Once and Future King*, London, Collins, 1952.(F)

RECORDINGS

(129) Jones, D., *Poets of Wales*, Argo PLP 1180.

(130) Jones, G., *Extracts from the Four Branches of the Mabinogion*, Oriel OR 002.

(131) *Matthews, C., *The Mysteries of Mabon*, Sulis Music, BCM 3721, London WC1N 3XX.

(132) Matthews, C. and J., *Walking the Western Way*, Sulis Music, BCM 3721, London WC1N 3XX.

(133) Purcell, H., *King Arthur*, Harmonia Mundi H, 252/53.

(134) Stewart, B., *The Underworld Journey*, Sulis Music, BCM 3721, London, WC1N 3XX.

(135) Williamson, R., *Music for the Mabinogi*, Ceirnini Claddaig CCF 10.

*This tape is a companion to *Mabon and the Mysteries of Britain*, incorporating songs, meditations and original music.

INDEX

Abaris, 150-1
Achilles, 45, 48
Admetos, 68-9
Afallach, 161, 166, 170, 175
Ahes, 86
Albion, 8-9, 174
Anna, 41, 86
Annwn, xii, 21, 23, 25, 26, 46, 48, 55, 63, 68, 70, 77, 78, 91, 99, 100, 106, 108, 109, 110, 111, 121, 153, 154, 156, 161, 164, 166; gates of, 107-10
anoethu, 93, 99, 100, 102, 106, 109, 111
Anu, 41, 86
Apollo, xi, 68, 69, 70, 94, 133, 147, 150, 151, 167, 169, 171, 174; Citharoedus, 151
Aquarian Age, 174, 183, 185, 186
Arawn, 21, 22, 23, 24, 25, 30, 60, 61, 63, 73, 78, 144
Arberth, 11, 21, 22, 23, 26, 27, 58, 60, 62, 63, 64, 162
Arianrhod, x, 5, 13, 73, 74, 75, 76, 78, 79, 80, 81, 82, 83, 85, 86, 87, 88, 89, 94, 121, 125, 128, 164, 165, 166
Aristaios, 147, 148, 167
Artemis, 145, 150
Arthur, King, xii, 5, 10, 13, 19, 25, 29, 40, 42, 48, 50, 53, 54, 55, 70, 78, 89, 91, 92, 95, 96, 98, 100, 101, 102, 103, 105, 106, 107, 108, 109, 110, 114,

123, 132, 148, 152, 154, 155, 156, 160, 162, 163, 165, 166, 167, 171
Assembly of the Noble Head, 40, 47, 66
Astraea, 170, 171, 183, 185
asvamedha, 33
Avalon, 54, 55, 96, 97, 111, 157, 161, 162, 163, 164, 166, 167, 171; King of, 161, 162, 165, 170

badger in the bag, 22, 28
Balor, 80, 84, 85, 86, 99, 104, 105, 108, 111, 117
Bedwyr, 92, 132
Beli (Belinus), 41, 73, 74, 86
Bladdud, 94
Blake, William, 9, 174
Blathnat, 49, 50, 98
Blodeuwedd, 5, 12, 50, 72, 76, 81, 83, 98, 148
Book of Invasions, 48
Bran, x, 11, 12, 19, 25, 30, 37, 55, 57, 62, 63, 65, 70, 99, 108, 121, 143, 158, 160, 165, 170
Branwen, 7, 38, 39, 40, 41, 42-3, 45, 46, 48, 50, 99, 143, 165
Branwen, Daughter of Llyr, x, 12, 30, 32, 37-55, 57, 59, 61, 63, 64, 101, 116
Bres, 98, 104
Briareus, 53
Bricrui, 41
Britannia, 8